The Invisible Diggers

A Study of British Commercial Archaeology

Paul Everill

HERIT ... SERIES No. 1

THE INVISIBLE DIGGERS – A STUDY OF BRITISH COMMERICAL ARCHAEOLOGY

Copyright: Oxbow Books and Paul Everill 2009

'Heritage' is an imprint of

Oxbow Books, 10 Hythe Bridge Street, Oxford OX1 2EW

A CIP record of this book is available from The British Library

ISBN: 978-1-905933-10-5

This book is available direct from

Oxbow Books, 10 Hythe Bridge Street,
Oxford OX1 2EW
(Phone: 01865-241249 Fax: 01865 794449)

and

The David Brown Book Company
PO Box 511, Oakville, CT 06779, USA
(Phone: 860-945-9329 Fax: 860-945-9468)

and from our website

via www.oxbowbooks.co.uk

Front: The watercolour image of the diggers is called 'Barrow Digging' by Philip Crocker and is reproduced with the permission of the Wiltshire Archaeological and Natural History Society.

Reverse: Image copyright of Dave Webb, from his 'Diggers Alternative Archive'.

Publication Design: Michael de Bootman.

Printed at the Short Run Press, Exeter.

CONTENTS

FIGURES

TABLES

ACKNOWLEDGEMENTS

I am, of course, utterly indebted to all of the archaeologists who have participated in the research process with me, both formally and informally, and who have helped shape this study. Sadly, and perhaps ironically, it is not possible to thank individually those who participated in the interviews and the online survey without sacrificing their anonymity, but I am very grateful indeed for their willingness to take part.

This began life as my doctoral thesis, and as such I owe a great deal of thanks to my PhD supervisor, Stephanie Moser, for her assistance, advice and enthusiasm throughout my research. I am also very grateful to John Schofield for reading some of my work and providing useful comments and encouragement; to Tim Hughes, Head of Training at RHS Wisley, for meeting me to discuss the similarities between archaeology and horticulture; to Tom Vannozzi, Consultant with 'The Leading Edge Market Research' for reading and commenting on aspects of my online survey; to Darren Glazier for reviewing my interview analysis chapters; and to Peter Hinton for commenting on my section on the IFA. Needless to say omissions, errors and opinions are entirely my own. I am also very grateful to Dave Webb, for allowing me to use a number of his photographs, and to Jon Hall and Vicki Herring for sending me some of their cartoons. I also wish to thank the family of the late Philip Barker for allowing me to include several pieces of his artwork.

On a personal note I would like to thank especially Paul 'Don' Donohue, Dom Barker, Nick Armour, Fraser Sturt, Chris Russel, James 'Zimbo' Cole and Mac for sharing their insight and experience, for helping me to keep my research relevant and for countless evenings in the pub. I also want to thank Karen Burnell for her support throughout the last few years, for helping me think about the questions I was asking in my research, and for saying yes to the most important question I've ever asked.

My biggest thanks are reserved for my parents, Joan and Alan, who made a lot of sacrifices so that this research could happen. They saw the value of this project when no-one else was prepared to fund it and it is simply not possible for me to express how grateful I am to them for their support. I hope they share some of the sense of achievement and, frankly, relief now that it is completed.

PREFACE

Since the increasing reliance on developers to fund archaeological work through the 1980s, and the implementation of Planning Policy Guidance Note 16 (PPG16) in 1990, British 'commercial' archaeologists have become increasingly distanced from their academic colleagues. This study examines the situation within contemporary 'commercial' archaeology and considers the challenges faced by those employed within that sector, including the impact of commercial working practices on pay and conditions of employment and the process of excavation and knowledge production.

Part One provides an historical background, documenting the development of 'developer-led' archaeology from its roots in the largely volunteer 'rescue' excavations. There is also a consideration of the perception of fieldwork as 'labouring', from the earliest excavations through to the present. Part Two presents the analysis of the data gathered for this study. Beginning with quantitative data provided by a survey of commercial archaeologists, a portrait is painted of the people employed in that sector before moving on to discuss the written submissions that many respondents included when submitting the survey. These chapters present and then develop certain key themes, and the subsequent analysis of extensive qualitative interviews with 28 participants allows these themes to be considered in far greater detail. The thematic analysis of the interviews is divided into two chapters – one considering the career paths of the participants and the other discussing their perceptions of the profession – and these sandwich the analysis of a participant observation study undertaken over two months in 2004/5. This study provides a fascinating insight into the working environment of commercial archaeologists and demonstrates how camaraderie and love of their job is often just enough to outweigh the adversity they face in the form of low wages, poor employment conditions and career prospects.

INTRODUCTION

This study is an exploration of archaeological practice. Its specific focus is on the relationships encountered and enacted by archaeologists within a neglected sector of the discipline in the UK – commercial archaeology. These include the physical relationship between the archaeologist and the archaeological remains, through which both are defined; the employer-employee relationship; and the inter-personal relationships that provide camaraderie and support. Whilst much has been written on the excavation process there is rarely discussion of the fragmentation of the role and specialisms of the commercial field archaeologist. Thus, despite academic reflections upon the nature of archaeological fieldwork (eg Tilley 1989; Cumberpatch and Blinkhorn 2001; Lucas 2001a, 2001b; Jones 2002; Edgeworth 2003) and an increasing recognition that the archaeological process is, to a certain extent, determined by the organisation and structure of the profession, there has been no systematic study of the commercial sector in archaeology. This neglect reflects the somewhat naïve assumption that the commercial practice of archaeology is inconsequential to the history and changing nature of archaeology; an omission which I intend to address during the course of this study.

A 'crisis' in commercial archaeology

> *Just as PPG16 transformed archaeology at a stroke, an effort of will and imagination could turn our current weaknesses inside out. We could convert our state of fragmentation, introspection and caution into one of coherence, buoyancy, and confidence for the future.*
> **(Richard Morris 1994)**

"I'm an archaeologist, my career is in ruins". This is more than just a bad joke, it is an accurate description of the position of the vast majority of commercial field archaeologists in Britain. The move towards predominantly developer-funded archaeology during the 1980s, and the now well-established system of competitive tendering, have forever changed the nature of the archaeological profession. Some argue, not without reason, that the introduction in 1990 of Planning Policy Guidance (Note 16), PPG16, which made archaeology a consideration of planning consent, has meant that there are currently more jobs and better wages than ever before for archaeologists working in that sector. It is also true that this explosion has created whole new ways in which archaeological practice is conceived and practised, from the 'desk-based assessment' to the 'field evaluation' of archaeological remains. Yet it is an undeniable fact that a

Figure 1: Never had such cr*p brickwork received such attention. © *Jon Hall*

Figure 2: Diggers alternative archive. © *Dave Webb*

large number of commercial archaeologists see a crisis being caused by the current system (Fahy 1987; Goodfellow 1990; Morris, R. 1993; Howe 1995; Sparey Green 1995; Hardy 1997; Anon 1998; Cooper Reade 1998; Denison 1999) and this crisis, if left unchecked, has significant ramifications for the whole discipline.

It is important to define what is meant by the term crisis in the context of commercial archaeology. In its broadest sense there is a fundamental problem in the structure and funding of archaeological work ahead of (re) development projects. Competitive tendering is recognised as providing no guarantee of quality, yet while it remains the system through which contracts are won it provides an incentive to reduce costs wherever possible. Compounding this is the fact that the monitoring of archaeological work is currently highly variable across regions of the UK, with no support given to curatorial archaeologists in the form of statutory minimum requirements for developer-led archaeology. Against this backdrop, the aim of this research is to examine specifically the impact on staff employed by commercial organisations. This is not to say that the wider problems will be overlooked, merely that they will be approached from the perspective of those whose working lives are affected by them daily in order to provide a unique insight into commercial archaeology.

The scale of academic fieldwork pales into insignificance when compared to the sheer enormity of the data and artefactual evidence produced by developer-led archaeology every year. Clearly an attempt to highlight, and suggest solutions to the current problems is overdue in both an academic and an ethical sense, for commercial archaeologists are finding it harder to perform their job to a level that they find satisfactory and ultimately the profession and the resource will both suffer. So what symptoms are the profession displaying that lead us to the conclusion that it is in crisis? Firstly, and most fundamentally, commercial archaeologists do not consider the pay and conditions of employment to be commensurate with the training and experience that they are expected to have. They watch every day as sites are inadequately excavated to keep developers happy and believe their own wages to be kept low to enable competitive tenders to be made to the same developers. They are very often unhappy with the skills of their managers, but are equally aware that many people entering the profession do not possess the necessary skills or basic field experience to perform the role. They become disillusioned when promotion and advancement seem unattainable dreams and many very able archaeologists leave the profession. They see the traditional perception of 'an archaeologist' being gradually whittled away leaving them perched precariously, relying on their ability to scavenge for the crumbs of responsibility and training that their employers are prepared to throw them. In the past an experienced professional field archaeologist was able to call upon a wide set of skills to carry out the complete range of site-based tasks. Excavation of features; broad diagnosis of artefactual and osteological material; interpretation of the function of the site; survey and even maintenance of equipment. These skills were almost invariably learned in a classic apprenticeship style. Senior archaeologists passed on their knowledge and experience to the next generation. This was correctly understood to be a crucial process and produced archaeologists that were well-rounded, multi-skilled and respected as experts. Clearly not everyone who picked up a trowel was destined to complete the cycle of apprentice to expert and the concept of full-time field archaeologists is a relatively new one. Appalling pay and conditions, then as now, also discourage many from remaining within the profession.

Figure 3: Diggers alternative archive. © *Dave Webb*

The mid to late 1980s saw the emergence of modern commercial archaeology in the UK. Also called at times 'Reactive', 'Professional', 'Contract' and 'Rescue' it has been placed by some in direct opposition to the values of 'Amateur' and 'Independent' Archaeology. Within Commercial archaeology the assessment of artefactual evidence is, more often than not, left to the specialist in the office. If an Osteologist is employed within their organisation the same will apply. If a survey is required, other than that of a simple Dumpy Level, some units rely on specialist staff. Some units have even removed photography from the armoury of site staff and placed that within a specialist department. Clearly specialists are required to glean the greatest amount of information from finds, samples etc., but the relationship should be between, for example, a pottery expert and site staff that feel competent to produce an initial assessment in the field. Having the skills to identify chronologies within artefactual evidence will clearly impact on the initial interpretation of a feature or site. However, interpretation is perhaps the most fundamental skill that is currently being removed from the professional realm of junior site staff. Some unit managers believe that the process of interpretation belongs entirely to the more senior staff within a project. This is clearly not only narrow-minded, but ultimately destructive to the profession because among today's disenfranchised site staff are those who will ultimately take up the reigns of unit and project management. In the market place of

Figure 4: Diggers alternative archive. © *Dave Webb*

modern British archaeology it is not financially viable, or worthwhile, for units to actively train and educate their staff. The 'Bread and Butter' site skills – excavation, recording and use of a Level – are taught on most university courses to varying extents. The new employee will be given a refresher if needed, having been observed by a supervisor or other site staff to judge the level of their ability, or they will be informed of the unit's idiomatic recording process if they have come from another unit. Beyond that there is rarely any effort made to expand the skills of staff. Senior staff, with the benefit of accumulated knowledge and experience, are no longer encouraged to pass this on as it has no measurable financial value. The skills of artefact analysis etc have been segregated from routine site activities and placed within the confines of the specialist's office. Occasionally junior staff will have the opportunity to pick up fragments of useful information when their more senior colleagues have the time to pass on their knowledge, but most often the accumulation of new skills will only be possible if the staff actively pursue the learning of them outside of their usual working day.

Figure 5: Diggers alternative archive. © *Dave Webb*

Surveys of commercial field archaeologists within the last few years have consistently shown that they are the lowest paid of all the so-called 'professionals' and that there is a striking absence of a formalised career structure with very few opportunities for promotion or 'professional development'. The question that we should be asking is what drives people to put up with these conditions when other disciplines would not even be able to attract staff in the first place. Further to that, and more crucially, we should be seeking to improve the situation so that field archaeology does not bleed away all of its experienced staff when they need a better paid and more stable environment within which to set up home and raise a family.

An indication of the mentality of many field archaeologists lies in an encounter the author had whilst working for the Museum of London Archaeology Service. Having come off site and gone to a local pub we were approached by a bank worker who had overheard us discussing archaeology. He asked a wide variety of fairly well-informed questions and said that he would love to leave his job

Figure 6: Fun with wheelbarrows. © *Jon Hall*

and work as an archaeologist. However, when told how much we earned his response was that he could not afford to do it, because, although he disliked his current job, the money would give him the opportunity to do what he really wanted once he had retired. Our reply, although it had not been considered until then, was that low wages and unstable job conditions were part of the sacrifice for doing what we really wanted to do before we retired. It seems likely that the vast majority of professional field archaeologists would agree that it is more than a job. It is a vocation. This attitude should not, however, be seen as an opportunity to keep wages low.

Reflections on fieldwork and 'practical archaeology'

This research, by virtue of the fact that it is looking at the experiences of commercial archaeologists, is concerned largely with the professionalisation of the discipline and the consequences of that development. Although there has been no other work with which one can directly draw comparisons there have been a number of studies that consider the impetus for, and effects of, professionalisation. Included amongst these works are those that look at the professionalisation of academic archaeology (Moser 1995). In some respects it might be tempting to transpose these works onto this subject of study, but it is clear that there is a gulf. When Moser refers to the central role of fieldwork within the discipline, she is actually referring to the way in which 'time served' in the field is used by some academics to legitimate their archaeological careers, in opposition to those who are considered purely theoretical. There is also a gender issue raised in her work which highlights the apparent masculinity of the field-archaeologist which is asserted through superficially 'male' roles of hard, manual labour; heavy drinking; and womanising. Some of these themes are satirised by Sellers (1973) and by an anonymous writer (1994) and are also present in the work of Elaine Morris (1991, 1992, 1994), Cane (1994), Gilchrist (1994) and Gero (1994), amongst others. Champion (1998) even discusses the historical 'invisibility' of female archaeologists. Yet many of these are considering the situation in academic archaeology, or at least often using data that has not taken into account the differences across the discipline. Gero (1994) writes that "women do less fieldwork than men, that women are discriminated against in participating more actively in fieldwork, and that in either fieldwork or analytic research, women receive less financial support than their male counterparts". However, in commercial archaeology, fieldwork can barely be described as an occasional activity, the undertaking of which increases the standing of the individual as a 'real' archaeologist. In fact the term 'fieldwork' is only necessary in order to define it in opposition to the normal, office-based routines of academia. When one considers commercial field archaeologists 'fieldwork' often becomes just plain 'work'. There are, however, some issues arising from other roles within professional archaeology and Cane (1994) describes how women are predominant in post-excavation work, finds specialisms etc. She believes that the normal promotion route is through site-based work and that this accounts for the lower numbers of women in management. Despite this Gilchrist (1994) states that she does "not believe that [commercial] archaeological employment discriminates against women in particular, but its present structure only encourages men and women who are free of personal responsibilities".

If professionalism is the definition of oneself and one's role through the imposition of various codes and charters and, therefore the regulation of entry into that profession as Moser (1995) suggests, is Wilshire correct when he writes that professions represent the "archaic initiational and purificational practices which establish the identity of group and individual member through exclusion of the unwashed and uncertified, for example, undergraduate students" (Wilshire 1990:xiii quoted in Robbins 1993: 24)? This statement represents professionalism as a quasi-religious state and sets up the conflict that characterised much of the 20th Century between religion and the secular world. It also leads to concern over "professionalism's replacement of morality with efficiency" (Robbins 1993). This is a perception that Robbins says is actually more ambiguous than it seems, representing, as it does, a flawed belief – that the rise of professionalism heralded the death of the intellectual in the second half of the 20th Century as free-thinkers became subsumed within the murky world of the 'academy'. Intellectualism as it was once understood required a large element of self-teaching, wide-reading and the ability (and capability) to offer critical thought on any number of contemporary issues. Over the last 50 years the trend towards professionalisation has seen universities become the prime loci for education and, as such, the true intellectual has become marginalized and disempowered.

Professionalism is actually a complicated state represented by differing definitions of the term itself.

> On the one hand, the professional is distinguished from the 'amateur' by the fact that he or she earns a livelihood by the given activity. This gives 'professional' negative connotations of self-interested, mercenary motive as opposed to the desirable alternative – historically based and limited to the leisure of certain social classes – of disinterested love of the activity or subject in and for itself. On the other hand, professions are often distinguished from other ways of earning one's livelihood – that is, from 'occupation' or 'trade' or 'employment' in general – as possessing a superior degree of learning or skill and/ or public utility and also, whether for these reasons or not, a superior social prestige.
> **(Robbins 1993: 34)**

Bruce Robbins in *Secular vocations: Intellectuals, professionalism, culture* (1993) is writing specifically about the shifting balance within literary and cultural criticism (although he does not believe in the 'fall of the intellectual' model, merely a changing cultural environment), but some of the points he raises are equally applicable to the changes within field archaeology. He asks "Have intellectuals, judged to be public, independent, and critical by virtue of stepping boldly outside their specialized competence, been replaced by professionals, characterized by their willingness to remain comfortably within their competence?" (Robbins 1993:x) He could be asking about the public role of archaeologists, once perceived as guardians of the nation's heritage and now trying to balance that with the demands of the commercial environment.

The language of this perceived conflict of interest is peculiar when one first confronts it. Intellectualism surely represents a benevolent force through which certain individuals, gifted with the tools and ability required, are willing and able to offer critical opinions on important issues of the day with the aim of improving our shared culture and society. Professionalism, one might believe, is the driving force by which other individuals, who are trained rather than perhaps specifically gifted, seek to undertake their work to the highest of standards and are bound by a set of guiding rules and principles. Many writers on the subject of intellectualism use a Yiddish term. Literally meaning 'air men', 'Luftmenshen' is used *to describe the principled poverty that is taken to distinguish true intellectuals from the professional journalists, literary scholars, and so on who have come later. Intellectuals seemed to live on air, and thus by poetic extension seemed as free as their ethereal element... Now, assimilated into institutions of one sort or another, they are salaried, pensioned, tenured, and they write accordingly. The Luftmenshen have been grounded. They have become an elite of specialists.* **(Robbins 1993: 7)**

Robbins himself ascribes to the intellectual a political setting that is more than likely left of centre, but when one transfers this to the discipline of archaeology, or indeed many other disciplines, the political imagery is somewhat different. The intellectual of the archaeological community, what one may once have called a 'Gentleman amateur', is more than likely supported by other means. Traditionally this support would have come from inherited family money, though it is more likely that these days that support will come from an unrelated, full-time 'day job'. In comparison, professionalism, in theory at least, gives those with an interest the opportunity to earn their living taking part in work that they love. The use of the word 'love' is deliberate here because, in field archaeology at least, no one can be accused of seeking professional employment for the financial rewards it entails.

A fascinating insight into the perceived conflict between 'intellectual' and 'professional' comes from Hawkes' (1982) biography of Sir Mortimer Wheeler, himself an example of the 'intellectual' archaeologist (though not in the true sense as he was employed by a number of different establishments during his illustrious career). While organising the "Parliament and Premiership" exhibition at the Museum of London in Lancaster House the then Prime Minister, Stanley Baldwin, donated his pipe. It was such a potent image of him (as Churchill's cigars were to be) that Wheeler wanted to use it in posters advertising the exhibition. He approached London Transport asking, unsuccessfully, if they could be displayed in carriage windows.

The affair of Baldwin's pipe serves as a reminder of a principle always observed by Wheeler in his handling of public relations. He was steadfastly against the employment of professionals, as much in the London Museum as on excavations. He extended this from PROs to guide-lecturers, having an especial horror of the parrot chatter of those who knew not what they told. Only those who fully understood what they were talking about should be allowed to interpret it for the public. **(Hawkes 1982: 115)**

The nature of invisibility

The physical relationship between professional archaeologists and archaeology, as discussed by Moser (1995, 1998), Lucas (2001a) and Yarrow (2003) is central to the experience of fieldwork, to the interpretation of archaeological features and to the production of 'knowledge'. However, this physicality is sometimes stripped of personality and individuality. Lucas is particularly critical of the way site staff are often treated in commercial archaeology.

In many ways, site assistants are completely interchangeable – he or she is not a person but a digging machine and although some assistants may be more efficient than others, their 'local knowledge' or personality is often ignored and certainly never mentioned in any contemporary manuals on fieldwork. **(Lucas 2001a: 9)**

HERITAGE RESEARCH SERIES NO. 1

This form of physical invisibility is created by a sense of 'interchangeability'. Site assistants become depersonalised on site, and feel overlooked and disenfranchised by their managers and professional body, the Institute of Field Archaeologists. Shapin (1989) makes a similar observation concerning scientific technicians, who are often almost completely overlooked. Using the historical example of Robert Boyle's laboratory, Shapin highlights the huge number of skilled technicians and assistants who worked there – often unsupervised – who were rarely referred to by Boyle in his writing. However, "the role of technicians was continually pointed to when matters did not proceed as expected. In such circumstances, technicians' labor (or rather, the incompetence of their labor) became highly visible" (Shapin 1989: 558). Boyle did acknowledge that he often made "experiments by others' hands" (Boyle 1772: 14 as quoted in Shapin 1989: 557) and, similarly, Knight (2002) observes that site assistants are almost invariably acknowledged collectively in reports and, furthermore, that they are apparently separated from an active involvement in the archaeological process.

> Strangely, and almost without fail, they would be mentioned not in connection with their work but in relationship to the dominant weather conditions during the excavation. The acknowledgements, it seemed, was a space where specialists would 'contribute', but site assistants had to 'endure'. **(Knight 2002)**

However, another form of invisibility is created during the actual excavation and recording of archaeological features and, subsequently, in the removal of the majority of site staff from the process of post-excavation analysis and interpretation. This is, perhaps, most evident during the creation of site photographs (Knight 2002; Bateman 2005), but includes many aspects of the management of an archaeological project.

> In terms of the excavation work that we carry out, we cannot find the words, and this is literally speaking, to describe to you how painful the process of cutting ourselves out of an archaeological imagination is? Or describe what a dangerous shattering of subjectivity there is in drawing and interpreting where you and others made something, but without you? And yet everything else is sectioned, planned and given a context. Do you know what it is like to always focus the camera in the shadows that reside after you deliberately push a colleague out of the frame, making them wipe out their footprints and pick up their work tools in the process of leaving? What kind of archaeology are these forced experiences for and who is it for? Why are we so professional about creating an archaeology devoid of us? **(McFadyen et al. 1997, as quoted in Lucas 2001a: 13)**

There have been a few attempts to restore the role of archaeologists across the full range of the archaeological process. These could be collectively termed 'reflexive archaeologies' (Hodder 2000; Andrews et al. 2000; Lucas 2001a) in which archaeologists are often encouraged to describe their personal involvement with the site through diaries. These diaries form part of the site archive, which demonstrates the processes which took place and the role of individuals in the act of excavation, as well as documenting the thought processes that led them to excavate a feature in a certain way. An extensive and deliberate collection of 'working shots' on the site cameras is also included in the archive. These approaches are intended to counter the "deferral of interpretation" (Andrews et al. 2000: 527) that many believe has been propagated by the Management of Archaeological Projects, Second Edition (English Heritage 1991). MAP2, as it is know, codified a system of management that separates excavation from interpretation, and thus, with interpretation deferred to a 'post-excavation' phase, it was also removed from the daily role of the 'site assistant'. The 'reflexive archaeologies' seek to redress the balance and restore the role of the site assistant within the interpretive process. They also recognise that this process begins, even before the first swing of a mattock, when the excavator has to make decisions on how best to deal with a particular feature – even deciding whether it is a 'natural' or 'archaeological' feature. Unfortunately such approaches are the exception rather than the rule, and contemporary commercial archaeology still often views 'diggers' as "digging machines" (Lucas 2001a: 9) rather than archaeologists.

Figure 7: Diggers alternative archive. © *Dave Webb*

Flannery (1982) also discusses the role of field archaeologists using the story of a flight home after a conference in San Diego. In the lounge of the 747 he encounters three other academic archaeologists whom he dubs the 'Born-Again Philosopher', the 'Child of the Seventies' and the 'Old Timer'. The former was an unpromising field archaeologist who discovered 'Philosophy of Science' and now spends his time generating laws and models for others to test. The 'Child of the Seventies' is characterised by amoral ambition, particularly when it comes to his publication record, while the 'Old Timer', the 'hero' of the piece, is a weather-beaten field archaeologist who has recently been forced to take early retirement. Commenting on the situation as he sees it, the 'Old Timer' uses the analogy of an American Football game.

> *"During Monday Night Football there are 22 players on the field, two coaches on the sidelines, and three people in the broadcast booth. Two of the people in the booth are former players who can no longer play. One of the people in the booth never played a lick in his life. And who do you suppose talks the loudest and is the most critical of the players on the field?"*

> *"The guy who never played a lick," I interrupted. "And the guys with him, the former players, are always saying things like, 'Well, it's easy to criticize from up here, but it's different when you're down on the field.'"*

> *"Well said, son," the Old Timer chuckled. "And I want you to consider the symbolism for a moment. The field is lower than everything else; it's physical, it's sweaty, it's a place where people follow orders. The press box his high, detached, Olympian, cerebral. And it's verbal. Lord is it verbal."* (**Flannery 1982: 270–271**)

Continuing his analogy the 'Old Timer' presses his concern that, in the future, there might be less people on the 'pitch' than in the 'booth', while those who choose to comment and criticise rather than 'play' have no real impact on the nature of the 'game'. He then concludes by saying

> *"But the players know that. Especially the contract archaeologists, and those of us who perennially work in the field. Because we have the feeling the guys in the booth look down on us as a bunch of dumb,*

sweaty jocks. And we're damn sick of it, son, and that's the God's truth." **(Flannery 1982: 271)**

A study of commercial archaeologists

In order to understand the nature of employment within the relatively young field of commercial archaeology three original sets of data were collected. These include interviews with 28 current or ex site staff; a participant observation study on a large urban site; and an online survey, which gathered key data on the demographics of, and opinions within the profession.

The interviews

Between April 2003 and August 2005 qualitative interviews with 28 participants (see Appendix for details) were conducted. 'Opportunistic' sampling was used, which, in practice, meant that only those who had freely expressed a wish to participate were interviewed and at times that were convenient and appropriate to the participant and their employer. Two units (who cannot be named as it might affect the anonymity of some of the participants in the study) were particularly helpful. The directors of one unit were keen to participate in this research themselves and volunteered to be interviewed. This had the effect of encouraging their staff to also take part, and meant that it was possible to conduct interviews during the working day with the support of the unit directors. The senior managers of the second unit were also supportive and it was possible to arrange a day visit to their offices and interview several volunteers from among their staff. The assistance of these two units provided 20 participants. The other volunteers were academic or commercial work colleagues. Sampling in this way enabled access to a wide spectrum of the profession. Participants included relatively inexperienced site staff through to unit directors and a 'County' Archaeologist; terrestrial and maritime archaeologists; field-based and office-based specialists; contractors and a curator. Each interview lasted, on average, between 45 minutes to an hour and was recorded on a micro-cassette recorder. During analysis of the interviews each one was listened to a number of times, before identification of the recurring themes and selection and transcription of the most appropriate excerpts to illustrate those themes. This data was analysed in two distinct chapters, where the general discussion of the career paths of archaeologists has been separated from their broader perceptions of the profession and its current condition.

The online survey

A second body of data was also needed to analyse contemporary commercial archaeology and this took the form of a survey of the profession. The Institute of Field Archaeologists (IFA) has previously attempted two surveys, published as Aitchison (1999) and Aitchison and Edwards (2003), with a third due to be published in 2008, but commercial archaeologists have often dismissed these results in the past as they are distorted by the inclusion of academic and other data. To address this quantitative data was collected – in the form of a

Figure 8: Diggers alternative archive. © *Dave Webb*

Figure 9: Diggers alternative archive. © *Dave Webb*

10

demographic survey – as a way of underpinning the qualitative research and relating it to the statistical realities of the profession. With this data it is also possible to document trends that have, until now, been perceived primarily in anecdotal terms. As an optional element within the survey online participants were encouraged to contribute written submissions outlining their comments and/or concerns regarding the profession or the research project. These submissions were analysed with the view to isolating common themes that represented broad feeling within the profession and were compared with those themes identified in the oral interviews. Excerpts from these written submissions form the basis of Chapter Four of this book.

Participant observation

In order to place the interviews and survey into context 'participant observation' data was also collected, which was undertaken whilst in full-time employment within an archaeological unit. Adopting the role of 'complete participant' (Burgess 1984: 80) a series of observations designed to characterise the relationships, patterns of behaviour and opinions of commercial archaeologists were recorded. These observations were recorded in the form of a daily field journal or diary, which was subsequently used to analyse the shifting focus of the observations. In this way it was possible to understand the changing experiences and mindset of commercial archaeologists employed on a large project. Edgeworth (2003) conducted similar research whilst employed on an archaeological site. His observations, which took place on a large 'rescue' project over the winter of 1989/1990, were intended to shed light on the excavation process through ethnographic analysis. However, because his work is concerned primarily with this process, the excavators themselves are portrayed rather one dimensionally. In contrast, the research undertaken for this study was not confined by trench edges and extends into the personal lives of excavators and their perceptions of their careers, their colleagues and the nature of their work. Because of the personal nature of much of this data the names of everyone involved were changed as well as all units referred to, and towns and cities where necessary.

Potential research themes

Prior to conducting the data collection and analysis a number of potential themes were identified and these are summarised below. Some of these, though not all, yielded the insights that were anticipated and many new themes arose as a result of the research.

Age and 'time served'

Commercial site staff seem to be aged, on average, between 21–30. The majority seem to work within the profession for two to five years before leaving to pursue further study or take on better paid, more stable employment. It seems that archaeology is very rarely seriously considered as a career option. The idea of having to raise families or settle down seem, to many, incongruous to the archaeological lifestyle and unachievable given the pay and conditions provided by employers. Those who remain within the profession often have to make a large set

Figure 10: Diggers alternative archive. © *Dave Webb*

Figure 11: Diggers alternative archive. © *Dave Webb*

Figure 12: Diggers alternative archive. © *Dave Webb*

HERITAGE RESEARCH SERIES NO. 1

Figure 13: Diggers alternative archive.
© *Dave Webb*

Figure 14: Diggers alternative archive.
© *Dave Webb*

Figure 15: Diggers alternative archive.
© *Dave Webb*

of sacrifices, or are able to support themselves with additional sources outside of work, occasionally even second jobs.

It is considered, as in many professions, that those who become managers were perhaps not the best field archaeologists and there is often friction generated by the decisions made within the office that affect site-based people and projects, especially when those decisions are seen to restrict their ability to undertake the fieldwork in a professional manner because of budgetary and temporal considerations.

Of particular interest from the outset was the length of time spent at each grade with a view to addressing questions such as: Is there a certain amount of experience required for promotion or is it more linked to 'networking' and self-promotion? It often seems that the bottleneck effect of many diggers with similar levels of experience attempting to fill one or two supervisory vacancies produces a situation in which the decisive condition is friendship with the right people. If archaeology is to continue as a profession it needs to be seen as professional and should reward staff on the basis of merit.

Pay and conditions

The IFA acknowledges that pay and conditions for professional archaeologists are unacceptable, but, when this research project began in 2002, had done little to alter the situation despite the leverage that it undoubtedly has within this sphere – though it should be noted that 2007 saw the biggest steps so far to address this, with the creation of an IFA 'Pay Benchmarking' working group designed to relate archaeological wages to comparable positions in other professions. A detailed study, it was felt, would demonstrate average wages and other employment benefits such as sick pay and holiday entitlement offered by units. These aspects of professional archaeology are not only fundamental to the experiences of those who work commercially, but also are a clear indication of the future problems of the discipline unless it is able to retain qualified and experienced staff. It is hardly surprising that many circuit diggers do not remain in the discipline when supervisory pay is often only an extra £20 a week or less.

Education and professional training

Until the 1990s an archaeological degree was not a prerequisite for employment. Some entered the profession through the old Manpower Services schemes and everyone learned the required skills through 'on the job' training. In recent years having a degree has become a requirement for many units when employing staff. However, while degrees in archaeology give staff a wealth of interpretative skills they often do not include enough practical fieldwork and with it the ability to use those skills in a meaningful way. This means that junior staff equipped with a degree often still need a lot of training. There is still no substitute for practical experience and a degree in archaeology does not necessarily make one a qualified archaeologist. The onus should be, in part, on universities to increase the practical component of their courses and perhaps to differentiate between academic and field archaeology. There is also a certain amount of friction between the two arms of the profession which is ultimately destructive. Academic field archaeologists are inclined to see commercial archaeology as a limited exercise without fully appreciating the constraints of the industrial/developmental context; the skills required to deal with multi-period archaeology; or the wealth of practical experience accumulated by those who work professionally.

Similarly, commercial archaeologists often believe that academics are spoiled by the concept of 'research' digging and that time spent excavating sites that are not under immediate threat of destruction when so much else is being lost is a foolish exercise in the long-term. Clearly there are elements of truth in both arguments, but ultimately everyone involved in field archaeology should be united by the need to salvage as much information as possible from sites that are under threat from development and some form of co-operation is required.

Figure 16: Diggers alternative archive. © *Dave Webb*

As a result of this research it was hoped that it would be possible to ascertain whether field staff felt they benefited from their educational background, and what changes should be made to improve the system, but also whether their employers make adequate provision for training. This should not just be training at a basic level, ie those skills required to merely do the day to day work, but also further training so that staff have the opportunity to make progress within the profession.

Political representation

As mentioned previously, many field staff have no access to support or representation from trades unions and feel they can not rely on the IFA which many believe to be run by a predominantly management-based council. The trade union PROSPECT (formerly IPMS) is slowly making progress in creating branches within archaeological units, but these are mostly within the larger, better established companies. In 2001 the Museum of London union branch organised strike ballots over pay and conditions and won several small victories for staff, but unionisation has been slow to spread and staff in smaller units tend to believe there is no point to membership. Ironically, in smaller units it is still sometimes the case that sick pay and holiday entitlement is limited and contracts are renewed on a monthly, or sometimes weekly basis. In some units junior staff are routinely laid off before Christmas and taken back on after the holiday break to get round the statutory holiday entitlement, though this is becoming less common. Field staff were asked about the need for unionisation and representation, in order to get an idea of the numbers who were already involved in an established union. Feeling for the IFA, which claims to represent field archaeologists at a national level, was also analysed and participants were asked what changes, if any, should be made to its structure.

Figure 17: Diggers alternative archive. © *Dave Webb*

Competitive tendering

While some unit managers are able to make a comfortable living from this set-up it has, by its very nature, kept wages low and in some instances led to claims of unprofessional practice with regard to fieldwork. It is

Figure 18: Diggers alternative archive. © *Dave Webb*

often debated whether a move to a regional structure would benefit archaeology and archaeologists in the long term (Walker 1996; Morris, R. 1998). It would lead to an environment in which national, standardised pay scales and improved conditions tied to governmental guidelines could be created for field archaeologists. Reasonable budgets could be required from developers to undertake field work without cuts having to be made in post-excavation analysis or staffing levels. One proposal favoured by some is the creation of regional franchises. This would see units tendering on the basis of long-term, best value, local expertise with minimum tenders set by the curators of that region to ensure undercutting could not impact too dramatically on excavation or post-excavation budgets, or on staff wages.

As part of this research the feeling of staff toward the current system was analysed along with the changes that they felt were necessary in order to maintain commercial archaeology as a professional discipline.

Gender and ethnic bias within the profession

Figure 19: Diggers alternative archive. © *Dave Webb*

Despite IFA data to the contrary personal experience indicates that, at junior grades, the male/female split is about equal and an accurate survey has finally determined the reality of the bias within this age group. It seems universally accepted, however, that there are less women staying in the profession and achieving supervisory positions. Does this represent a gender-based glass ceiling, or is it merely that the absence of a career development structure in commercial archaeology means that the majority of those currently working at junior grades will leave because they have no hope of promotion?

It is also clear to anyone who has worked in the profession for any length of time that the number of ethnic minorities in commercial archaeology is almost negligible at junior grades and possibly non-existent higher up. Is this a mirror of society as a whole, in which the 'heritage sector' struggles to create a spirit of 'inclusiveness'? Whose heritage are we excavating and preserving? If it is defined as the national heritage is this further proof that as a nation we are as divided ethnically as we ever have been? How do we begin to improve the situation, or is heritage ultimately bound up in essentially racist concepts of the past and social development and are archaeologists, like many museum visitors, predominantly white and middle class?

Personal reflections

My own career is fairly representative of the experiences of those who work in commercial archaeology in a post-PPG16 Britain and a personal overview at this point will also demonstrate the position from which the research was approached. My first excavation was in 1989 when, at the age of 16, I found a place on a training dig at Wroxeter, Shropshire, as part of my 'work experience' requirement at school. Having got the bug I decided I should pursue an archaeological career and went to university with that intention. Graduating in 1994, however, the fragile economy had slowed the rate of development and jobs within commercial archaeology seemed consequently hard to come by. My university had provided two months of training excavations (more than most courses in Britain at that time), but despite this I found it impossible to find work. One unit offered me a place on the condition that I worked as a volunteer for six months, but with student debts to pay off I had to turn it down. As time passed my archaeological

CV became dustier and less relevant. By 1997 I was working as an office 'temp', but found work as a site assistant on a summer research excavation. Following this I returned to study part-time for an MA, continuing to work as a site assistant on the same annual project. During the winter of 1999/2000 a development boom was approaching full swing. Having completed my course I had no trouble finding work in Ireland, where a six-year plan for road construction was being funded by the European Union. Travelling initially to Co. Clare I found that I was one of many young British archaeologists that had been attracted to Ireland. Most of us were employed on a strictly 'project-specific' basis, which meant that at the completion of the job we were no longer required by the archaeological unit. Despite this a few of us managed to avoid redundancy by moving to other units just in time.

One of the other advantages of employment in archaeology, no matter how short the contract, is that you find yourself within the network. The people you work with have come from many different units and most of them retain contacts. Prior to the phenomenal success of the "British Archaeological Jobs Resource (BAJR)" website – which grew from modest beginnings in 1999 – most diggers relied on word of mouth for the news on who was currently recruiting. An archaeological site hut when redundancies are looming is the most effective job centre. This is how I came to hear that the Museum of London was looking for archaeologists. Following a mobile phone conversation from a field in the middle of Co. Tipperary to the City of London in June 2000 I was offered a 'Fixed Term' Contract to start in two weeks time. I worked a week's notice then flew home, found a bed at a friend's house in Greenwich and started work on a huge urban site on Fenchurch Street.

Across the City large developments requiring the intervention of archaeologists were beginning and my employment at MoLAS was secure, on a renewable three-month contract, for a year and a quarter. At the end of that time it was clear that large projects were beginning to dry up and there were threats of redundancies time and again, none of which proved necessary. However, the managers would clearly not be able to continue to find work for all the people that had been taken on during the height of the boom, on top of which I felt it was a good time for me to leave London. The Cambridge Archaeological Unit was advertising on "BAJR" for experienced staff so I e-mailed my CV to them. The following day they phoned and offered me a job to start in a fortnight. So, again, I worked a week's notice and then had a week to find somewhere to live in Cambridge before starting work on a huge gravel quarry in the middle of the Fens in August 2001. Again employed on a renewable three-month contract I worked there for a year, before leaving Cambridge to begin work on my PhD. Over the course of my research I worked for several more units to help cover living costs and, following the completion of the PhD, was employed full-time by the Southampton City Council Archaeological Unit.

During this time the most money I ever earned was around £15,000 per year with the Museum of London Archaeology Service. That was mostly because of London weighting, plus a promotion to Assistant Supervisor, that together amounted to an extra £3,000 per year. On average my earnings were between £11,000 and £12,000 per year. In an article in the Daily Mirror on pensions, published on the 22nd January 2003 the future plight of those currently working in archaeology was highlighted.

Among the worst hit are the low paid and those doing short-term contract work for whom there is no company pension and who are earning too little to save for themselves. Nathan Chinchen is a 26-year-old archaeologist from Swanage in Dorset.

'Most of my contracts are for six months or less and even if I get work for a full year I earn only £11,000.' He tried out the pensions calculator on the TUC website which suggested he might afford to save £15 a month. That would give him a pension well short of £50 a week at 65. So he would have to rely mainly on the state pension when he retires. **(Daily Mirror 2003)**

Possible findings

The vast majority of those employed in commercial archaeology realise that the situation is a challenging one. It is hoped that the end product of this research will be a piece of work that achieves at least the following targets:

1   Through analysis of the historical background to the emergence of commercial archaeology to understand its implications both for 'the archaeology' and for those employed within it.

2   By allowing site staff an active input to the research the conclusions will be more holistic, rather than focusing on a few central issues that are already widely researched.

3   Through thorough research on the current state of the profession to provide a theoretical framework for improvements that can be made by the IFA, employers, the unions and the Government to ensure that in the future the quality of the archaeological work is of an unquestionably high standard, but more urgently that the practice of professional employment is one that ensures the 'structural' integrity of the discipline for the present and future professionals.

The book is divided into two parts. Part One presents background material in order to place the analysis of data in Part Two into context. Chapter One provides the historical background to a consideration of contemporary commercial archaeology by looking at legislative developments and the move from 'rescue' archaeology towards developer-led projects. Chapter Two provides further background by considering the current position of 'site assistants', or 'diggers', within the commercial sector. Chapter Three, the first chapter of Part Two, contains an analysis of the survey data. This quantitative study establishes the demographics of commercial archaeology and, furthermore, through analysis of opinions expressed in response to some questions, provides a number of themes which are expanded upon in the qualitative work in the rest of the book. This begins with Chapter Four, in which excerpts from the written submissions to the survey are analysed thematically, and a similar method is used in Chapter Five to discuss the qualitative interviews – with a focus on the background,

Figure 20: Diggers alternative archive. © *Dave Webb*

experiences and career paths of the participants. The analysis of the participant observation study in Chapter Six examines some of these themes still further, by using a single site as a case study and by considering employer–employee and interpersonal relationships, as well as the nature of the work being undertaken and its effects on site staff. In Chapter Seven the interviews again provide the data as the perceptions commercial archaeologists have of their profession are discussed thematically, before the key points of each chapter are again summarised in the Conclusion and the findings presented.

PART
ONE

CHAPTER ONE
The Origins of Professional Archaeology

Figure 21: Origin of the risk assessment. © *Jon Hall*

Introduction

Much has already been written on the legislative, public and professional developments that have created contemporary commercial archaeology (eg Breeze 1993; Hunter et al. 1993; Lawson 1993; Biddle 1994; Carman 1996; Chadwick 2000; Wainwright 2000). While this topic could form the focus of a research project in its own right, the history of commercial archaeology is outlined in this chapter in order to understand the background and nature of the 'professional' environment within which the subjects of this research are sited. The working lives of British contract archaeologists in 2008 are a direct result of the evolution of Rescue Archaeology and the shifting priorities of politicians, and this has produced complex and often contradictory narratives within the profession. This chapter aims to provide the reader with a sense of context, and an appreciation of why many of the participants have very individual interpretations of what it means to be a commercial archaeologist and why, therefore, personal expectations are often so different.

In format this chapter will deal separately with the legislative components of Ancient Monument Protection and the Town and Country Planning Acts, which led ultimately to the publication of PPG16 (Planning Policy Guidance, Note 16) in 1990. PPG16 itself is covered in more detail – as it effectively established and enshrined modern, developer-led, contract archaeology – as is MAP2 (The Management of Archaeological Projects [2nd Edition]), which was produced by English Heritage in 1991 in order to standardise the excavation and post-excavation process. Alongside these sections 'Rescue' archaeology will be discussed from its amateur and research-led roots prior to the Second World War – through the radical changes initiated by the (re)development boom in the 1950s and 60s – to the emergence of commercial archaeology.

Ancient monument legislation

In 1882, following decades of concern over the condition of some of Britain's archaeological and historical remains, the Ancient Monuments Protection Act became "the first conservation measure passed by the British Parliament." (Breeze 1993: 44). An initial 'schedule' of 24 Monuments (John Schofield pers comm), located across Britain, formed an appendix to this Act and these subsequently came under State Guardianship – though remaining the property of private landowners. General Pitt Rivers was appointed as the first Inspector of Ancient Monuments in 1883 with a mandate to preserve, analyse and understand the archaeological remains in his charge (Pugh-Smith and Samuels 1996: 6). Several Parliamentary Acts, culminating in the Ancient Monuments and Archaeological Areas Act 1979, have subsequently superseded the 1882 legislation, but the basis remains the same.

Under the terms of the 1979 Act the relevant Secretary of State (since 1997 this means the Secretary of State for Culture, Media and Sport) is responsible for the Scheduling of Monuments of national importance in England. Since the devolution of some powers from Westminster in 1999 the Secretaries of State for Wales and Scotland no longer perform this role. Currently Cadw, established in 1984, undertakes these duties as the Historic Environment Division of the Welsh Assembly. Historic Scotland, created in 1991, performs the same role for the Scottish Executive (ie the Ministers of the Scottish Parliament). Since the creation of English Heritage in 1983 it has advised the relevant department (currently DCMS) on key issues including the Scheduling of Monuments and areas of archaeological importance. This also, significantly, includes the granting of Scheduled Monument Consent (SMC), which has to be obtained from the Secretary of State before any works that might damage or destroy the monument can be undertaken.

The Secretary of State may grant consent for the execution of such works either unconditionally or subject to conditions, or can refuse outright. The consent, if granted, expires after five years. Compensation may be paid for refusal of consent or for conditional consent in certain circumstances, in particular if planning permission had previously been granted and was still effective (Sections 7–9). Failure to obtain SMC for any works of the kind described in Section 2(2) is an offence, the penalty for which may be a fine which, according to the circumstances of the conviction, may be unlimited. Provision is made for the inspection of work in progress in relation to SMC (Section 6 (3), (4)). Successful prosecutions of parties who undertook works without consent or broke SMC conditions have occurred. **(Breeze 1993: 48)**

By January 2006, there were 17,700 Scheduled Monuments - covering some 36,000 archaeological sites – listed by the DCMS in England. There can be no doubt that the Ancient Monuments and Archaeological Areas Act of 1979 and its predecessors have protected and preserved a lot that would otherwise have been lost to us. However, some commentators believe that when faced with real crisis the Act was essentially powerless (Biddle 1994), and that

> *After several decades of reaction to archaeological crises and escalating expenditure by central government on rescue archaeology, it was not the Ancient Monuments and Archaeological Areas Act 1979 which solved the problems. Rather it has been the creation of English Heritage by the National Heritage Act 1983 and the publication of Planning Policy Guidance Notes "PPG16" in 1990 and "PPG15" in 1994 which have done more to safeguard the long-term future of archaeological remains in Britain.*
> **(Pugh-Smith and Samuels 1996: 7)**

Planning legislation before PPG16

Planning policy in Britain did not become a major concern for the Government until the rapid expansion of towns and cities following the industrial revolution created certain health issues. These problems were invariably related to the density of housing and in 1844 the Royal Commission on the Health of Towns published its first report. In 1848 two Acts were passed by Parliament that were to be the first of many relating to town planning. The first, the Public Health Act, set up local health boards in areas where the conditions were deemed unacceptable, either by the higher than average mortality rate or by a petition of local people. These local boards "were granted powers to ensure that both existing and new houses were provided with water and drainage" (Blackhall 2000). The second Act, the Nuisance Removal and Disease Prevention Act, made it a legal requirement for new housing that they should not rely upon open ditches for drainage. The Nuisances Removal Act 1855 extended this to the provision of adequate toilet facilities, drainage and ventilation in order to ensure that a house was suitable for human habitation. There were several more Acts in the late 19th Century that expanded on this theme of ensuring a lower limit for the quality of housing in order to deal with public health issues.

The first legislation to introduce modern town planning schemes was the Housing, Town Planning etc Act 1909. This enabled (or, in large towns, required) local authorities to create town-planning schemes that were subject to approval from the Local Government Board, or Parliament itself. These schemes "allowed the definition of zones in which only certain types of buildings would be permitted" (Blackhall 2000). This Act also incorporated and expanded earlier requirements for sanitation with regard to new housing.

The Town and Country Planning Acts

In 1932 Parliament passed the first of a long line of Town and Country Planning Acts. Significantly, it extended the concept of planning schemes to non-urban environments and to the redevelopment of urban areas. The Acts of 1943 and 1944 were concerned predominantly with the rebuilding of those areas badly damaged by the war, but by 1945 the thoughts of Government were focused on building a better Britain for its exhausted population. This led to the embracing of the concept of New Towns in the New Town Act of 1946 and the creation of Green Belts[1] in the TCPA, 1947. In this modern vision for Britain, the population was to be decentralised from the overcrowded and war-ravaged urban centres and the spread of these areas was to be controlled to keep them discreet. Many young families were moved from London Boroughs to market towns in the South East under Town Expansion Schemes.

The Town and Country Planning Act 1947 repealed nearly all of the previous legislation. Planning decisions were removed from the shoulders of local authorities and centralised at a time when industries and utilities were also being nationalised. Central government implemented a system of town and country maps to be produced by local planning authorities. These were to use a standard system of scale, notation and colour coding and would demonstrate land use. For the first time the concept of planning 'zones' was abandoned in favour of 'land allocation', whereby the primary land use of certain areas is decided by the planners. It is, however, more flexible than the older system of 'zoning' as it does not rule out some secondary uses for the land (ie shops in residential areas). This system is still used in Britain today. The TCPA 1947 also took some rights away from individual landowners. It would no longer be possible for someone to develop on his or her own land without prior approval from the State. Furthermore those individuals who did not receive permission were not eligible for compensation, while those that did were required to pay in tax the difference between the value of their land before and after the granting of planning permission (known as the windfall gain).

The Planning Acts of 1953, 1954, 1959 and 1960 made minor amendments to the TCPA 1947 and all of this legislation was consolidated in 1962. However, the next significant Act was the TCPA 1968. The 1950s and 1960s had seen a period of extensive slum clearance and rehousing along with the increasing involvement of private developers in the redevelopment of town centres. The 1947 Act proved to be prohibitively slow in relation to the speed at which development was moving. The TCPA 1968 amended the twenty-year-old system of plan making and approval and installed a two-tier structure in some local authorities. Within the areas affected by this new legislation county councils were responsible for producing the broader plans as required by the TCPA 1947, which still required governmental approval. At the same time district councils produced more detailed and technically up-to-date local plans, which, significantly, required the participation and approval of local people. The Local Government Act 1974 created new metropolitan counties and the two-tier system of planning was extended to the whole country.

The incoming Conservative government of 1979 was keen to encourage developers and redevelopment and saw the current planning legislation as a significant barrier to economic progress. By 1986 the Government had introduced Enterprise Zones, Urban Development Corporations and Simplified Planning Zones, all of which were designed to assist in the redevelopment of run-down areas by removing large portions of the planning requirements. It had also abolished the development land tax (the windfall gain payable by landowners under the

---

[1] *Contrary to popular opinion the primary function of a Green Belt, as it was established in the TCPA 1947 and as is still the case (PPG 2), is to control the outward expansion of urban areas. This has the effect of encouraging regeneration and redevelopment within those areas and ensuring that nearby towns do not merge into one another. A secondary aim was to protect the surrounding countryside and preserve the character of historic towns. Because of this "declared boundaries of existing green belts can be altered if circumstances require such a change." (Blackhall 2000)*

TCPA 1947) as a further encouragement to developers and by its abolition of the metropolitan county councils it removed a whole tier of planning requirements in the cities. It was during this period that the Government began trying to reduce local authority expenditure by encouraging private investment. For much of the 1980s "planning was 'developer led' because of the government's determination that private investment should not be stifled by the planning system. Where local planning authorities refused planning permission, their decisions were frequently overruled by the then Secretary of State" (Blackhall 2000). However, it would be a shift in government policy towards a tightening of planning controls at the end of that decade that would eventually lead to the creation of the Town and Country Planning Act 1990 and the Planning Policy Guidance Notes (PPGs) that are associated with it.

Archaeology before PPG16

From research to RESCUE

Prior to the outbreak of the Second World War archaeological fieldwork was almost invariably an academic exercise. Whether or not it was 'institutionally' academic the act of excavation was designed to recover objects or, later, to answer specific research questions. So-called 'Rescue' archaeology in this period was often just a matter of retrieving artefacts and bones once the contractors had excavated their trenches. "The research worker or the good amateur archaeologist was usually too engrossed in his particular problems to watch building sites or to undertake an excavation of a site for no better reason than that it was going to be destroyed" (Rahtz 1974).

The war saw two very important changes within archaeology. Firstly the widespread construction of large defence installations, such as airfields and other bases, brought the destruction of archaeology by development to the attention of the government, which was required to act under Ancient Monument legislation. 450 airfields had been constructed on 300,000 acres of land and 55 Research excavations had been financed as part of the process (Wainwright 2000). Secondly, with more important things to deal with, research excavations were largely curtailed. The result was that government-sponsored rescue excavations provided employment for trained staff.

After the war the Ministry of Works, through the Ancient Monuments Inspectorate, began to take on greater and greater responsibility for the funding of rescue excavations. The pace of development in the 1940s and 1950s that had been encouraged and controlled by the Town and Country Planning Acts of this period was, to some extent, reflected in the increase of state-funding for archaeology. This funding was still woefully inadequate. By the 1960s the widespread destruction of archaeological sites by developers was a cause of great concern amongst archaeologists (Addyman 1974; Barker 1974a; Thomas 1974). In 1963 the Royal Commission on the Historical Monuments of England published a list of 850 monuments, which were thought to be at risk. As Geoffrey Wainwright (2000) recalls, "The response by Government... was to appoint three directors of rescue excavations within a structure headed by John Hamilton... I returned from India in 1963 to be recruited by Arnold Taylor – the then Chief Inspector of Ancient Monuments – and to join Brian Davison and Ian Stead (see Figure 22) as the Government digging team."

Figure 22: Ian Stead, front centre, with his dig team a St Albans, 1966. © *Ian Stead*

Most rescue excavations were undertaken by local amateur groups that had been able to negotiate some time before development. Only a small number of these were lucky enough to receive funding. In the case of Scheduled Ancient Monuments government agencies struggled to organise adequate excavation prior to development. Brian Philp (2002) recalls an incident in 1964:

> *When Stuart E. Rigold, Inspector of the Ministry of Public Buildings and Works, telephoned to say that the Faversham Royal Abbey site was due for development and, due to an administrative oversight, needed instant excavation as it was a Scheduled Ancient Monument. It seems that the only four known full-time excavators in England were 'otherwise engaged', though I suspected holidays abroad, convenient conferences and allergies to mid-winter digging were more likely.*

A similar episode occurred in 1969 when Sir Mortimer Wheeler invited Brian Philp and his Kent team to assist the desperate efforts of archaeologists to excavate as much material as possible ahead of the groundworks at York Minster. Richard Morris (1999) describes the same project from the time of his involvement in 1971.

> *When engineering works started, the initial provision for archaeology was ridiculously small, and much historical material was lost during the several years it took to marshal sufficient funds to assemble a team which could keep pace with the repairs....We sometimes worked round the clock and were invariably working against it. Night shifts were occasionally relieved when the sub-organist came in to practice, on one occasion obliging with requests from 'The Sound of Music' in the small hours.* **(Morris 1999: 15)**

Projects such as these were the rule rather than sad exceptions and it was this desperate situation that forced archaeologists to come together. Six likeminded fieldworkers – John Alexander, Philip Barker, Martin Biddle, Barry Cunliffe, Peter Fowler and Charles Thomas – called a meeting at Barford, Warwickshire in February 1970. A second meeting was held in Newcastle in November of that year to accommodate those field archaeologists based in the north. Between them over eighty excavators attended the two meetings and proposals were put forward to tackle the problems within archaeology. The first stage was to hold a public meeting. "This meeting took place on 23 January *[1971]* in the Senate House of London University. Over seven hundred people attended, making this the largest archaeological gathering ever held in this country. The most encouraging feature was that the average age of those attending was about thirty" (Barker 1974b). This meeting was an opportunity to talk about the proposals from the first two meetings and to put them to a wider archaeological community.

The immediate result of this meeting was the formation of RESCUE. Initially based at an office in Worcester with a core administrative staff of permanent employees, RESCUE was intended to raise funds through subscriptions and donations. From its conception its principal aims, as voted for at the public meeting, were to:

1   *use every means to make the public aware of the rapidly accelerating destruction of our archaeological heritage;*

2   *press for revision and extension of existing legislation concerning archaeological remains, and seek new legislation where necessary;*

3   *seek greatly increased funds for basic field survey work and recording and for rescue excavation and its publication;*

4   *improve and extend field archaeological training at all levels;*

5   *in general, help to record and preserve the physical remains of Britain's past, with particular reference to the changing character of the natural environment;* **(Barker 1974b)**

The initial impact of RESCUE was heartening. The level of Government funding for rescue archaeology rose dramatically from £133,000 in 1970 (Barker 1987) to £450,000 in 1972 and £800,000 in 1973 (Barker 1974b). However, despite the efforts of RESCUE and increased media and public interest in archaeology, this level of funding increase could not be maintained by central Government. By 1986 it had more or less plateaued at £5,000,000 (Barker 1987). The early success of RESCUE was able only to slow the crisis and from the early 1970s it was clear that rescue archaeology needed some degree of financial independence from the Department of the Environment if it was to survive in any meaningful way.

The manpower services commission 1974 – 1987

Shortly after the creation of Rescue and the associated increase of government subsidies to archaeology, the Manpower Services Commission was created. It was a response to the economic troubles of the early 1970s and from 1974 it provided jobs and training for the long-term unemployed. Archaeology, with its high labour requirements, was ideally suited to this and featured heavily in the Community Programmes run through the MSC after 1980.

> *The Community Programme (CP) is designed for adults of 25 and over who have been unemployed for 12 of the preceding 15 months, (and have been unemployed in the two months preceding the start of the project), and for people aged 24 and over, who have been unemployed for six months previously.* **(Green 1987)**

By 1986 the MSC provided funding of £4.8 million for archaeology, compared to £5.9 million from the Historic Buildings and Monuments Commission (Crump 1987), and in September 1986 there were 1,790 places on archaeological projects through the CPs. On top of the dependence archaeology developed for MSC funding there were a number of side effects to this relationship.

> *Ironically, one positive 'spin-off' from MSC involvement in archaeology is that volunteer rates may have gone up in some areas to bring them into line with CP wages. Also, as site safety is one of the areas monitored by MSC, standards have to be rigorously maintained. The provision of safety clothing and foul weather gear by MSC also marks an improvement except where unscrupulous sponsors spend this part of the 'capitation grant' on machine time and volunteers.*
> **(Crump 1987)**

There were also some criticisms of the effect that the MSC was having, both on archaeologists and the unemployed that it was designed to help. The old 'circuit' had been replaced by CP projects and there were concerns that recent graduates were finding it harder to find work in archaeology. There were also concerns that the average CP wage of £67 a week meant that the CP workforce was not encouraged to have a commitment to the project and supervisors spent as much time policing the site as excavating it (Crump 1987).

However, despite this there is no doubt that MSC funding was vital to archaeology and when the commission was scrapped in 1987 it left a huge hole. During the 1980s the relationship between archaeological units and developers had become more solid and the void left by the MSC was to become increasingly filled by funding from developers.

The Institute of Field Archaeologists

Formed in 1982, the IFA was established to define the standards required of professional archaeologists. RESCUE: The British Archaeological Trust and others had, since 1971, been successful in raising the profile of archaeological work, and in pushing for greater financial assistance from the State. However, by the mid 1970s there was a feeling amongst many senior British archaeologists that a body needed to be established that would support and encourage the growing professionalism within the 'rescue' sector. In 1974 an early attempt by the Council for British Archaeology to create such a body was brought to a grinding halt by the negative reaction of academic and amateur archaeologists, who "saw, or thought they saw, a threat to their own interests in the introduction of a national lobby of full-time professionals" (Hobley 1987: 41). However, in 1978 Philip Barker, one of the driving forces behind the creation of RESCUE, enlisted the support of a 'Management Studies' expert who observed that field archaeology was poorly managed and in need of modernisation.

> *Philip Barker, with Trevor Rowley, immediately "grasped the nettle" and in early 1979 put field archaeology on the road to professionalism by establishing the Association for the Promotion of an Institute of Field Archaeology – APIFA. Thus the recognition of the need for modern management skills in archaeology made this initial and important contribution to the establishment of an Institute.*
> **(Hobley 1987: 41)**

Barker asked 36 archaeologists to each submit 20 names and this approach produced 400 invited members of the newly established APIFA (Hobley 1987). In total over 500 archaeologists were to join the APIFA and from these a committee was set up which was to determine the form of the proposed body. Philip Barker and Brian Davidson, amongst others, wanted to see the new Institute lead the way in raising standards in the field in order to protect the archaeological remains from bad practice.

> *But for others it was the archaeologists that needed protecting. For them, IFA was to be a trade union, cherishing the livelihood of the workforce, the circuit diggers who had come in from the cold and were anxious not to return there. For others again it was to be the voice of authority; a new platform from which to direct British archaeology. Neither the CBA nor the SoA represented the field professionals. IFA was to become the right hand of the profession, like the RIBA for architects.* **(Carver 2006)**

Ultimately, however, the debate was won by those archaeologists, like Philip Barker, that wanted an organisation that would set standards for all areas of archaeological practice and the IFA was born.

> *The consensus view was published as the Memorandum and articles of association and Code of conduct of its designated successor, the Institute of Field Archaeologists (IFA). Elections were held and APIFA handed over responsibility to the first Council of the new Institute of Field Archaeologists in December 1982.* **(IFA 2006: 12)**

The Code of conduct was officially ratified at the IFA's Annual General Meeting in June 1985 and has been amended at eight subsequent AGMs. The current Code, approved in 2002, consists of five governing principles that are intended to ensure the highest standards of professionalism, integrity and ethical conduct amongst members of the IFA. Each principle is supported by a number of rules, outlined in full in the Code of conduct. The five principles are as follows.

PRINCIPLE 1	The archaeologist shall adhere to the highest standards of ethical and responsible behaviour in the conduct of archaeological affairs.
PRINCIPLE 2	The archaeologist has a responsibility for the conservation of the archaeological heritage.
PRINCIPLE 3	The archaeologist shall conduct his/her work in such a way that reliable information about the past may be acquired, and shall ensure that the results be properly recorded.
PRINCIPLE 4	The archaeologist has responsibility for making available the results of archaeological work with reasonable dispatch.
PRINCIPLE 5	The archaeologist shall recognise the aspirations of employees, colleagues and helpers with regard to all matters relating to employment, including career development, health and safety, terms and conditions of employment and equality of opportunity. **(IFA 2006: 14–16)**

sites have been preserved either by record, following excavation, or by being left in situ by developers who have been made aware of the significance of the archaeological remains on their land. It has created a new archaeological process (Biddle 1994) that includes a 'Desk-based assessment' — an initial stage to assess the likelihood and extent of archaeological remains on a site. This utilises the Sites and Monuments Records (SMRs) held and maintained by each county, as well as often incorporating reports generated by non-invasive methods such as Geophysical survey and field walking. The Desk-based assessment is used to determine the most appropriate response to development as well as to inform developers of the likely additional costs. Next the relevant County or City 'Planning Archaeologist' can, if it is deemed appropriate, place an 'archaeological condition' on planning permission. This might be merely a 'Watching Brief' in case, against expectation, important remains are discovered during groundworks, or it might be an 'Evaluation' which seeks to sample the site by placing a number of trenches across it prior to groundwork commencing, in order to ascertain the exact extent of archaeological remains. If important remains are discovered during an 'Evaluation', or if the site contains an already known area of archaeological importance (as is the case in a number of historic towns and cities), the 'Planning Archaeologist' can order a full excavation of the site ahead of groundworks.

On urban sites in particular the excavation might be undertaken in phases, with the archaeologists moving into an area after demolition of existing buildings and before the teams of groundworkers can start preparing the area for the construction phase. This requires close co-operation between all elements of the project, with a complex timetable of start dates and deadlines that leave little room for flexibility. In an environment in which the extent of archaeological remains might not be known until the natural deposits are reached this inflexibility can be problematic and can often lead to some, low priority areas of archaeology being sacrificed so that others can be fully excavated. Despite this, PPG16 represents a vast improvement in the protection afforded to archaeological remains.

> *Archaeological remains should be seen as a finite and non-renewable resource, in many cases highly fragile and vulnerable to damage and destruction. Appropriate management is therefore essential to ensure that they survive in good condition. In particular, care must be taken to ensure that archaeological remains are not needlessly or thoughtlessly destroyed. They can contain irreplaceable information about our past and the potential for an increase in future knowledge. They are part of our sense of national identity and are valuable both for their own sake and for their role in education, leisure and tourism.* (DoE 1990)

Richard Morris (1994), in a brief review of the effects of PPG16 four years on, writes that it

> *has brought undoubted benefits to archaeology. It has provided a framework for locating development away from archaeologically sensitive areas; and it (quite reasonably) requires developers to pay for any reconnaissance needed. It thus frees public money from the exigencies of rescue archaeology, to be spent in more measured ways.*

He also notes, however, that it has generated a new set of problems for the profession, principally that the system of competitive tendering does not always deliver the highest quality archaeological work; that local authority Sites and

Monuments Records (SMRs), which support the system, are not statutory and are often under funded; that units keep running costs down by largely employing young archaeologists on short-term contracts; and that PPG16 was never designed to generate a research output so the academic component of 'rescue' archaeology had all but disappeared. Chadwick, writing some years later expands upon Biddle's concerns. He points out that not only were there some problems at the start, in cases where large projects were given pre–PPG16 planning permission, but also that:

> Reliance upon developers may leave some archaeological projects vulnerable to financial changes. The Lower High Street in Southampton remains unfinished thirteen years after archaeological work began, following the bankruptcy of the development firm. In Doncaster, the cancellation of Department of Transport (now Highways Agency) funding for a road scheme meant that the regionally important medieval North Bridge site was only written up as a basic archive report, with minimal specialist analysis. Full publication was refused. The nearby Church Street excavation found evidence for several phases of Roman fort, the Anglo-Scandinavian burgh defences, the Norman castle defences, and later medieval buildings and a tannery. DoT funding ended long before an archive report could be produced. The local council, the Highways Agency or English Heritage evinced no interest in completing and publishing these sites from a much neglected, historic northern town. **(Chadwick 2000)**

'Grey literature'

This is the term given to the reports published by contracting archaeological units under PPG16 requirements and is a deeply misunderstood phenomenon. It is surprising how often 'grey literature' is cited by those criticising commercial archaeology's failure to contribute to research. Another common misinterpretation of the term 'grey' is that it simply does not exist. In reality, every contract unit in the UK will have shelves full of their own reports. The relevant SMR should also have most, if not all – depending on storage space – or at the very least will have added the information to their SMR details. Although often the reports are limited in terms of detail, due to financial constraints, it is often only ignorance of their existence that prevents them being more widely utilised. Bradley (2006) is the first high profile academic to examine the phenomenon of 'grey literature' in detail. He began his project believing that there are two distinct cultures in British archaeology and that the pace of contract archaeology was such that synthesis of all the commercial reports needed to bring academic studies up to date was not possible. However, by the time he had finished his research he appears to have developed a missionary zeal for 'grey literature' and one can only hope that other academics follow suit.

> If I can characterise the project as a whole, I would say this. I began in a state of dejection at the way in which field archaeology seemed to be out of control. I concluded with the feeling that if two people (one of them working part-time) could assimilate the prehistoric evidence in just three years, my pessimism had been misplaced. What appeared to be a barrier was first a challenge and then an opportunity. Why did we lack the confidence to realise this before? **(Bradley 2006)**

Curators: *responsible for the conservation and management of archaeological evidence, eg county archaeological officers.*

Contractors: *those undertaking work, eg field units.*

Clients: *those paying for the work, eg developers, English Heritage.*

Consultant: *those offering independent advice.*
(Lawson 1993)

These terms had first been coined during discussions within the Institute of Field Archaeologists in the late 1980s, but PPG16 was to set these relationships in stone. The relationship between contractor and client has been discussed above, particularly with reference to the quality of work that this has sometimes produced, but other, ethical, issues have also been raised elsewhere. Cumberpatch and Blinkhorn (2001) express their concern that

> *The owner of an area of land containing archaeological deposits cannot be said to enjoy complete rights over the disposal of archaeological assets in any sense other than the narrowly legal as other groups can make competing and equally valid claims. Local communities may, for example, have good reason to claim prior moral rights in a piece of land which holds values other than the purely financial, and in such a situation it is far from clear that the archaeologist has any moral imperative to act as an agent for one party over another.*

In terms of the ethics of archaeology it is hard to disagree with them and clearly the value of archaeological remains can not, and should not, be measured in fiscal terms or seen as merely an obstacle in the path of development. However, it is certainly the case that, until PPG16 is superseded and most probably even then, commercial archaeology will remain a service provider in a competitive market with all the limitations that that entails.

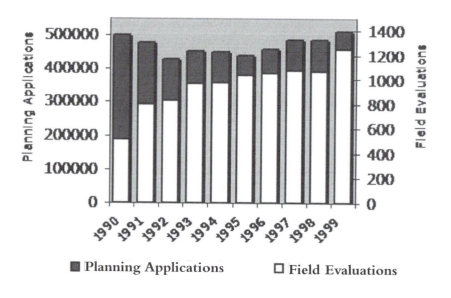

Figure 24: Number of recorded field evaluations carried out in England annually 1990–99 in relation to the number of planning applications. *(Data taken from Darvill and Russell 2002)*

MAP2

In 1991 English Heritage published The Management of Archaeological Projects (2nd Edition), commonly known as MAP2. Though recently superseded it established a number of key requirements for archaeological projects and set a new benchmark. It followed a number of other reports, published since the mid 1970s, that had been concerned with ensuring the adequate publication of archaeological material. The Frere Report of 1975 had proved to be impractical in requiring total publication of all data in so-called Level three reports, and the Cunliffe Report of 1982 lent towards "critical selection of data" (English Heritage 1991). The main purpose of MAP2 was to stress the importance of a 'critical review' stage throughout the management of an archaeological project, not purely to ensure an appropriate publication, but so that the whole process was responsive in the face of changing requirements.

> *This revised document puts forward and describes in detail a model for the management of archaeological projects. The most innovative part of this model is identified as 'assessment of potential for analysis' (phase three [Figure 25]) and this has received detailed treatment because the importance of a formal post-excavation review phase has become evident. It is intended that this management framework will operate side by side with a framework of academic priorities which will help to estimate archaeological value. These priorities will of necessity change as the successful completion of well planned projects contributes to the growth of the academic database.*
> **(English Heritage 1991: para 1.5)**

The assessment phase referred to above is essentially concerned with gauging the degree to which the data-collection phase will contribute to broader archaeological knowledge. From that point it is possible to reassess what further work (finds, environmental analysis etc) might be required to gain the most from the site under study. MAP2 also places emphasis on ensuring that appropriate funding is secured for each phase, and warns against taking funds allocated to one phase to use in another. It gives the specific example of diverting funds from production of the site archive to use in the event of fieldwork proving more costly than anticipated (English Heritage 1991: para 5.3). In many respects it is hard to envisage how English Heritage could monitor every project in such detail, apart from those which it was funding directly. Although MAP2 remains sound guidance, the suspicion would have to be that a large number of commercial and academic projects do not stick rigidly to it and that archaeological management is often still an ad hoc, reactive process. It is also criticised for codifying the separation of the excavation of interpretation phases (ie post-excavation analysis of finds) which discourages reflexivity and leads to a sense of disenfranchisement amongst site staff (Lucas 2001b). Having said that, it does set a benchmark for archaeological publication at various stages throughout a project and it emphasises the importance of updating the relevant SMR.

Conclusion

British commercial archaeology in 2008 is far from being the 'evolutionary' pinnacle of archaeological and legislative practice. It is merely a waypoint at which this research found itself sited. Having said that, with the PPGs currently under review in the Office of the Deputy Prime Minister and the archaeological

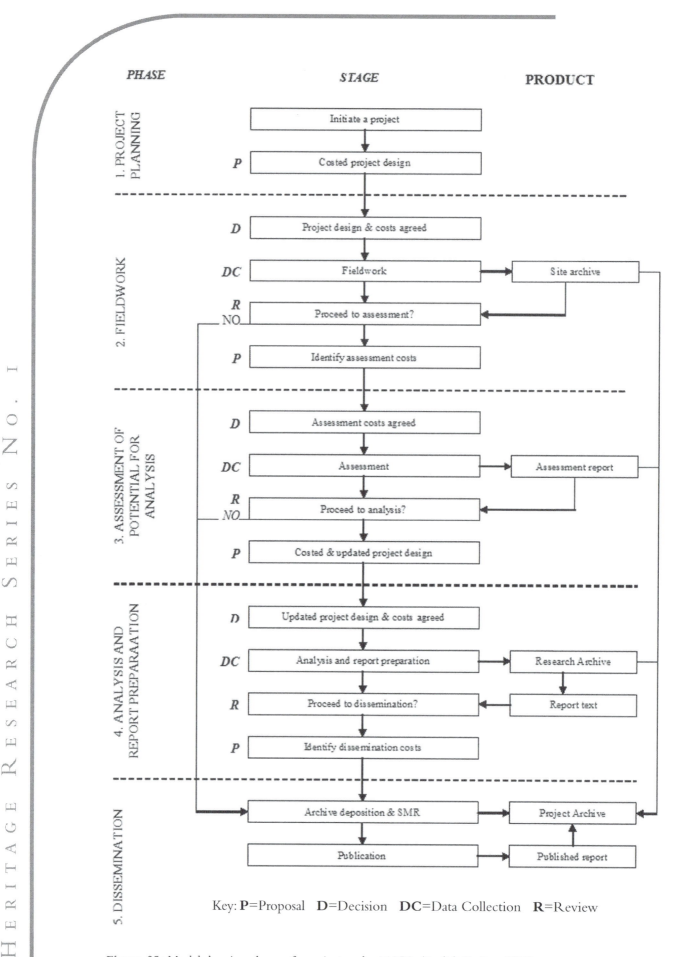

Figure 25: Model showing phases of a project under MAP2. *(English Heritage 1991)*

Key: **P**=Proposal   **D**=Decision   **DC**=Data Collection   **R**=Review

profession waiting with baited breath to see what changes might be made to Planning legislation by the current Government, 2008 could be something of a crossroads for contract archaeology. An undermining of PPG16 would change the landscape irrevocably and could effectively put an end to the profession before it had got past adolescence. A strengthening of the principles of PPG16, combined with a renewed emphasis on research as a core component of archaeological work (and ensuring adequate funds are made available to undertake such work) would be a simple step forward.

Contemporary commercial archaeology in the UK has evolved from a state in which unpaid practitioners reacted to the threat posed to archaeological remains by developers. The legislation which was supposed to protect nationally important remains was weak and ultimately bypassable and it was only the endeavour of teams of itinerant 'rescue' diggers that salvaged anything from the process. The increasing rate of (re)development forced some of those 'enthusiasts' to try to eke out a living on the "subsistence level wage" (Philp 1974) available by becoming full-time archaeologists. County units and regional trusts emerged through the 1970s, funded largely by lobbying central Government for greater financial support. By the late 1980s the State could no longer support these demands and 'rescue' archaeology was effectively privatised and made subject to market forces. Since the 1980s 'professionalism' has been increasingly highlighted by elements within contract archaeology, principally the Institute of Field Archaeologists and the managers of units, as large numbers of organisations vie for market share.

Opinions remain divided between those who now see 'commercial' archaeology as a separate and distinct discipline with a professional foundation and those who believe that it is essentially an academic discipline that does not belong in an open market. It is not a simple dichotomy, however. There are a multitude of shades of grey and this study will demonstrate some of the common themes within many of the personal narratives – both those consciously expressed during interviews and in written submissions and those made evident through surveys and participant observation.

CHAPTER TWO
Invisible Labourers?

Figure 26: Cheesy director.
© *Vicki Herring*

Introduction

When considering the many reasons that may account for the current status of commercial archaeologists it is difficult to pinpoint one overriding factor. In Chapter One it was shown how the profession evolved from a culture of volunteering and was thrust into a competitive market-place. Perhaps its value is yet to be adequately established, however thinking in terms of value has associated concepts of production. It is clear that the archaeological 'end product' is not always understood let alone ascribed any kind of genuine value by the contractors who employ archaeological units. Since 1990 the explosion of commercial units - supported by the implementation of PPG16 and the subsequent role of archaeology within the planning process – should have more markedly improved the situation for the employees. It is perhaps easy, and certainly tempting, to blame the current system of competitive tendering for keeping wages low. Clearly this does play a part, but it seems that in many debates on these issues we are misunderstanding some pivotal truths about the profession. In simple terms the unit archaeologists have been disenfranchised by the system – a system of management codified by MAP2 (1991) – which separates the excavation, interpretation and post-excavation elements. Those same people have been let down by employment practice that requires them to have a relevant degree, yet does not ensure that the degree courses have an adequate practical training component (Everill 2007a).

So the situation can be summarised thus – a graduate from an average university arrives at an average commercial unit with little or no on-site experience. The skills they may have learned lean towards the interpretative side of the job. Yet that is not their responsibility, nor is it particularly useful without the associated site skills. The degree becomes, to varying extents, worthless. Even in 1987, with the profession still very much in its infancy, it was clear that

> *Few, if any, of the* [degree] *courses were really seen, by those on them, as providing the necessary background for archaeological employment. One major factor in this was argued to be the perceived conflict between an archaeology degree as a general academic education and as an archaeological training. Put crudely, some archaeology degrees have little or no value for a student rash enough to want to follow a career in archaeology in Britain.* **(Joyce et al. 1987)**

This situation has frequently been commented on (eg Millet 1986; Hunter 1987), but never been addressed. Almost twenty years later brochures advertising the Archaeology Department in Southampton to prospective Undergraduate students highlight its 'transferable skills' at the expense of specific archaeological training.

> *Because of archaeology's scope and the range of different practical, analytical and academic skills it requires, we believe that an archaeological degree offers one of the best general Arts degrees currently available. Our degree programmes aim to produce graduates with a full set of skills in:*
>
> - *Analysing and interpreting numerical data.*
> - *Preparing written reports and studies.*
> - *Making oral presentations to small and large groups.*
> - *Use of information technology.*
> - *Using different types of information critically.*
> - *Team work and time management.*
> - *How to think and problem-solve.*
>
> *These are skills that are essential for a career in archaeology, but also prepare you for a wide range of different careers.*
> **(University of Southampton 2004)**

It is unsurprising then that the junior field archaeologist has become not an inheritor of the world of Sir Mortimer Wheeler et al, but merely an enthusiastic, skilled labourer. When Shortland (1994) discusses how geologists in the field defined themselves, not through their perceived origins as Gentlemen Amateurs, but almost unconsciously through their roots in mining, it throws up an interesting question. How do commercial field archaeologists define themselves? Perhaps not through their perceived or actual roots, but through the relationships they develop on site, not with their colleagues so much as with those 'others' with whom they share their workplace. Field Archaeologists of the 1920s defined themselves in opposition to the labourers on their site, whether they be culturally separate through nationality as in, for example, Woolley's (1930) work in Mesopotamia or through class as on any of the large field projects run in the UK which utilised large numbers of workmen. This relationship was class-based and often Imperialistic. The modern British commercial archaeologist has more in common with the scaffolders and bricklayers of a large construction site, all being required to wear the same Personal Protective Equipment (PPE), often only being distinguishable by the colour of their hard hats or the logo of their respective employer on their high visibility vests. Perhaps, in the same way as Shortland's geologists, commercial archaeologists see their roots lying more squarely with the labourers of the large-scale research digs than with the educated 'gentlefolk'.

Identifying the commercial archaeologists

A number of small surveys were undertaken on the archaeological profession during the 1990s (Spoerry 1991a, 1991b; Wood 1991; Morris, E. 1992; IFA 1995; Turner 1996, 1997, 1998; Moloney 1998). However, RESCUE had been conducting its own occasional survey since 1978/79. Spoerry (1992, 1997) synthesises some of this earlier data when writing about the 1990–1 and 1996 RESCUE surveys. The total number of curatorial and rescue archaeologists in 1978–9 was estimated to be about 1600, of which 663 were 'permanent' posts. By 1986–7 the total figure had grown massively, due in no small way to the Manpower Services Commission, to 2900, though only about 600 of these were permanent. The end of the MSC saw numbers drop by 1990–1 to about 2200 archaeological staff, though permanent posts had risen to 860. The 1996 survey indicated an overall figure of 2100 jobs and suggested that the profession had achieved a certain stability. In terms of pay the surveys indicate that "In 1990–91 three quarters of archaeological staff were paid less than £12,000 a year. In this same period the national average salary (both sexes) was about £13,200 a year." (Spoerry 1992). If one looks at the figures, however, and removes the permanent posts that most likely do not represent 'site staff' then in actual fact over three quarters were earning less than £10,000 in that period. "In 1995–6 just over three-quarters of archaeologists were paid less than £16,000 a year, when the national average earnings (both sexes) was about £17,500 a year." (Spoerry 1997). One can again safely assume that archaeologists in the field were well below even that figure.

Seeing the need for more research English Heritage commissioned the Institute of Field Archaeologists and the Council for British Archaeology to produce a survey of organisations in the UK that employed professional archaeologists (Hinton and Aitchison 1998). Entitled "Profiling the Profession" (Aitchison 1999) the study had seven initial objectives which were:

1   *To identify the numbers of professional archaeologists working.*

2   *To analyse whether the profession is growing, static or shrinking.*

3   *To identify the range of jobs.*

4   *To identify the numbers employed in each job type.*

5 *To identify the range of salaries and terms and conditions applying to each job type.*

6 *To identify differences in employment patterns between different geographical areas.*

7 *To help those seeking to enter the profession.*
   (Aitchison 1999)

The survey identified 349 relevant organisations and these were divided into 10 categories including 'Archaeological Contractors' and 'Other Commercial Organisations', but also University departments, local government staff and independent consultants. Of the estimated 93 contracting organisations, employing approximately 30% of the total archaeological workforce, 51 responded to the postal questionnaire. This questionnaire required each unit to give details of their work and their staff as it stood on the 16th March 1998. There was some disbelief amongst the staff of commercial organisations when the published results demonstrated that the average salary for all full-time archaeologists was £17,079. This figure is clearly influenced by the inclusion of academic staff, consultants and other more highly paid members of the profession. However this relative distortion of results becomes particularly relevant in comparison with other related occupations.

In Table 2 the archaeological profession occupies a place above construction industry workers, but below the managers and other related specialists. However closer inspection reveals that had 'Builders, building contractors' been put together with 'Managers in building and contracting' – in the same way that all Archaeologists had been lumped together – their average salary would well exceed that of archaeologists. The organisers of the survey could justifiably argue that their aim was not to specifically study any one group within the profession but

PROFESSION	Average gross earnings
University and polytechnic teaching professionals	£30,179
Civil, Structural, municipal, mining and quarrying engineers	£28,286
Architects	£25,882
Town Planners	£25,887
Managers in building and contracting	£25,689
Building, land, mining and 'general practice' surveyors	£24,495
Draughtspersons	£19,745
Scientific technicians	£19,641
Librarians and related professionals	£19,010
Archaeologists	£17,079
Road Construction and maintenance workers	£16,904
Construction trades	£15,512
Builders, building contractors	£15,345
Other building and civil engineering labourers not elsewhere categorised	£13,843

Table 2: Full time salary comparison with other occupations. *(after Aitchison 1999)*

Position	Average full-time salary	Temporary contract	Permanent contract
Site Assistant	£10,094	73%	27%
Supervisor	£12,830	53%	47%
Finds Officer	£14,966	25%	75%
Project Officer	£15,060	43%	57%
Project Manager	£19,434	30%	70%
Director	£22,629	29%	71%
Average of all	**£15,835.5**		

Table 3: Average archaeological salaries. *Data taken from Aitchison 1999*

Position	Average full-time salary	Increase since 1998	Temporary contract	Permanent contract
Site Assistant	£12,140	20.26%	82%	18%
Supervisor	£14,290	11.38%	41%	59%
Finds Officer	£18,422	22.42%	35%	65%
Project Officer	£18,049	19.85%	17%	83%
Project Manager	£22,433	15.43%	12%	88%
Director	£27,148	19.97%	14%	86%
Average of all	**£18,747**	**18.22%**		

Table 4: Average archaeological salaries. *Data taken from Aitchison and Edwards 2003*

to provide an overall picture. It is interesting, however to look at the information relating directly to those employed within the commercial sector of archaeology in March 1998 (see Table 3). Data from the follow-up survey, published four years later (Aitchison and Edwards 2003)[3] do show an encouraging rise in the average full-time salaries over the preceding five years (see Table 4), but this is against a backdrop of substantial increase in other sectors that actually sees a relative fall for the entire archaeological profession in terms of salaries (see Table 5). These figures would seem to suggest that the contracting organisations have been experiencing a period of growth and increased profit, which has been reflected in the salaries of staff. This is perhaps in contrast to the rest of the archaeological profession, which saw a far smaller wage increase in the same period.

There are also interesting statistics relating to age and gender within contracting organisations which demonstrate the relative youth of the profession (77% are aged between 20 and 40 in 1998 and 66% in 2002) and the under representation of females in the commercial workplace. There is a significant female domination of the 'Finds Officer' roles (see Table 6) as previously discussed.

The 2003 study of the Archaeology Labour Market (Aitchison and Edwards 2003) also included, for the first time, data on disabled employees and on the ethnic diversity of the profession. This demonstrated that there is actually very little diversity at all, with 99.34% of archaeologists being white (compared to 92.1% nationally), while only 0.34% of staff were defined as disabled (compared with 19% of the total working population).

[3] *At the time of writing a third survey was in preparation, see Aitchison and Edwards 2008.*

HERITAGE RESEARCH SERIES NO. 1

PROFESSION	Average gross earnings	Increase since 1997/98
University and polytechnic teaching professionals	£34,791	15%
Architects	£34,426	33%
Managers in building and contracting	£33,924	32%
Civil, Structural, municipal, mining and quarrying engineers	£31,527	12%
Building, land, mining and 'general practice' surveyors	£30,275	24%
Town Planners	£27,064	5%
Draughtspersons	£23,227	18%
Scientific technicians	£23,157	18%
Librarians and related professionals	£22,728	18%
Road Construction and maintenance workers	£20,183	19%
Builders, building contractors	£19,277	26%
Archaeologists	£19,161	12%
Construction trades	£18,809	21%
Other building and civil engineering labourers not elsewhere categorised	£17,455	26%

Table 5: Full time salary comparison with other occupations. *(Aitchison and Edwards 2003)*

APPAG

In 2003 the All-Party Parliamentary Archaeology Group (APPAG) published its first report entitled "The Current State of Archaeology in the United Kingdom". Formed in 2001, APPAG advertised for 250 word submissions from organisations and individuals with an interest in archaeology, receiving 267 in total. It also questioned representatives from certain key bodies at a number of committee sessions. The published report was detailed and wide-ranging, with a large number of recommendations – not least that an absence of one, clear, non-governmental lobby group has created a confusing muddle of different voices that results in little being achieved. However, in Part 3, section B, the topic of "Archaeology as a Career" is discussed. It is essential to quote large sections here as this represents, to date, the single most important analysis of the profession by an external body.

> *28. The submissions emphasised the plight of archaeologists as insecurely employed, poorly paid and generally itinerant, as demonstrated by Aitchison's report Profiling the Profession (1999). This is in large part due to the effects of the system of competitive tendering … A mobile casual workforce is inevitably excluded from training opportunities where they do exist. The absence of proper training prohibits promotion to more secure senior posts. There is no clear career development path and, in most cases, neither universities… nor employers appear to consider it their role to prepare archaeologists for professional practice. This is largely due to external financial pressures, with developer funding dominating and contributing sums approaching £75 million per annum; but it is also because archaeology only has a weak professional structure.*

> *29. Although archaeology is a graduate profession this is neither reflected in the career opportunities nor in remuneration. Often those*

Position	Male (1998)	Female (1998)	Male (2002)	Female (2002)
Site Assistant	69%	31%	67%	33%
Supervisor	57%	43%	66%	34%
Finds Officer	27%	73%	36%	64%
Project Officer	68%	32%	69%	31%
Project Manager	79%	21%	77%	23%
Director	75%	25%	72%	28%
Average of all	**62.5%**	**37.5%**	**64.5%**	**35.5%**

Table 6: Gender differentiation within the profession. *Data taken from Aitchison (1999) and Aitchison and Edwards (2003)*

who work in excavation units are treated as site technicians who simply record archaeological deposits rather than as archaeologists who are capable of interpreting them. The current fragmentation of the profession is already exacerbating those problems…

31. … Training is vital if archaeology is to achieve high professional standards and it needs to be linked to career development, providing benchmarks for salaries which reflect the true worth of the multifarious skills of the profession.

Recommendation

32. There is an urgent need to improve pay and conditions for employment in field archaeology so that they are commensurate with graduate entry level in allied professions such as local authority planning officers, civil engineers and university lecturers… In the longer term, the current fragmented commercial unit system which has resulted from competitive tendering should be replaced with a more stable regional, or more local framework of archaeological organisations. (**APPAG 2003**)

Comparisons with horticulture

A survey of other professions reveals that commercial archaeology is not alone in its current predicament. In an article in The Garden, the Journal of the Royal Horticultural Society, Catherine Fitzgerald (2003) comments on the situation in horticulture from the point of view of a student at the RHS Garden, Wisley.

Many people never consider horticulture as a possible career. Perhaps this lack of encouragement is related to the fact that most horticulturalists earn unacceptably low wages. For example, a gardener is unlikely to earn more than £12,000 in the first year of a new job, whilst most head gardener positions attract about £18,000. Compare this with the average UK wage of around £24,000, take into account the training and experience such a position requires, and something is seriously wrong – even when the employer provides accommodation. The benefits of a healthy, relatively stress-free lifestyle are small compensation, but the profession is not always as idyllic as we might like. Gardeners work outside in all weathers, for long hours, often doing monotonous or physically demanding tasks. But for those with passion, interest and commitment, the opportunities are there.

Horticulture is often a vocation more than a career, followed by people who would not want to do anything else, however poor the pay.

The similarities with archaeology are clearly very striking. Tim Hughes (pers. comm.), the Head of Training at the Royal Horticultural Society Garden at Wisley, puts the current situation down to a number of factors. Although horticulture is a broad umbrella, like archaeology, and covers a number of very varied professions from laboratory-based sciences to hard and soft landscaping, the professional gardeners are in much the same position as professional archaeologists. Trainees at Wisley Gardens start on £11,000, while a 'Junior Gardener' earns £14,000. These salaries are slightly higher than average because the RHS is a national organisation. Despite this Mr. Hughes has seen an increase in people in their 30s leaving lucrative jobs in the City to retrain as gardeners. He puts this down to a lifestyle choice and that the perception of gardening is of a low-stress, healthy profession which outweighs the low wages in the minds of many people. The gender split of new entrants is currently approximately 50/50, and ethnically it is predominantly white. It seems that there are fewer women in the higher positions, perhaps leaving a very physical profession to have families. Mr. Hughes suggests that the ethnic make-up is due to the distinctly European origins of gardening and that the culture of the job is only slowly beginning to appeal to a broader section of society. He believes that the motivations for remaining in gardening are the camaraderie, pride in the job and the fact that it is a small, comfortably insular profession. The retention rate of staff in gardening seems to be better than in field archaeology. It seems that those entering into a career in gardening do so with their eyes open and with an awareness of the peculiarities of the job. He also stated that the flexibility and fluidity of the profession and scope for promotion is something that encourages people to remain in the job.

The issue of relevant training is also something that is particularly pertinent. In gardening, 15–20 years ago, one would study for an Ordinary National Diploma (OND). This required one year of practical experience prior to starting the course, followed by one year of college. There was then a further year of practical experience before the final year of college. The contact time at college was 9am to 5am, five days a week, with occasional weekend duties on top. Clearly this produced qualified gardeners with a large amount of practical experience. Today the relevant course is the BTEC National Diploma. This includes no practical experience and the contact time is only 16 hours a week – so students can still claim Income Support if necessary. Ten years ago NVQs were introduced in an attempt to plug the gap in practical experience, but they are not hugely liked within the profession (Hughes pers. comm.). The current feeling amongst the gardening community is that the majority of the training courses focus too much on the theoretical element at the expense of practical skills. This is also the case in archaeology, but the difference is that Further Education courses, such as those available to would-be gardeners are to some extent defined by the industry to ensure that the content is relevant. The current pressure is to increase the practical element so that the current skills shortage can be filled. In archaeology the vast majority of courses are in Higher Education, and the individual universities define these programmes of study. Of course in that situation the driving concern of the university is to fill the courses and to make money.

Mr. Hughes also raised another interesting point with regard to the perception of gardening as a career. Traditionally Careers Advisors at school, when dealing with children who were perhaps weaker academically, would point them towards a 'land-based' career. Equally, archaeology may be glamorised in the minds of the public, but the actual physical act of excavation remains subject to some historic prejudices. Ask someone to name a famous historic gardener and their answer would most likely be one of the renowned designers of large private gardens. The hands-on, physical gardeners were generally servants. Even today advertisements for gardening positions at private houses often include family accommodation and the possibility of domestic work in the main house for the partner (see Horticulture Weekly; www.growing-careers.com; www.englishcountrygardeners. co.uk for examples). So it seems that even qualified and experienced gardeners are still seen very much as part of the system of servitude when it comes to pay and conditions. To quote Tim Hughes "Working with your hands and working with the land is still seen as labouring" and this is equally applicable to field archaeologists.

A tradition of labouring: The Parkers of Heytesbury

Archaeology has a long history of utilising labourers in fieldwork and it is difficult to find fault with Tim Hughes' assessment that this sort of work is still seen as labouring – regardless of the skills, experience and qualifications required. Indeed, it is very interesting to note how little has changed since Colt Hoare and Cunnington conducted their fieldwork in Wiltshire, two hundred years ago. The excavations of William Cunnington (1754–1810) and Sir Richard Colt Hoare (1758–1838) are widely regarded as being pioneering early forays into the field and include the first known use of a trowel in fieldwork. In many respects Cunnington and Colt Hoare were an unlikely pairing. Colt Hoare was a classically educated aristocrat, while Cunnington was a merchant and tradesman who had taught himself about geology and archaeology by reading widely (Cunnington 1975).

As Cunnington and Colt Hoare embarked on their fieldwork the former, charged with managing the day to day activities, took on local labourers. Contemporary practice was to leave the labourers to the hard work and to receive the finds from them afterwards.

> *Cunnington from the first wanted more than this, though he never thought it necessary to be present all the time. He did the next best thing, however, and within a few years had trained two skilled diggers, Stephen and John Parker, on whom he and Hoare might rely to report where and how the finds were made as well as make them.*
> **(Cunnington 1975: 13)**

Having first hired them around the turn of the century, the relationship between Cunnington and the Parkers, a father and son team, is known to have extended beyond purely a work-related one. In 1802 he intervened when Stephen Parker junior, John's brother, was tried and convicted of sheep stealing.

> *Heytesbury March 14th 1802*
>
> *Sir,*
>
> *Compassion to old Parker, the bearer of this, is the cause for my troubling you at this time. His son, Stephen Parker, I understand lays under condemnation in Winchester gaol; and tho' he perhaps justly merits the awful sentence pronounced upon him, yet from the circumstances of his not having been guilty of a murder or those crimes to the State in which case it would be almost criminal to pardon, I sincerely intreat you will in compassion to this much distressed family, have the goodness to speak*

to the judge and endeavour to alter his sentence to transportation.

I am with great respect,

Wm Cunnington.
(Cunnington 1975: 69)

Due in no small part to the weight the words of a man like Cunnington carried, Stephen Parker's sentence was commuted to transportation. This episode aside the first mention of the Parkers in an archaeological context was in one of Cunnington's many letters to Colt Hoare. These letters were essentially reports on the excavations that Cunnington and the Parkers had undertaken, and would later be edited by Colt Hoare to provide a substantial part of the text of Ancient History of North and South Wiltshire which he published in volumes between 1810 and 1819. In November 1804 Cunnington wrote with details of the excavation at Sherrington long barrow

> *Stephen and John have been at work on the Sherrington barrow all last week… Mr Wyndham paid us a visit at the barrow; he was of opinion that this must have been a Saxon barrow. Against this opinion Stephen, and John, and myself entered our protest. We had no objection to the interments on top of the barrow being Saxon or what they pleased; but contended it was a British tumulus. The floor of ashes and charred wood, cist, pieces of pure British pottery found in the barrow, the skeleton of a pig and other animals, also a large bird interred together, influenced us to maintain this opinion in opposition to Mr Wyndham and Mr Lambert.* **(Cunnington 1975: 67–8)**

In an extremely socially stratified age it was not deemed acceptable for the Parkers to be have an "opinion in opposition to two learned gentlemen" (Cunnington 1975) and Colt Hoare edited Cunnington's account to remove this contentious element. Despite this attitude the Parkers were becoming renowned

Figure 27: The Parkers working under the supervision of Cunnington and Colt Hoare from an 1805 watercolour by Philip Crocker called 'Barrow Digging'. *(Reproduced with the permission of Wiltshire Archaeological and Natural History Society)*

and widely respected for their skill. In 1807 Colt Hoare's friend Iremonger was preparing to excavate barrows near Winchester, Hampshire. He had already invited Colt Hoare to join him when he wrote to him again at the end of June.

You will I trust not think me guilty of great intrusion in requesting the assistance of your Wiltshire labourers on this occasion, for my Hampshire men have disgraced themselves by their exorbitant demands; and I am confident the expenses of their journey will be amply repaid by their superior skill and alacrity. **(Cunnington 1975: 107)**

In the light of this letter it is possible to see the team of Colt Hoare, Cunnington and the Parkers as a very early 'contracting unit' in which their expertise was sought and, in at least one instance, paid for. In the context of the 'Ancient Wiltshire' volume and the excavation work that provided the data for it Colt Hoare was, in the modern sense, the Project Manager, Cunnington was the Site Director and John and Stephen Parker were, respectively, the Site Supervisor and Excavator. Writing in 1975 Piggott remarked on their similarity to the research units that were then predominant.

With Hoare as patron, planning the work as a whole, Cunnington as excavation director in the field, Crocker as surveyor and draughtsman, and Stephen and John Parker as skilled diggers, this Georgian archaeological research unit worked for nearly a decade. **(Piggott 1975: 238)**

When extra labourers were required the Parkers were responsible for raising and supervising a team. In this sense it is telling that little or no attention has been paid to the Parkers in modern archaeological historiographies. Despite this it is clear that Colt Hoare and Cunnington held the Parkers in high esteem, largely because of their enthusiasm and aptitude for the work they were undertaking. This is highlighted particularly in another letter from Cunnington to Colt Hoare, dated 25th October 1807.

I was on tiptoe expecting Stephen and John on their arrival with your account of the October meeting. They were highly delighted in narrating their discoveries. Had John found a purse of guineas, he could not have been better pleased. **(Woodbridge 1970: 210)**

It is also highlighted more strikingly in a footnote to the first part of the 'Ancient Wiltshire' series. Colt Hoare had already dedicated it to Cunnington and the hard work he had contributed to the project, but he then takes the unusual step – in the context of the age – and refers to the Parkers directly.

John Parker and his father Stephen, natives of Heytesbury, have been constantly employed by us in all our operations; and to the former we feel much indebted for many interesting discoveries of British settlements and other antiquities. Dr Stukeley has recorded the merits of Reuben Horsall, the town-clerk of Abury; and why should I not do equal justice to those of our Heytesbury pioneers? **(Colt Hoare 1810: 97 quoted in Cunnington 1975: 69)**

The death of William Cunnington marked the end of these excavations and the Parkers presumably returned to their previous lives. John Parker however, as an old man, was able to give Pitt-Rivers information about a barrow he excavated for Cunnington and Colt Hoare (Cunnington 1975:69). To the end of his life and beyond he and his father would remain unsung heroes of the early years of archaeological excavation.

The tradition continues

Of course Cunnington and Colt Hoare were not the only people to employ labourers on archaeological sites. Pitt Rivers utilised large numbers during his work and observed the importance of skilled workmen during excavation, despite an apparently low opinion of the 'moral' character of those in his employ on Cranborne Chase.

> *From 10 to 19 men were employed in the excavations, consisting chiefly of men of the neighbourhood, who happened to be out of employ, and consequently could not be expected to prove themselves amongst the most efficient of their class. No more useful organization could be established for archaeological purposes, than that of a permanent Corps of efficient workmen. So much depends on the intelligence and experience of the men, in observing the seams of soil, the silting, and other deposits, in distinguishing made earth from undisturbed ground, and in recognizing at a glance, whilst turning over the soil, objects that are of value as evidence of date, many of which are overlooked by workmen who are engaged in these operations for the first time, that too much attention cannot be given to the proper training of excavators.*
> **(Pitt Rivers 1892: 23–24)**

Sixty years later another former military man, Sir Mortimer Wheeler, described the structure of the projects of his day in Archaeology from the earth (1954). He also emphasises the importance of skill and experience in his workmen, though deems it to be essential only in the foreman.

> *The foreman is the sergeant-major. He has proved himself as a digger and should be the best workman on the site. He may assist in the uncovering of especially fragile or important objects. But he must, above all things, be by nature capable of controlling his men with fairness and scrupulous fairness… One or more of Sir Leonard Wolley's Iraqi foremen, I believe, used to travel voluntarily some hundreds of miles every year across the desert in order to rejoin his old chief's staff during subsequent work near Antioch. Such friendships are amongst the highest reward that a director can desire. They bridge the class-room and help to link inferred fact with basic earthy knowledge.*
> **(Wheeler 1954: 139)**

In Braidwood's account of the planning of an archaeological expedition in Iraq, she reveals a more insidious view of the workmen.

> *There were other villages in the past that produced skilled diggers. But their people, unlike the Shergatis, were not used for excavation work during the war. Consequently, none of the younger generation had an opportunity to learn how to dig and the villages lost their tradition. The Shergatis are now, to all intents and purposes, a closed guild of craftsmen. They are likeable people as individuals and they are*

competent. As a group, however, they have a large nuisance value: they feel they are indispensable and thus make many demands on a dig. **(Braidwood 1959: 71)**

Even more recent works on archaeology hark back to these days to emphasise the new 'professional' status of archaeologists in contrast to the labourers of old.

Archaeology has come a long way since the days of the grog-swilling, barrow-digging men. Archaeologists now find themselves not only in their traditional bastions, the universities and museums, but also in county planning departments, computer centres and construction camps. But the professionals are only the tip of the iceberg – a mere 500 or so of them in the British Isles. **(Miles 1978: 109)**

"No-one knows the labourer" (Sturt 1912)

The irony of the current situation in commercial archaeology appears to be that educated 'professionals', often from Middle Class families, are not only perceived as an element of the 'Labouring' class, but also freely adopt some of their characteristics. The relationship between the Middle and Working Classes has, of course, been a source of conflict and unease for almost as long as they have existed.

The elements of bitter class war frequently mark the attitude of middle-class people towards the labouring class. It seems to be forgotten that the men are English. One hears of them spoken as an alien and objectionable race, worth nothing but to be made to work... By becoming wage earners solely, the villagers have fallen into the disfavour of the middle-classes, most of whom have no desire than to keep them in a sufficient state of servility to be useful... The animus of which I am speaking is almost a commonplace. In truth, I have heard it expressed dozens of times, in dozens of ways... that the English labouring classes are a lower order of beings, who must be treated accordingly. **(Sturt 1912 quoted in Snell 1985: 8)**

It is appropriate to begin this section with a quote from Sturt, a Middle Class socialist (Sturt 1941: 52). From his position as an employer and neighbour to the 'labouring class' George Sturt, under the pen name George Bourne, writes *Change in the Village* in 1912. He has a particularly insightful view of the lives of the ordinary people around him and, despite a certain historical naivety of his own, goes some way to correcting the romanticised images created by Hardy and other contemporary writers.

A reader of [Hardy's] *'The Dorsetshire labourer' (1883) would imagine that the massive yearly turnover of population described there, at the time of the yearly hiring fair, was a near universal experience of labour in late nineteenth-century Dorset. But this would be quite misplaced. Even in the hey-day of the yearly hiring system, in the early eighteenth century, it had been the unmarried farm-servants who were generally hired by the year. Married men (in eighteenth-century terms, 'labourers') settled for the more precarious employment of a day or weekly hiring, although remaining far more immobile than unmarried labour. Certain classes of married farm labour (eg shepherds or carters) might still be yearly hired – but they were the exception.* **(Snell 1985: 394)**

HERITAGE RESEARCH SERIES NO. 1

53

Sturt argues that a shift from a peasant economy based around the common land to a wage earning, labouring life has forever changed the lives of the people, but also the structure of the village. Beginning with the enclosure of the common land the position of the 'peasants' becomes increasingly precarious. Previously they were able to keep cattle and had time to grow their own crops in sufficient quantities that a regular income was not required. The 'peasant' was therefore often self-supporting, or rather the community of peasants was, and the perception of them and their role in the wider society was coloured by this. Subsequently they become 'wage-earners' and consumers. Their position in the community is now firmly established as being at the bottom of a system of consumption that today characterises our own society. They become dependant on others for their livelihood and welfare, whether that be through employment or the often inadequate provisions available to them during times of hardship and ill-health.

> To a greater or lesser extent, most of them were already wage-earners, though not regularly. If a few had been wont to furnish themselves with money in true peasant fashion – that is to say, by selling their goods, their butter, or milk, or pig-meat, instead of their labour – still, the majority had wanted for their own use whatever they could produce in this way, and had been obliged to sell their labour itself, when they required money. Wage-earning, therefore, was no new thing in the village; only, the need to earn became more insistent, when so many more things than before had to be bought with the wages. Consequently, it had to be approached in a more businesslike, a more commercial, spirit. Unemployment, hitherto not much worse than a regrettable inconvenience, became a calamity. Every hour's work acquired a market value. The sense of taking part in time-honoured duties of the countryside disappeared before the idea – so very important now – of getting shillings with which to go to a shop.
> **(Sturt 1912: 89)**

It seems in some way that Sturt is characterising the shift in perceptions of 'productivity' as the main reason for the apparent decline in the stature of the labouring class. The intimate knowledge of rural/agricultural ways - and the often romantic view held by Sturt that they were in some way part of the soil and seasons upon which they relied – is replaced by the daily struggle to pay bills and buy food. Clearly it is hard to believe him in his description of an apparently idyllic village life prior to enclosure. It does seem that there may, however, be some truth in the shift that he describes in the capacity for the peasants to support themselves, and consequently the way in which others perceived them within the community.

His relationship with one labourer in particular, Bettesworth his aging gardener, is described in much detail in *Memoirs of a Surrey Labourer* (1907). In this we discover that Fred Bettesworth, like many of his generation and 'class' has turned his hands to most things over the years. He enlisted as a young man to fight in the Crimea, something he hesitates to discuss – particularly with regard to a little trouble he got into when going into the French lines in search of rum. He has also worked many years in gravel pits, with horse and donkey carts and in the building trade. By the time the book was written he is an elderly man, struggling to care for his wife who is infirm and forced, against his nature, to seek parish relief for the cost of placing her in the local infirmary where she eventually dies. The details of many conversations between Sturt and Bettesworth are related and one forms an impression of mutual respect. Clearly Sturt is constrained by his social position in his understanding of some of the issues and he apologises to his readers when discussing Bettesworth's predilection for 'a glass of beer' – lest they be offended. Sturt also describes, however, Bettesworth's sense of community and propriety. On one winter's day, Bettesworth, exhausted already through caring for his wife and his regular work in Sturt's garden, attempts to persuade a group of younger men to help him spread sand in the icy lane.

> *February 13th 1900*
>
> *Already he had done a longish piece of it himself, but much remained to do. Several men had 'went up reg'lar busters,' and 'children and young gals' on their way to church had fallen down. It would be a public service to besprinkle the path with sand. So Bettesworth made his suggestion to his neighbours – 'four or five of 'em'. They was hangin' about: hadn't nothin' to do.' But no. They shrugged their shoulders and walked away. It was no business of theirs. They even laughed at the old man for the trouble he had already taken, for which no one would pay him. And now, in telling me about it, it was his neighbours' want of public spirit that annoyed him. They had not come up to his standard of the behaviour meet for a labouring man.*
> **(Sturt 1907)**

It is also obvious, however, that Bettesworth is no angel. In his youth he was quick to use his fists, and even now he is able to 'put down' a lout who accosts him in the public house. Yet what comes through most strongly is his essential decency and worth. Sturt describes him as ill educated and often ignorant of world events, but he is not a stupid man (he expresses regret that he never learned how to read). When his curiosity is roused, as it is by reports from the Boer War and Nansen's voyage in the newspapers he follows events keenly, despite having to have them read out to him. He describes how his visit to the public house on a Sunday night is his way of 'enlightening his mind' and here the local labouring men swap advice on crops. He is also a repository of knowledge about the village of Bourne, its populace and the agricultural practices that had so long been a part of everyday life. He sees the changes in employment practices and rails against the apparent decline of skills and trades. He also witnesses the changes coming, as old ways die, replaced by incomers from the towns ignorant of what had passed before.

> *October 7th 1899*
>
> *With a rapidly increasing population empty cottages are scarce, as Bettesworth now found. Moreover, his choice was restricted. There were reasons against his going to the upper end of the valley. It was more newly peopled by labourers from the town, who had never know, or else had lost, the older peasant traditions which Bettesworth could still cherish – in memory, at least – here in the more ancient part of the village. Of course, that was not how he explained his distaste; he only expressed a dislike for the society of the upper valley. 'They be a roughish lot up there,' he would say.*
> **(Sturt 1907)**

In his later years, being unable to adequately look after his ailing wife and their home, he becomes a disreputable figure – particularly amongst the women – on account of the extreme sordidness of both. At the end, however, having been taken in and looked after by his nephew's family, he is visited by a number of 'gentlefolk' who have heard what a proud and (generally) upstanding man he was when younger. A Colonel residing in Bourne, who hears of his Crimean service, goes out of his way to arrange a veteran's pension for him and another gentleman has whiskey delivered to him (for medicinal purposes). Sturt himself promises the old man that he will pay him enough of a pension to keep him out of the workhouse when it becomes clear that he is too frail to continue working and visits him every few days as he lies dying. Bettesworth's standing amongst the labouring men at all times seems to remain high and he is regarded with respect by most of them. He eventually dies on 25th July 1905.

> *July 28 (Friday)*
>
> *… A week earlier…when I parted from him, he seemed too ill to take his money – too unconscious, I mean. I offered it to his niece, standing at the foot of the bed; but she said, glancingly meaningfully towards him, 'I think he'd like to take it, sir.' So I turned to him and put the shillings into his hand, which he held up limply. 'Your wages,' I said.*
>
> *For a moment he grasped the silver, then it dropped out on to his bare chest and slid under the bed-gown, whence I rescued it, and, finding his purse under the pillow, put his last wages away safely there.*
> **(Sturt 1907)**

George Sturt was not the first to attempt to understand the lives of labourers, though he was the most successful of his contemporaries. Fifty years before Sturt began his journals, Crewe (1843) wrote that the changes in the Poor Law and subsequent 'means testing' meant that a "very unjust and unfavourable opinion of the character, habits and practices of the Agricultural Poor would be created at their expense". Around that time Somerville was undertaking interviews with labourers and published a series of insightful dialogues in 1852. In this example he is talking with a road labourer who is earning eight shillings a week.

> *'It be not much, be it?'*
>
> *'No, it is not much. How do you manage to live?'*
>
> *'Not well; and there be three more – wife and two children. We had another boy, but he died two weeks aback; as fine a boy as you could wish to see he wur, and as much thought on by his mother and I; but we ben't sorry he be gone. I hopes he be happy in heaven. He ate a smart deal; and many a times, like all on us, went with a hungry belly. Ah! We may love our children never so much, but they be better gone; one hungry belly makes a difference where there ben't enough to eat…'*
>
> *'you must have a very hard struggle to keep yourselves alive?'*
>
> *'Ees, hard enough. It makes one think on doing what one would never do, but for hunger…'*
>
> *'He, the late Lord I mean, was a clergyman – was he not?'*
>
> *'I've heard he wur once, but I don't know much of what he wur, 'cept that he transported me.'*
>
> *'Transported you! What for?'*

'For poaching. I got seven year; and wur killed near almost. And they killed my brother at once – knocked his skull to pieces.'

'Who – the gamekeepers I suppose? Did you make much resistance?'

'No; I heard them fall on my brother, and I wur fifty yards from him. And when I wur hiding, they came and took hold on me, and beat in my skull. Here you can feel with your hand; out of that part, and this, and this, eleven pieces of bone were taken. I never wur expected to live for a long time. No, I never made no resistance; for they had broken my head and killed my brother afore I knew they saw me...'

He wishes, he says, and prays to God, that he could now for himself and family at home have such an allowance of food as he had in the West Indies when a convict.

'We had a terrible good living', this was his expression, 'by as ever I had for working in England. Fresh beef three times a-week, pork and peas four times a-week... father died soon as I wur gone – one son killed, and me a'most, and then transported, wur too much for him to stand. Ah! He wur broken hearted...'
(Somerville 1852: 37 quoted in Snell 1985: 384)

This excerpt highlights not only the extreme hardships faced by many of the 'labouring poor' in that period, but also the value of asking the right questions of the right people if one is to understand those hardships. Somerville, one can reasonably assume, was not only in the minority by virtue of his desire to understand the lives of labourers, but also because of his methodology, which went far beyond the purely observational.

Conclusion

Qualitative work such as Somerville's interviews and Sturt's observations of Bettesworth's later life are early examples of the kind of sociological research that was undertaken with commercial archaeologists for this study, and which will be presented in detail in the following chapters. Important to note, however, is the fact that it was not intended in this chapter to claim that site-based staff are 'merely' labourers. On the contrary, the intention was to demonstrate that, traditionally, archaeological fieldwork has often been discounted as 'merely' digging. Tim Hughes' (pers. comm.) comment that "Working with your hands and working with the land is still seen as labouring" is a wonderfully succinct summary of the situation. The actual process of excavation is often grossly underestimated and rarely, if ever, granted the standing of a 'specialism'. In actual fact it is highly specialised. Stephen and John Parker's social status meant that they could never, even if they wanted to, escape the 'Labouring Class'. Yet their training, experience and expertise meant that they were the foremost field archaeologists of their day. They were the first and archetypal 'Invisible Diggers'.

PART
TWO

CHAPTER THREE
Profiling the Vocation

Figure 28: The science.
© *Jon Hall*

Introduction

In order to ensure that this research was grounded in a detailed understanding of the profession it was important to augment the qualitative data obtained through semi-structured interviews and participant observation with quantitative data gathered from a questionnaire-based survey of professional, commercial archaeologists. The objective of obtaining representative data was addressed by encouraging individual archaeologists to respond, rather than by asking each unit to complete one questionnaire regarding all their staff. The latter was the method used in both Institute of Field Archaeologists' (IFA) surveys of the profession (Aitchison 1999; Aitchison and Edwards 2003), see Chapter Two – which has resulted in a suspicion amongst site staff that the under 30s were under-represented in both these surveys – being overlooked as 'temporary' staff. This issue was addressed by creating an online survey and encouraging participants to take part, the result being that a more accurate profile of the profession has been generated.

Previous surveys

The IFA's surveys of British archaeologists (Aitchison 1999; Aitchison and Edwards 2003) and the Society for American Archaeology's survey of its members (Zeder 1997) provide interesting insights into the profession, with many aspects shared by UK and American archaeologists. For example, Aitchison and Edwards (2003) demonstrate that the staff in UK commercial organisations are 64.29% male and 35.37% female. Zeder's (1997) figures for US professional archaeologists (ie all non-student archaeologists) are 64% male and 36% female. A male dominated profession might be expected, but it is impossible to satisfactorily account for these near identical figures on both sides of the Atlantic. Morris (1992), reporting the results of the IFA's 'Equal Opportunities in Archaeology Working Party' survey, also states that women account for only 35% of archaeological staff in Britain. She suggests that the problem lies in explicit and implicit sexism in the archaeological workplace, with few women achieving promotion to management positions. This is perhaps due to a perception that men are physically and mentally better equipped for excavation, while women tend to be best suited to finds work. Morris suggests that this state of affairs, combined with a widespread feeling that promotion to management should be achieved through extensive field experience, means that senior posts are largely male-dominated.

In both the UK and USA the ethnic diversity of staff is also a concern, with very few archaeologists reporting a non-European ancestry. 99.34% of all British archaeologists in the IFA survey were white, while 98% of the SAA's respondents classed themselves as being of European descent. That does include, however, the 9% who answered 'other', the majority of which Zeder believes to be Canadians objecting to the classification of 'European American'. Benjamin (2003) notes that "Black and Asian students number 69 out of 1940 students on archaeology, heritage and museum related courses [in the UK], just 3.55%." He suggests that this is largely due to the perceived lack of relevance to those individuals and communities of white, European heritage. Benjamin also notes that Black and Asian undergraduates are statistically more likely to study subjects that lead to stable, well paid careers.

The methodology of each survey was quite different, with the IFA sending questionnaires to each organisation employing archaeologists and asking for all their staff to be listed on one form, while the SAA sent a questionnaire to each of its members. Some in the IFA now believe that many of their responses did not include junior staff on 'fixed term' contracts, as the managers of some units did not see them as anything more than temporary staff and thus they were not included on the form. Zeder also concedes that

> Our sample of private sector archaeologists comes primarily from the ranks of mid- to upper-level management. Strikingly absent are crew members, crew chiefs, and field directors, despite the likelihood that these people out number higher-level managers. It is further likely that crew positions are filled by younger people (both students and nonstudents) just starting out in their careers in archaeology. Apparently

these people tend not to join the SAA. The disenfranchisement of this possibly quite sizable group of archaeologists from the major professional organization of the discipline is an important topic. **(Zeder 1997: 11–12)**

In order to produce a more comprehensive understanding of the profession it is clear that efforts need to be made to include junior staff in such a survey. This issue of inclusivity and, therefore, ensuring a response from a representative sample was a prime concern in the design and advertising of the survey undertaken for this study.

Methodology

The first step in collecting data for the online survey was to establish a web space. Having already subscribed to Yahoo! Geocities for personal web space it was decided to utilise the extra space available there to create a dedicated 'Invisible Diggers' website. The domain name www.invisiblediggers.net was purchased from oneandone.co.uk and an option called URL masking was selected, which essentially redirects the browser to the real website whilst retaining the domain name in the address bar. These decisions were made predominantly due to cost considerations. The website was advertised in "The Digger" Newsletter, on the "BAJR" website, in "RESCUE News" (Everill 2003a, 2003b) and in flyers which were sent to every commercial unit in the UK for which an address could be found.

The first stage of the on-line presence was launched on the 15th March 2003. Initially it functioned as a 'guest book' underneath an outline of the research. It was hoped that a brief introduction to the project would encourage archaeologists to speak freely about the situation they found themselves in and to raise points regarding the future directions in which they hoped commercial archaeology might develop. It soon became clear that this was too open-ended, and a number of archaeologists replied that they were not sure what information was actually sought. Thus the result was that, despite having 825 hits on the website in the first month, the actual number of 'submissions' was disappointingly low. Having originally discounted the idea of a questionnaire approach – feeling that any survey that involved check-boxes and yes/no answers might be seen as leading people towards certain responses – a compromise option was chosen in October 2003 and the website was relaunched. This time a series of basic demographic and professional questions were included that would, at the very least, give an idea of which sections of the profession had which opinions towards their job. When selecting the phrasing of certain key demographic questions the objective of providing data directly comparable with the most recent IFA data was always borne in mind. Underneath those questions a 'comments' box was included with the hope that some of the questions might provoke participants to think about their careers and their expectations sufficiently to want to provide more detail. This approach was much more successful and in the first nine months there were over 130 responses (by then the website had received 2,145 hits since the very first launch). The IFA suggests that 2358 archaeologists work in commercial organisations in the UK, but these include non-academic educational and other service providers (Aitchison and Edwards 2003: 20). My estimate of about 2,100 staff employed within commercial units in 2003 is based purely on data from 'contracting' organisations provided by Current Archaeology magazine and individual unit's websites. If that figure is accurate 130 responses represented a

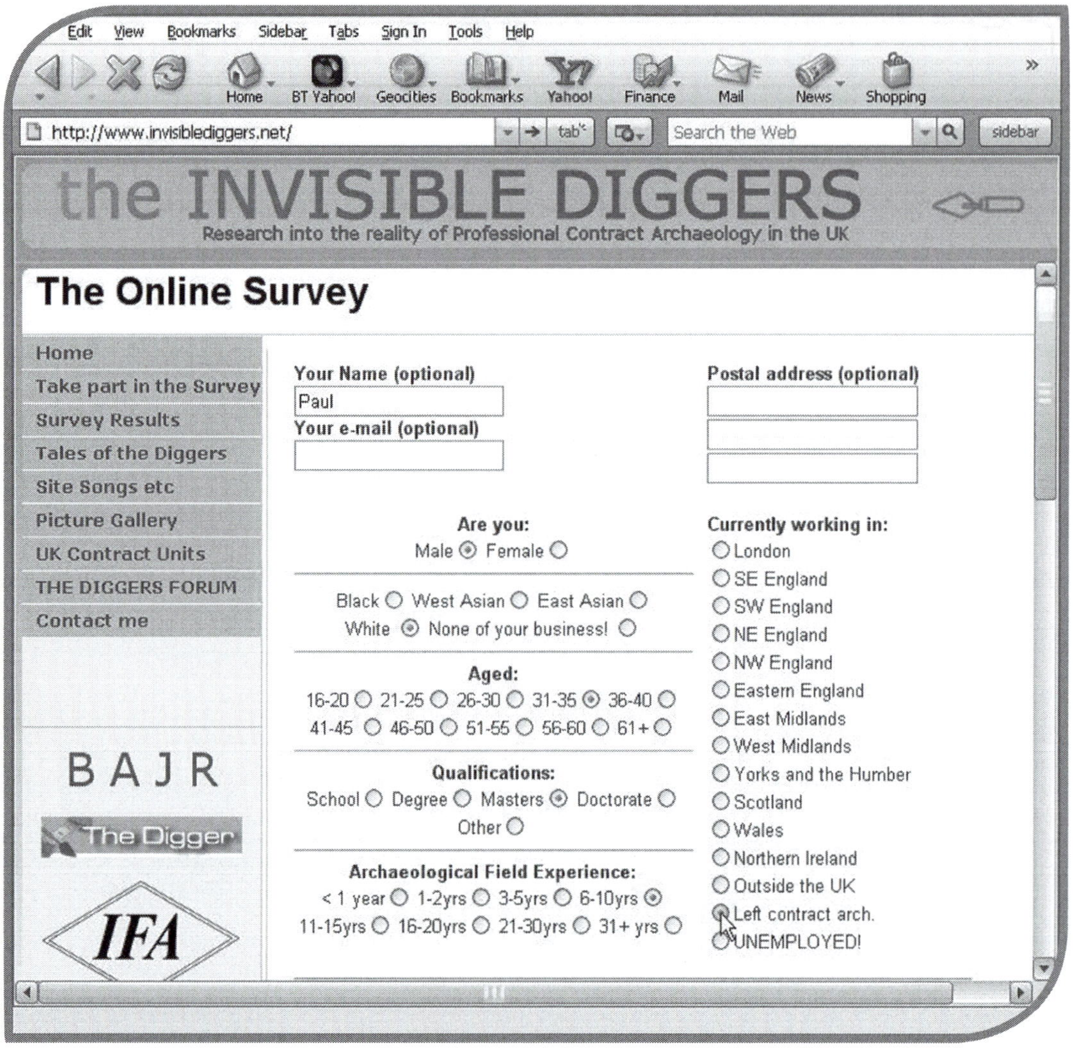

Figure 29: Screenshot of online survey. *(part one)*

healthy 6.19% sample. By the time the online survey was closed down in June 2005 the website had received almost 3,500 hits with 329 survey responses representing a statistically significant 15.67% sample of the profession.

Over that two year period the website evolved to include a series of site songs sent in by archaeologists as well as interim results from the survey and excerpts from written submissions. The format of the website also improved over that period, gaining a coherence which perhaps it did not have to start with. Always central to the website, however, was the Online Survey. This was a fairly simple HTML form that participants could complete and then submit. Figures 29, 30 and 31 show the options available.

By clicking the 'SUBMIT' button their selections were coded and e-mailed to a project address in the following format:

> Name = x
> Gender = Male
> Race = White
> Age = 31–35yrs old
> Qualifications = Masters
> Arch Experience = 3–5yrs
> Currently working in = SE England
> IFA Membership = Yes (AIFA)
> Union Membership = Yes (Prospect)

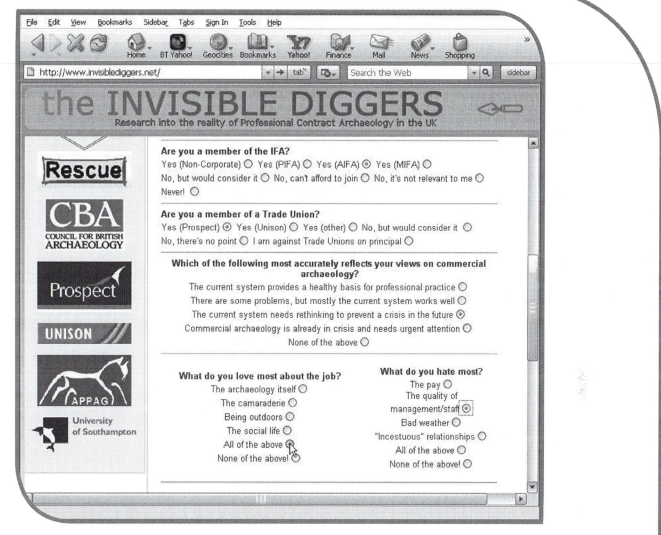

Figure 30: Screenshot of online survey. *(part two)*

Views on commercial arch. = It's in crisis

Job pros = All of the above

Job cons = All of the above

one word or phrase summary of archaeology = Bloody good fun!

How much longer do you intend to work in commercial archaeology?
= I'm trying to get out now!

Comments = It's the people you work with that often make or break
a site, and sometimes the only thing that gets you through the winter
is the camaraderie and the "après–dig" spirit that is still around in some
units.

subject = 'Invisible Diggers' Survey Results

REMOTE_HOST: 152.78.89.83

Having received the data the forms were saved in a Microsoft Word document.
The 'free text' submissions were retained as a separate MS Word Document,
and excerpts from these submissions are discussed in Chapter Four. The coded
demographic data was entered into a Microsoft Access database so that queries
could be run to analyse the data and pull out significant relationships and this
forms the basis of this chapter.

Statistically speaking, 329 responses means that there is a 95% confidence that
the margin of error is +/− 5.4% (Table 7). This means, in practice, that if 50%

HERITAGE RESEARCH SERIES NO. 1

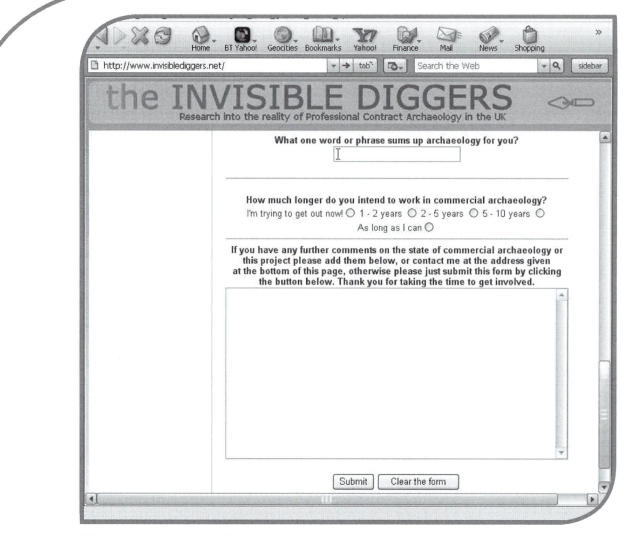

Figure 31: Screenshot of online survey. *(part three)*

of the respondents answer positively to a question in the survey, there is a 95% certainty that the actual percentage that feel that way lies between 44.6% and 55.4%. Tom Vannozzi, Lead Consultant with 'The Leading Edge Market Research', was approached for a professional assessment of the survey results and stated that a sample this size would be considered of real value in a standard Market Research study. In fact, had the survey achieved 1000 responses the margin of error at this confidence would only drop to 3%. This highlights not only the effectiveness of this approach, but also more importantly, the accuracy of the results in comparison to previous surveys of the profession. The only aspect that needs to be considered is that, because it was possible to take part in the survey over a prolonged period, these results do not reflect a 'snapshot' of the profession over a week in one given year. However Mr. Vannozzi states that

> *In fact this is a positive as it ensures that the responses to the survey were not swayed by any short-term environmental factors. That is to say, if something had happened which might effect the views of the archeological community over a short term period (such as a negative news story for example) then that could have a disproportionate effect on the survey results. By having a long survey period, the short-term impact of events is ironed out and the results could be seen as being more accurate.* (**Tom Vannozzi, pers comm**)

		At 95% confidence margin of error	At 99% confidence margin of error
Sample size:	329		
Percentage:	5	2.4%	3.1%
Percentage:	10	3.2%	4.3%
Percentage:	20	4.3%	5.7%
Percentage:	30	5.0%	6.6%
Percentage:	50	5.4%	7.2%

Table 7: The 'margins of error' for the online survey results.

The Results

Age, gender, ethnicity and geographical location

The questions that dealt with the basic demographic data produced some very interesting results, although they fall broadly within the range that one might have expected. The gender bias in the profession correlates almost exactly with the IFA's own figures (Table 8), but the ages (Table 9) − and in particular analysis of age by gender (Table 10) − demonstrate a different profile within the profession. This survey suggests quite clearly that the under 30s were massively under represented in the IFA survey. It is possible that that age group were more motivated to take part in this project and are thus over represented here. However, with an average number of years commercial field experience of 7.49 years, an average age of 32.37 years, and taking into account the predicted 'margin of error', the respondents to this survey are much more likely to be representative of the entire workforce.

Being able to study the under 30s in detail for the first time produces some fascinating results. Despite the profession being almost two thirds male, it seems that the 'under 25' age group is predominantly female. This was certainly a common perception of commercial archaeology, but until now it was not possible to demonstrate it statistically. It is also possible to show the relative youth of the profession, and the relative rate at which male and female staff leave. Figure 32 shows quite clearly that the number of female staff drops off at a reasonably rapid, but constant rate from the early 20s to about the early 40s when it levels off. There is a slight increase in numbers in the 46–50 age group before it continues to fall off, but less steeply. This increase, against the general trend, might be a result of the influx of staff during the Manpower Services Commission's involvement in archaeology and will be discussed later. By contrast the profile for male staff shows that there are more in the 26–30 age group. Although the number also decreases

			IFA data on commercial organisations (Aitchison and Edwards 2003)
MALE	212	64.44%	64.29%
FEMALE	117	35.56%	35.37%

Table 8: The gender bias, compared to data in Aitchison and Edwards 2003.

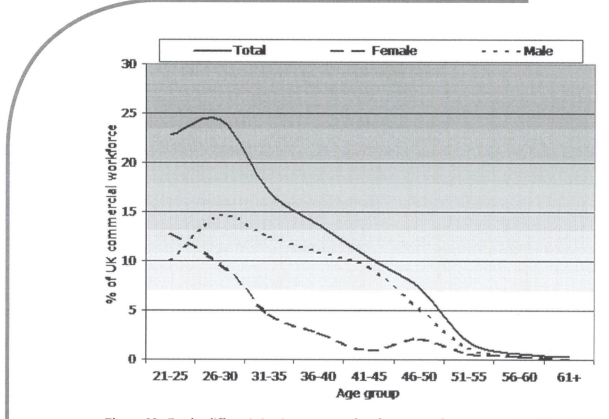

Figure 32: Gender differentiation in contract archaeology across the age ranges. *(see Table 10)*

with age, it is not until their early 40s that the rate of decline is as steep as that for women in their 20s. This levels off slightly from the early 50s.

There are a number of possible reasons why women leave the profession at a faster rate than men, especially during their 20s and 30s, though it must be assumed that starting a family figures very highly. It may also be possible that some female staff see less of a future for themselves in the profession than their male colleagues, because of the nature of the work or because of perceived or actual sexual discrimination (Morris 1992; Lucas 2001b: 7–8). With the data available it is only possible to speculate on this issue. Similarly the responses to the question of ethnicity are largely open to interpretation. The data from this survey (Table 11) supports the IFA's analysis that the profession is overwhelmingly white. This may be due to a number of factors. However, it seems likely that Benjamin (2003) is correct in his assessment that archaeology is perceived as a white, middle class interest that does not encourage the participation of other ethnic or social groups. It is also seen as having a low value in terms of a stable career and earning potential, which may discourage ethnic minority students from families that encourage high professional achievement. Sadly, despite a few initiatives to encourage greater participation, the entire heritage sector is often seen as concerned only with 'white' heritage.

The geographical spread of the UK workforce is also largely as one might expect (Table 12). The English Heritage regions (plus Scotland, Wales and Northern Ireland) were used in the IFA survey and here, but direct comparison with the IFA's data is not possible. The online survey also included responses from those who listed themselves as unemployed, as well as a number currently working outside the UK or who did simply not answer that question. However, broadly speaking, both sets of data tell the same story. Around a fifth of UK commercial archaeologists were currently working in southeast England. This, of course, correlates to the greater number of planning applications in that region (Darvill and Russell 2002). This

AGE	TOTAL		Age range totals	IFA data on commercial organisations (Aitchison and Edwards 2003)	
	Number	%			%
16–20	1	0.3%	0.3%	< 20	0%
21–25	75	22.80%	47.12%	20–29	31%
26–30	80	24.32%			
31–35	56	17.02%	30.7%	30–39	35%
36–40	45	13.68%			
41–45	34	10.33%	17.62%	40–49	25%
46–50	24	7.29%			
51–55	6	1.82%	2.43%	50–59	8%
56–60	2	0.61%			
61+	1	0.3%	0.3%	> 60	1%

Table 9: The age of commercial archaeologists, compared to data in Aitchison and Edwards 2003.

AGE	TOTAL		FEMALE		MALE	
	Number	%	Number	%	Number	%
16–20	1	0.3%	1	0.3%	0	0%
21–25	75	22.80%	42	12.77%	33	10.03%
26–30	80	24.32%	32	9.73%	48	14.59%
31–35	56	17.02%	15	4.56%	41	12.46%
36–40	45	13.68%	9	2.73%	36	10.94%
41–45	34	10.33%	3	0.91%	31	9.42%
46–50	24	7.29%	7	2.13%	17	5.17%
51–55	6	1.82%	2	0.61%	4	1.22%
56–60	2	0.61%	1	0.3%	1	0.3%
61+	1	0.3%	0	0%	1	0.3%

Table 10: The age of commercial archaeologists by gender.

data suggests that the rest of the regions are in three groups: those with 7% to 9% of the workforce (southwest England, London, Scotland, Yorkshire & Humberside and the East Midlands); those with 3% to 5% (northeast England, northwest England, Eastern England and the West Midlands); and Wales and Northern Ireland with less than 2%. An astonishing 9.12% of survey respondents were unemployed at the time they submitted their form, though three quarters of them were trying to stay in the profession (see the section on career plans below).

Field experience and qualifications

Any survey of commercial archaeologists should include educational background and experience in the field and the data generated by these aspects of this survey

ETHNICITY			IFA data on all archaeologists (Aitchison and Edwards 2003)
Black	0	0%	0.18%
W Asian	0	0%	(South Asian) 0.05%
E Asian	1	0.30%	0.14%
White	291	88.45%	99.34%
Blank	4	1.22%	
No Response	33	10.03%	

Table 11: Ethnicity of commercial archaeologists, compared to data in Aitchison and Edwards 2003.

CURRENTLY WORKING IN...	Number	Percentage of total	IFA data on commercial organisations (Aitchison and Edwards 2003)
SE England	64	19.45%	21%
SW England	29	8.81%	15%
London	27	8.21%	15%
Scotland	25	7.60%	7%
Yorks & Humber	24	7.29%	8%
E Midlands	23	6.99%	5%
NE England	15	4.56%	7%
NW England	13	3.95%	5%
E England	12	3.65%	2%
W Midlands	10	3.04%	4%
Wales	6	1.82%	8%
N. Ireland	3	0.91%	1%
Unemployed	30	9.12%	
Others (inc. blanks)	48	14.59%	

Table 12: Geographical spread of respondents.

has been particularly interesting. Having already discussed the age profile of the profession, analysis of the number of years of field experience (Table 13) further establishes that the vast majority of commercial archaeologists leave the profession after only a few years. Furthermore, despite now being in a minority, those with school or other non-Higher Education qualifications have by far the greatest average number of years field experience (Tables 14 and 15). Figure 33 shows graphically the dramatic drop in staff numbers after five years experience. This correlates to the similar drop in numbers from the late 30s onwards seen in Figure 32. It may be surmised that it is often at this stage of their career that junior site staff are considering promotion or leaving the profession altogether. It is also very interesting to note that the general trend – ie that staff numbers are inversely proportional to field experience, and that the archaeological profession

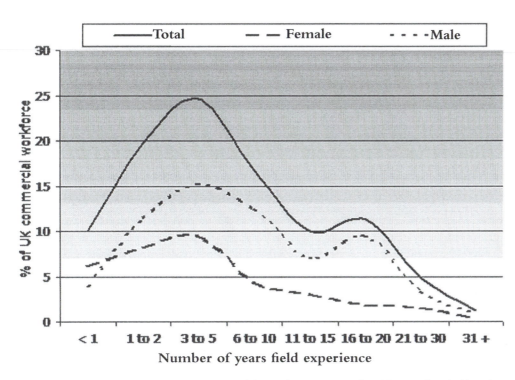

Figure 33: Field experience within the workforce, shown as a total and by gender. *(Table 13)*

has a more or less pyramidal structure to it – has an exception at the 16 to 20 years field experience stage.

Though one can not be certain, it seems possible that this represents those archaeologists who entered the profession during the Manpower Services Commission era, when staff numbers were at their highest, and have subsequently retained their employment – and their interest – against the general trend. Certainly the dates coincide and it seems the most likely explanation. However, it is clear from Figure 33 that this group are predominantly male, yet in Figure 32 there is a similar increase in female staff, against the trend, within the 46–50 year old age group. It is plausible that this may also reflect the MSC era (though it may be women returning to work once their children have grown up) and it might indicate that while male staff from that period remained in the field, accruing more experience, many of their female contemporaries subsequently shifted to specialism-based work.

FIELD EXPERIENCE	TOTAL		FEMALE		MALE	
	Number	%	Number	%	Number	%
<1yr	33	10.03%	20	6.08%	13	3.95%
1–2 yrs	65	19.76%	27	8.21%	38	11.55%
3–5 yrs	81	24.62%	31	9.42%	50	15.20%
6–10 yrs	55	16.72%	14	4.26%	41	12.46%
11–15 yrs	33	10.03%	10	3.04%	23	6.99%
16–20 yrs	37	11.25%	6	1.82%	31	9.42%
21–30 yrs	16	4.86%	5	1.52%	11	3.34%
31 + yrs	4	1.22%	1	0.30%	3	0.91%

Table 13: Commercial field experience shown as a total and by gender.

QUALIFICATIONS OF COMMERCIAL STAFF			IFA data on professional archaeologists (*Aitchison and Edwards 2003*)
DEGREE	159	48.33%	58%
MASTERS	113	34.35%	21%
PhD	17	5.17%	10%
OTHER	14	4.26%	–
SCHOOL	13	3.95%	10%

Table 14: Education of commercial staff, compared to data in Aitchison and Edwards 2003.

FIELD EXPERIENCE and QUALIFICATIONS	Number of individuals	Years field experience (*Total*)	Years field experience (*Average*)
SCHOOL	13	163	12.54
OTHER	14	156	11.14
PhD	17	163	9.59
DEGREE	159	1197	7.53
MASTERS	113	707	6.26
NO RESPONSE	13	79	6.08
All Participants	**329**	**2465**	**7.49**

Table 15: Commercial field experience of staff related to their education.

IFA and trade union membership

In this section the intention was to gauge the level of support for the Institute of Field Archaeologists and for the movement toward unionisation which has gathered some momentum in recent years. Opinion towards both seems greatly divided (Table 16). Although 35.26% are members of the IFA, 34.64% expressed negative feelings towards the organisation, ranging from being unable to afford the membership fees, not considering it relevant to them or outright refusal to even consider it. Only fractionally more than one in every four commercial archaeologists under the age of 30 are members of the IFA (Table 17). Having already established that this represents nearly half of the workforce the IFA could be said to be an inverted pyramid, with MIFA ('Member of the IFA' – normally Project Officers and above) over-represented and PIFA ('Practitioner of the IFA' – ie junior site staff) grossly under-represented. The 31–40 age group is more representative of the national figures with 34.65% being members, while of the 41–50 and 51–60 age groups about half are members. Regionally, Wales stands out with the highest percentage membership of the IFA, though the disproportionately low response rate from archaeologists based in Wales might make this figure unreliable (Table 18). This may also be the case with regard to the data from Northern Ireland, which produced no IFA Members at all. Interestingly, of the top five regions for the size of the archaeological workforce (Table 12), only Scotland figures in the top five regions for membership of the IFA.

The data relating to Trade Union membership is similarly revealing (Tables 19 and 20) as only 27.36% answered that they were in Prospect, Unison or another

ARE YOU A MEMBER OF THE IFA? (TOTAL 116 – 35.26% YES)		
Yes – Non corporate	13	3.95%
Yes – PIFA	31	9.42%
Yes – AIFA	37	11.25%
Yes – MIFA	35	10.64%
Would consider	98	29.79%
Can't afford to join	44	13.37%
Not relevant	41	12.46%
Never!!	29	8.81%

Table 16: IFA membership.

IFA MEMBERS BY AGE		Percentage of age group that are IFA members – all grades
21–25	18	24%
26–30	25	31.25%
31–35	16	28.57%
36–40	19	42.22%
41–45	19	55.88%
46–50	13	54.17%
51–55	3	50%
56–60	1	50%
61 +	1	100%

Table 17: IFA membership by age group.

union. 24.01% indicated that they had no intention of joining because they were either against Trade Unions on principle, or saw no point in becoming members. However, 47.42% of respondents revealed that they would consider joining a union. In comparison to the IFA which seems to have a problem appealing to younger archaeologists, it might be surmised that Prospect, the Trade Union for private sector archaeologists, and Unison, which represents local authority employees, simply have a problem recruiting members which might be addressed through concerted effort and the raising of, what is currently, a low profile within the profession. However, it is also possible that only a direct threat to their jobs would encourage many of that 47.42% to actually join a union, by which time it may or may not be too late. The task facing both the IFA and the Trade Unions is to turn passive support into actual members. Turning once again to the regional data (Table 21) the situation is the reverse of the IFA, as three of the top five regions by workforce are also the most unionised. This is in many ways unsurprising as Prospect deliberately pursued 'union recognition' in the biggest units first, and a number of those account for the greater size of the regional workforce. It also seems likely that this represents the different perceptions of the IFA and the unions, ie that you join the IFA in order to get a (better) job, and you join a union to protect or improve your current job. On that basis it is logical that the bigger, more stable units have a higher percentage of union members. This partial mutual exclusivity is somewhat underlined by Figure 34, which shows regional membership of the IFA and the Unions, as well as the percentage of the regional workforce which are members of both.

HERITAGE RESEARCH SERIES NO. 1

Region	IFA members – all grades	Percentage of regional workforce
Wales	5	83.33%
NW England	9	69.23%
W Midlands	6	60%
Scotland	13	52%
E England	5	41.67%
Yorks & Humber	10	41.67%
SW England	12	41.38%
London	10	37.04%
SE England	23	35.94%
NE England	3	20%
E Midlands	3	13.04%
Unemployed	2	6.67%
N. Ireland	0	0%

Table 18: IFA members as a percentage of regional workforce.

ARE YOU MEMBER OF A TRADE UNION? (TOTAL 90- 27.36% YES)		
Yes - Prospect	59	17.93%
Yes - Unison	8	2.43%
Yes - other	23	6.99%
Against it on principle	17	5.17%
No point	62	18.84%
Would consider joining	156	47.42%

Table 19: Trade union membership.

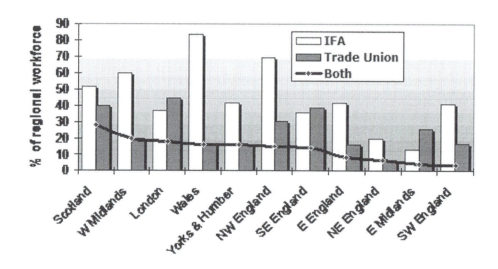

Figure 34: IFA and union members as a percentage of regional workforces. (see Table 23)

UNION MEMBERS BY AGE		Precentage of age group that are union members
21–25	7	9.33%
26–30	23	28.75%
31–35	20	35.71%
36–40	14	31.11%
41–45	13	38.24%
46–50	9	37.5%
51–55	3	50%
56–60	0	0%
61+	1	100%

Table 20: Trade union membership by age group.

Region	Trade union members – all unions	Percentage of regional workforce
London	12	44.44%
Scotland	10	40%
SE England	25	39.06%
NW England	4	30.77%
E Midlands	6	26.08%
W Midlands	2	20%
Unemployed	6	20%
SW England	5	17.24%
E England	2	16.67%
Wales	1	16.67%
Yorks & Humber	4	16.67%
NE England	1	6.67%
N. Ireland	0	0%

Table 21: Trade union members as a percentage of regional workforce.

Perceptions of the profession and individual career plans

Having established the basic demographic profile of commercial archaeology and then considered the extent to which the IFA and the unions had been successful in recruiting members, the next logical consideration is the relationship that staff have with their profession. In a number of ways this section is the most crucial in any assessment of the current state of commercial archaeology, but it builds upon the foundations laid by the previous sections. The question 'Which of the following most accurately reflects your views on commercial archaeology?' allowed for five responses, which were designed to cover all possible perceptions without leading respondents towards any particular answer.

- The current system provides a healthy basis for professional practice.
- There are some problems, but mostly the current system works well.

Region	Percentage of regional workforce who are IFA members	Percentage of regional workforce who are Union members	Percentage of regional workforce who are members of both
Scotland	52%	40%	28%
W Midlands	60%	20%	20%
London	37.04%	44.44%	18.52%
Wales	83.33%	16.67%	16.67%
Yorks & Humber	41.67%	16.67%	16.67%
NW England	69.23%	30.77%	15.38%
SE England	35.94%	39.06%	14.06%
E England	41.67%	16.67%	8.33%
NE England	20%	6.67%	6.67%
E Midlands	13.04%	26.08%	4.35%
SW England	41.38%	17.24%	3.45%
N. Ireland	0%	0%	0%
Unemployed	6.67%	20%	0%

Table 22: Percentage of regional workforce who are members of both the IFA and a trade union.

- The current system needs rethinking to prevent a crisis in the future.
- Commercial archaeology is already in crisis and needs urgent attention.
- None of the above.

The response to this question was one of the most striking aspects of the entire survey, with 76.60% of the profession feeling that commercial archaeology was either already in a crisis, or would be if nothing were done to change the current system (Table 23). This is the first time that this groundswell of opinion has been identified and offers a vivid contrast to some of the rosier pictures of the profession painted by some unit directors in recent years (eg Lawson 1993: 149). It was not entirely possible to define what the respondents meant by 'crisis', or, indeed, precisely what they understood by 'the current system'. In phrasing that question it was intended that 'the current system' should be taken to mean the system of developer-led, competitive tendering through which commercial units gain most of their work, and which is, therefore, ultimately responsible for the employment practices within those units. 'Crisis' is harder to define and it may be that each respondent meant something different by it. However, it can be taken as a broad indication that many in the profession feel that commercial archaeology is unsustainable in the current environment, either through the loss of skilled staff or a perceived reduction in the quality of the work undertaken as a result of market forces (for more detailed discussion of these topics, see Chapter Four which contains excerpts from the written submissions).

Despite this largely negative perception of the profession the vast majority of staff clearly still want to stay in the job for as long as they can (Table 24), with only fractionally under a third of staff currently trying to find alternative work or planning to within two years. Even when one takes into consideration only those

VIEWS ON COMMERCIAL ARCHAEOLOGY		
It's in crisis	134	40.73%
It needs a rethink to avert crisis	118	35.87%
It's mostly okay	62	18.84%
It's doing well	5	1.52%
None of the above	9	2.74%

Table 23: Views on the current condition of commercial archaeology.

respondents who stated that they felt that the profession was already in crisis, or needed a rethink to avert a crisis, it is only a slightly reduced majority that intend to remain in commercial archaeology for as long as they can (Table 25). Similarly, even those regions in which a high percentage of the workforce feel negatively about the state of the profession (Table 26), still demonstrate a high number of staff who intend to remain within it. Table 27 shows a breakdown of the results by age and gender. On the left are percentages of each age group, by gender, who are trying to leave the profession now, or plan to within two years. On the right is the corresponding percentage that intends to stay in the profession for as long as they can. These figures demonstrate that the under 30s are the most dissatisfied group, particularly the 21–25 year old male staff. After the age of 30 the percentage of both genders aiming to stay in the profession increases dramatically. This is more or less what one might expect and follows on from the figures already discussed, which show the huge drop in staff numbers after around five years field experience and at about the age of 30. 80.64% of the 21–30 age group believe that the profession is in crisis, or needs a rethink, but it seems likely that, for this age group, a primary concern may be that they do not feel that their careers are progressing or their work recognised and rewarded. It is very interesting to consider the figures for what one might consider to be the major 'push' and 'pull' factors in commercial archaeology (Tables 28 and 29). These show that aspects such as the archaeology itself (ie the actual remains and the process of excavation), simply being able to work outdoors, the camaraderie and the social life score very highly, with 44.68% responding that they love 'all of the above' about their jobs. However, where single aspects were highlighted the archaeology itself was far and away the most important element. When asked what they hated most, around a quarter answered 'all of the above' to a choice of the pay, the quality of people employed in the profession (both digging staff and unit management), incestuous relationships (ie the sexual as well as professional relationships that can get quite complicated in any small profession, and particularly within individual units) and bad weather. Pay was the standout single issue with 35.87% of respondents choosing to highlight that alone, but the quality of staff/management also featured prominently. Table 30 compares the responses in the Love/Hate questions with the responses to the question regarding how long the individual intends to remain in the profession. This database query was performed to see if there were any particular issues that were retaining staff, or driving them away. At first glance it seems that there is little to be gained from this data, as there are no striking push or pull factors apparent. However, those who choose to highlight 'the archaeology' as the single element they loved about their jobs were also those most keen to remain in the profession, with only 10.53% trying to find alternative employment. The other interesting figures to come out of this suggest that, apart from those who indicated that they 'hated' all of the options, or highlighted the quality of staff/management as the single issue they disliked about the profession, none of the single issues of this small selection were really responsible for driving people away. In fact even the issue of pay still scored a high percentage of respondents who intend to stay in the profession as long as they can, while those of this group who indicated that they were currently trying to leave formed a lower percentage than those who highlighted the majority of single issues in response to the question of 'what do you love about the job?'. This apparent paradox merely indicates that single issues are not enough to drive people away from the profession when the strength of feeling towards it remains high, but actually the highest percentages of people trying to leave the profession were those whose answer, when asked what they loved most about it, did not include 'The Archaeology'.

Conclusion

The average British commercial archaeologist is a white male, 32.37 years old, with a degree and 7.49 years of 'contract' field experience. This will probably come as no surprise to most people in the profession, nor will many of the other statistics presented here. Despite this the importance of this survey should not be underestimated. It represents the most significant survey of demographics and opinions within the UK commercial sector to be targeted at the individuals employed therein. It means that what had previously been merely anecdotal is now supported by sound quantitative data. It portrays a profession with an exceedingly high turnover of staff, many of whom becoming disillusioned and choosing to leave after about five years. It also vividly shows that there is still a core of staff remaining from the Manpower Services era that must clearly have retained their enthusiasm for the remains and process of archaeology, as well as retaining their jobs through some difficult years. For the first time the true level of discontent with the current system within which commercial units operate can

HOW LONG DO YOU INTEND TO STAY IN CONTRACT ARCHAEOLOGY?		
As long as I can	189	57.45%
Trying to get out now!	60	18.24%
1-2 years	41	12.46%
2-5 years	20	6.08%
No response	12	3.65%
5-10 years	7	2.13%

Table 24: Individual career plans.

Those who think the profession is 'IN CRISIS' or 'NEEDS A 'RETHINK' answered in the following way when asked how much longer they intend to stay in commercial archaeology –		
As long as I can	133	52.78%
Trying to get out now!	54	21.43%
1-2 years	32	12.70%
2-5 years	17	6.75%
5-10 years	6	2.38%

Table 25: Negative views on the state of the profession compared to the career plans of individuals.

Region	Percentage of regional workforce who believe that the profession is "in crisis" or "needs a rethink"	Percentage of regional workforce who are trying to leave commercial archaeology now, or plan to within two years	Percentage of regional workforce who intend to work in commercial archaeology as long as they can
E Midlands	91.30%	39.13%	47.83%
W Midlands	90%	40%	60%
Unemployed	86.67%	26.67%	0%
Wales	83.33%	16.67%	66.67%
Yorks & Humber	79.17%	16.67%	70.83%
London	77.78%	33.33%	51.85%
Scotland	76%	32%	60%
E England	75%	25%	58.33%
NE England	73.33%	40%	60%
SW England	72.41%	24.14%	62%
SE England	71.88%	35.94%	50%
N Ireland	66.67%	66.67%	33.33%
NW England	53.85%	23.08%	76.92%

Table 26: Regional views on the state of the profession compared to the career plans of individuals.

AGE	Male	Female	TOTAL	Male	Female	TOTAL
16–20	–	100%	100%	–	0%	0%
21–25	48.48%	26.19%	36%	45.45%	50%	48%
26–30	43.75%	40.63%	42.5%	45.83%	43.75%	45%
31–35	24.39%	26.67%	25%	63.41%	53.33%	60.71%
36–40	33.33%	11.11%	28.89%	66.67%	77.78%	68.89%
41–45	12.90%	33.33%	14.71%	83.87%	33.33%	79.41%
46–50	11.76%	28.57%	16.67%	76.47%	57.14%	70.83%
51–55	0%	0%	0%	75%	50%	66.67%
56–60	0%	0%	0%	0%	100%	50%
61+	100%	–	100%	0%	–	0%

Table 27: Age and gender breakdown of those planning to leave the profession within the next two years (on the left) and those intending to stay as long as they can (on the right).

be observed. 40.73% of contract archaeologists believe their profession is already in a crisis, and a further 35.87% believe that a crisis is inevitable unless changes are made. This overwhelming response cannot be ignored if the profession is to mature and yet, with both the IFA and the unions failing to recruit effectively from under represented sections of the profession, it can be no surprise that this message is not being heard.

WHAT DO YOU LOVE ABOUT COMMERCIAL ARCHAEOLOGY?		
Archaeology	133	40.43%
Being outdoors	19	5.78%
Camaraderie	11	3.34%
The social life	2	0.61%
All of the above	147	44.68%
None of the above	15	4.56%

Table 28: Aspects of the profession viewed most positively.

WHAT DO YOU HATE ABOUT COMMERCIAL ARCHAEOLOGY?		
Pay	118	35.87%
Quality of staff/ management	60	18.24%
Incestuous Relationships	21	6.38%
Bad weather	13	3.95%
All of the above	87	26.44%
None of the above	27	8.21%

Table 29: Aspects of the profession viewed most negatively.

There is a great diversity of perceptions regarding the work itself (Table 31), but the bottom line is that it is a love of 'archaeology' that keeps most people in the profession, even when there are a number of aspects, such as the pay, that are a cause for concern. Many of these themes are elaborated upon in the qualitative data presented later, adding depth to the basic themes identified through the quantitative analysis.

Question	Answer	Percentage of that response group who also answered the following way when asked how long they intend to stay in the profession	
What do you love about commercial archaeology?	All of the above	As long as I can	50.34%
		Trying to get out now!	18.37%
	The Archaeology	As long as I can	63.27%
		Trying to get out now!	10.53%
	Being outdoors	As long as I can	31.58%
		Trying to get out now!	47.37%
	Camaraderie	As long as I can	54.55%
		Trying to get out now!	27.27%
	Social Life	As long as I can	50%
		Trying to get out now!	50%
	None of the above	As long as I can	53.33%
		Trying to get out now!	33.33%

Table 30: Key push and pull factors.

What do you hate about commercial archaeology?	All of the above	As long as I can	41.38%
		Trying to get out now!	27.59%
	Pay	As long as I can	59.32%
		Trying to get out now!	13.56%
	Quality of staff or management	As long as I can	55%
		Trying to get out now!	28.33%
	Incestuous relationships	As long as I can	76.19%
		Trying to get out now!	4.76%
	Bad weather	As long as I can	69.23%
		Trying to get out now!	0%
	None of the above	As long as I can	81.48%
		Trying to get out now!	7.41%

Table 30: Key push and pull Factors. (*continued*)

1=	FUN	3.34%
1=	FRUSTRATION or FRUSTRATING	3.34%
1=	(THE) PAST or HISTORY	3.34%
4	INTERESTING	2.74%
5	FIND(ING) or DISCOVERY	2.13%
6	HARD or HARD WORK	1.82%
7	BAD PAY or UNDERPAID	1.52%
8	DIRT(Y)	0.91%
9=	EXCITING	0.61%
9=	ADVENTURE	0.61%

Table 31: Top ten keywords used in the 'one word summary of commercial archaeology'.

CHAPTER FOUR:
In their own words – Tales of the Invisible Diggers

I enjoy the intellectual and physical challenges of archaeology but most of all I find that I enjoy the company of archaeologists. There is a common theme of maverick intelligence which delights me.

(Anonymous submission to the online survey in 2004)

HERITAGE RESEARCH SERIES NO. 1

Figure 35: Paperwork.
© *Jon Hall*

Introduction

Following on from the quantitative data in the previous chapter we now move on to the qualitative data generated by the online survey, in which commercial archaeologists account for their situation and attitudes towards the profession in their own words. The combination of extracts from personal submissions and examples of creative writing serves to generate a more holistic representation of the profession than could otherwise be produced. This functions as an important platform from which to approach the interview analysis, where key themes are covered in more detail.

This chapter is accompanied with examples of Philip Barker's artwork. Barker was the author of Techniques of Archaeological Excavation (1977) – dedicated "To all who have dug with me" – and was, for a number of years, the Director of the excavations at Wroxeter, in Shropshire. The former was the first textbook many archaeologists ever bought and the latter was the training ground for hundreds of aspiring excavators. Philip was also one of the founding members and Secretary of RESCUE: The British Archaeological Trust, in 1971 and therefore played a pivotal role in the raising of public awareness and the increase of Government funding for rescue archaeology. However, before embarking on his renowned career in archaeology in 1960, he was an art teacher in Shrewsbury. Many of his later works are directly inspired by his passion for archaeology, which is a further reason for their inclusion here. Also included are cartoons by Jon Hall and Vicki Herring. The former a digger of many years experience; the latter a digger now turned archaeological illustrator. Both have documented some of the idiosyncrasies of the profession, and those who work within it, and their work reflects the broader perceptions that diggers have of themselves.

Thematic analysis of the submissions

The need for increased professionalism and organisation

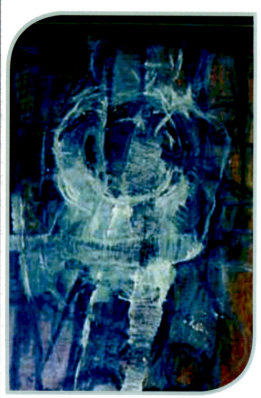

Figure 36: Philip Barker
UNTITLED *c* 1971.

A major theme amongst those who chose to complete a written submission during the online survey was that of the need for commercial archaeology to start acting like a profession. Many archaeologists expressed the view that the 'archaeology as a lifestyle choice' attitude once prevalent was preventing it from 'growing up'. The following excerpts demonstrate that archaeologists perceive there to be a lack of organisation and structure within the profession, which they felt was characterised by poor quality management and business practice and the inadequate training of graduate archaeologists now entering the profession:

Time to wake up from Selkirk-esque delusions about the state of British archaeology; someone drove a big yellow D8 and box through that ivory tower years ago. Short of full statutory protection for the archaeological resource (ain't ever going to happen) PPG16 and it's proposed successor and the commercial sector are here to stay.

This said, it's time for the profession to become a profession, and time for the IFA to truly start setting standards in practice and pay rather than protecting the commercial interests of two or three major contracting companies. It's time for our supposed professional body to curb some of the wilder excesses of commercial archaeology; where commercial pressures compromise the archaeology and where it is acceptable for the workforce to be paid the pitiful wages, under the shocking employment conditions, currently prevalent.

Until British archaeology abandons the amateur ideals of the 1970's and seeks to reposition the profession within the construction industry as a professional service, nothing will change – wages will remain low, contractors and consultants will continue to compromise the archaeological resource for tiny profit margins, careers will be virtually impossible to maintain, employment will remain temporary and peripatetic, diggers will continue to leave the profession after two or three years to get proper jobs and the "invisible digger" will remain – poor, disenfranchised and constantly looking for a way out. (**Respondent 116**)

Commercial archaeology currently works by exploiting the lowest-paid practitioners. Prices are kept artificially low by paying ludicrously low wages and providing very poor conditions for excavators. Commercial archaeology needs to become professional, whereby there are recognised job grades with recognised pay rates, either linked to local government pay rates or university pay rates. If the pay rates are standard, it will be easier to assess whether the price will allow the necessary work to be done, and it will ensure that companies bear the brunt of pricing rather than the people working for them. (**Respondent 38**)

Commercial archaeology is badly managed, with management practices that would not be tolerated in other industries. (**Respondent 45**)

In my view, the basic problem in archaeology relates to the profession's inability to provide a living wage compatible with modern society. The units have considerable scope to increase wages and their day rates if they act in unison, over time. The rates charged by units are laughed at by most other professions. As someone who regularly employs archaeologists I would have no qualms about paying more for a quality service. Unfortunately, archaeology is beset by a low-pay mentality and lack of real business experience.

The IFA's constant interference, through the setting of appallingly low pay rates does not help. In my view, they should either seek to significantly enhance pay or stop promoting low pay.

Overall, archaeology is a profession in a constant crisis. Many experienced, talented and motivated people leave archaeology early in their careers and consequently little talent makes its way up the chain. The profession needs to develop clear career structures, significantly enhanced pay scales and a more professional approach to other professions. (**Respondent 71**)

Figure 37: Philip Barker UNTITLED *c* 1989.

At the risk of sounding like my Dad (once in a lifetime eventuality, I hope!), some organisation is needed to get things sorted. From top to bottom, bottom to top, back to front, and inside out. Pay, conditions, management, employment rights, career structure, the whole ethos of commercial developer funded archaeology and units. (**Respondent 82**)

It's not the job, it's everything else! Pay, conditions, we have no professional pride, something needs to change before too many good people leave because they can't take it anymore. (**Respondent 90**)

Training and experience in commercial archaeology is pretty poor. Very few projects or units seem to be able to afford to train newer people or graduates and quite frankly the majority of graduates simply can't excavate. This is partly inherent in archaeology as you learn so much on the job but some basic techniques are often missing – if I see one more person put a north arrow on a section drawing I'll sob. This sort of thing should be drummed in at degree level and then in the commercial sector we can help them gain the experience of the variety of features and how they have formed but not need to go over or teach the essential techniques. This would be ideal but of course most jobs taken on by units are costed relatively low in order to win the work and this leaves no room for on site training, or if this can be done it is through necessity, ie not having anyone on site with a clue of what they're doing. When I started in archaeology I was taught much of what I know from 'old hands' but this segment of the working population seems to be very small now. Management is another serious problem area. Many managers lack management skills and simply try and manage by common sense with varied results. The management level in any commercial organisation has the most effect on the archaeology and

the workforce and there are so many intrinsic problems including: personal power playing, insufficient experience (skills may be there but little experience to reinforce it), a remoteness from the actual projects themselves and in several instance a distinct lack of interest in the archaeology itself! **(Respondent 93)**

We need to be professionally organised – more people in the union, better training and wages. There are people I know who still get laid off over Christmas and go from week to week on weekly contracts – we are a disorganised bunch from top to bottom and no wonder developers and architects run rings round us and don't take us seriously. The price of an archaeological condition on a developer's budget is measly and we are still scraping around doing things in ever-tighter budgets to that 'fixed price'. **(Respondent 121)**

Figure 38: Philip Barker UNTITLED *c* 1998.

These excerpts highlight a widespread feeling that commercial archaeology can not begin to raise wages in the industry until it is able to charge higher rates for professional work. Respondents highlight the low opinion that other 'developer-led' professions have of many archaeological units and the case is made for an improvement in this image through higher standards throughout the profession. There is a perception that developer's budgets would stretch to an increased rate for archaeological work, but only if the efficiency and quality of that work was increased proportionately. There is also a strong sense of frustration amongst those respondents who wish to be treated more professionally by their own employers, and amongst those who see new staff lacking in the requisite skills. For many the answer lies in a strengthening of the Institute of Field Archaeologists and for it to regulate standards in the profession more effectively than it does currently.

Pay and conditions

Pay and conditions are an intrinsic part of any professional working environment. Without adequate remuneration and contracts that recognise the need for some stability in their lives, many commercial archaeologists do not feel that their employers view them as 'professionals'. If the units feel like that then it is hardly surprising that they are accused of not charging developers a proper 'professional' rate (see above). However, the submissions reveal that it is actually the conditions of employment that are more of an issue to commercial archaeologists than the pay.

I think the pay and conditions for diggers are appalling. I do not understand how anyone can exist at the lower end of the profession and have a reasonable quality of life. The present structure of commercial archaeology is no good for diggers and commercial archaeological organisation also have their problems. There is certainly no easy answer and I don't know what it is. **(Respondent 15)**

Self-employment is still widespread up here in Scotland. I cannot claim global knowledge but one of the big four companies takes all its diggers as self-employed, with a preference for recent graduates. All its employees are supervisor or above. There are known to have been sites where all site staff have been self-employed. One of the units in the chasing pack of medium companies seems to have virtually no employees, and of the small companies most take on diggers only as self-employed. I do think this is a blistering sore in the Scottish market that some are trying to resolve. Sadly there is a pool of diggers who appear happy to keep this status quo, as they feel advantaged by it. I think they are mistaken and they are following an inherently risky practice that is probably illegal. The self-employed diggers believe they are getting a cash rich deal (higher day rates, less tax, less NI etc) but really they get only marginally more money in hand, have a ropey tax history (as they could be assessed as 'employees') and never seem to have any personal insurance cover to safeguard themselves. **(Email respondent)**

Anyway, I still love my job, and can see its value but as I get older sometimes think maybe I should have made my 'millions' first and then taken this on as a hobby! **(Respondent 1)**

I see little prospect of change for those tied to archaeological companies who are frustrated by current commercial practice. The problems arise from the historic legacy of the charitable structure of many archaeological organisations. The majority of archaeologists in field archaeology are employed by not-for-profit organisations, who seek to control market share through the provision of high labour volumes at cheap rates, practicing competitive strategies that protect their interests. **(Respondent 37)**

I think the main problems are bad pay, poor career structure, lack of long term prospects and also the fact that a great many units do really bad archaeology. **(Respondent 40)**

I feel frustrated that we teach so many enthusiastic students in archaeology at our UK universities, but there are so few jobs waiting

HERITAGE RESEARCH SERIES NO. I

for them at the end of three years hard slog. And when you do find the jobs they are generally badly paid and worst – such short contracts. I can well sympathise with those that leave the profession eventually, not because they no longer have a passion for this subject, but because they just cannot live a proper life. (**Respondent 44**)

Where do I start. My feelings on the subject are still pretty raw having been rendered penniless, homeless and jobless, just because I was dedicated and stuck at it, believing one day I would find a niche (ie permanent position). I have watched countless incompetents and liars be promoted above me, and then had to help cover up their inevitable mistakes to protect the reputation of the company. At the same time I have seen countless talented and dedicated people be patronised and exploited for the profit of a small number of unit directors. I worked for over six years in the north of England as a field archaeologist and latterly as self-employed human bone specialist. When the specialist work dried up I was offered a digging job at £55 per day on a two-week contract by a unit for which I had given my all. I truly believe if I was male and buddied up to the bosses I would have been far more successful in my career. (**Respondent 59**)

We need to squeeze out the cheapskates who pay low wages: ultimately their activities harm individuals and are responsible for the appalling loss of talent which haemorrhages out of the archaeological world every year. (**Respondent 119**)

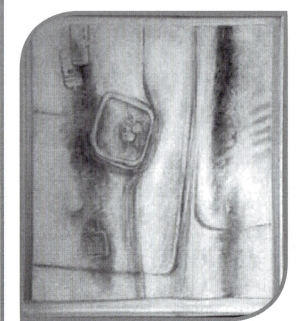

Figure 39: Philip Barker UNTITLED *c* 1980.

I think there is an appalling brain drain in archaeology, whereby as soon as someone becomes sufficiently knowledgeable and experienced, they are desperate to leave, because they have also experienced the bad pay and conditions, lack of job security, and a feeling that no-one (whether it be county council curators, developers, or the odd cowboy unit) really cares about the archaeology, so why should we…It's happening to myself and numerous colleagues, and no doubt will affect the next set of keen graduates a few years down the line. Still, we archaeologists love nothing more than a good moan, and if there was nothing wrong in our jobs then what would we complain about? (The price of beer?) (**Respondent 129**)

In the summer it's the best job in the world, in winter you feel like you've been sent to a Russian Gulag, but out of the many and varied jobs I've done in my time, nothing comes close to the camaraderie and the large amount of cool broad-minded people you meet digging and it is a low stress job unlike many other professions. Instead the stress is when you have got home filthy, haven't got to the bank, have f★★k all money and have just got a postcard from your mates with 'proper jobs' who are living it up somewhere hot on full pay. (**Email Respondent**)

It is clear from these excerpts that many commercial archaeologists have a love/hate relationship with their jobs. There is an overwhelming sense of frustration amongst those respondents who clearly have, or had, a real passion for their subject, but who are now forced, by low pay, short-term contracts and poor employment practices, to re-evaluate their careers. One respondent even cites sexism in the workplace as a contributing factor to her leaving the profession. There is also frustration amongst those who see large numbers of talented staff being driven out of the profession and a concern that the current turnover of staff is unsustainable.

Respect: archaeologists or unskilled labourers?

Not being treated as a professional is one accusation levelled by commercial archaeologists and this might manifest itself in a number of ways, as has already been demonstrated. However, in extreme examples some find themselves completely invisible to their managers and some even claim that they are not allowed to 'be' archaeologists.

> I work in Ireland. Over the years I have found loads of sites and archaeological material during monitoring. I have written reports on said sites and material. My name appears nowhere!! How frustrating. **(Respondent 52)**

> I found the title 'Invisible Diggers' rather apt. In my opinion a lot of the problems within British Archaeology, ie poor pay and career opportunities amongst others are caused by our fellow professionals engaged in unit management and consultancy posts. The attitudes displayed by many of these people towards field staff (especially those on short term contracts) beggars belief at times. Site visits are a prime example. A horde of 'Experts' accompanied by management suddenly drop onto your trench, totally ignore the excavators, and loudly make pronouncements regarding the work people are in the process of completing. Usually no input is requested from the excavation staff, obviously because we are some lower species of pond life who aren't intelligent enough to have an opinion. This is not a morale boosting moment for many people. **(Email respondent)**

> From time to time I do enjoy the job but my main enjoyment comes more from the people I work with rather than job satisfaction. It is a physically demanding job as well as mentally and the conditions we have to work in are often appalling. This generally does not make for an environment conducive to 'enjoyment'. A lot of the time, in fact most of the time, people are kept in the dark in every respect of the job and you often have no idea of what is going on, either on site or in the unit in general. The diggers are always the last to know about anything, including where they will be from day to day.

> Organisation is not a strong point in any unit that I have ever worked for and there seems to be an overwhelming lack of communication throughout the profession. People need to be included in every aspect of the workings, as presently different levels of staff are very isolated. For example, once you have finished a site, the diggers never hear about reports, finds or what the significance of the site is in a larger picture. This adds to the feeling that diggers are disposable people who are basically paid to dig holes and no more. **(Email respondent)**

HERITAGE RESEARCH SERIES NO. I

There is, however, a very important and interesting counter-argument that characterises some of the feeling of those who have managed to make a career in the profession.

Admittedly, I have some experience of working with and for people whose expertise leaves a great deal to be desired, but I have a suspicion 'twas ever thus – particularly after having attempted to use now material collected in the Good Old Days. I received exactly the same lack of formal training currently bemoaned, but got where I am – an occasionally successful businessman, and very good technician – because I wanted to know how to be better, and listened to people when they told me. Often in terms of canine invective, I must admit. Continuing Personal (or Professional) Development is something that must first come from the intended recipient. You can lead people to mud, but you can't make them think.

I think we need to develop a sense of perspective, which recognises what a real crisis is. We are lucky enough to be working in an industry whose clients are forced upon it by national and international law. The level of skill, expertise and individual responsibility required of those of us who start out as diggers is minute, and does NOT compare with architects, surveyors, or any of the other white collar trades so blithely bandied about. It does not even compare with the requirements of many of the trades within the construction industry. Diggers are groundworkers, and we get paid better basic than they do, and generally enjoy better conditions.

That is not to say that the situation is perfect, or that conditions are good enough – but they are improving, and constantly, and no thanks to the legions of Public Bar Lawyers who most vociferously criticise the efforts others make on their behalf. The bulk of improvements made in the conditions, pay and recognition received by diggers have been provided by the very competition that so many of them decry. There are currently far more diggers, earning far more money, and living far better lives than there were in 1990. I was one of them. End of story.

These excerpts characterise the occasionally polarised positions of commercial archaeologists. On the one hand there is an argument that diggers are completely overlooked by their managers, that they are treated as nothing more than labourers and given none of the respect that they feel they are due. On the other hand is the sense that the improving situation does currently allow site staff to expand their skills and expertise in order to earn greater respect. Whilst they may both be accurate to varying degrees, the suspicion has to be that for staff at a lot of units there are few, if any, such opportunities to make themselves visible and to become something more than a labourer in the eyes of their managers.

Digger apathy

The 'Public Bar Lawyers' referred to above are almost certainly a factor of every profession to varying degrees. For some reason, however, 'Digger Apathy' is a recognised condition within the profession. This is almost certainly because the size of the workforce and the young and malleable nature of the profession mean that real change is achievable if only people chose to get involved. It seems that those who see no future for themselves in the profession have no interest in trying

Figure 40: Digging. © *Vicki Herring*

to change the system, much to the frustration of those that do. Of course it is far more complicated than that with opinion divided on the role of the IFA and the Trade Unions and whether even the desire to improve things is enough. The first two excerpts are spectacular examples of the two extremes, though the second demonstrates that many commercial archaeologists do not understand that the role of the IFA was never intended to be one of a trade union or equivalent.

> *Commercial field archaeologists need to stop moaning and start joining the IFA and Prospect in order to raise their pay to a decent level. If archaeologists don't do this, things will never improve as there are too many mugs willing to work for a pittance.* **(Respondent 66)**

> *The IFA is basically lip service and have little political (labour and worker's rights essentially) clout. I currently see no real need to join. I can fight my own battle for better wages and working conditions and take an active role in changing perspectives toward 'diggers', wages, and job security rather than joining an organisation such as the IFA. If the IFA really wants to be considered a serious organisation, they need to do more for archaeologists rather than print a few new pamphlets telling me how to be an archaeologist.* **(Respondent 92)**

> *As for the IFA, I am not a member and personally view it as an employers association that does not best serve the interest of the vast majority or archaeologists. However, membership is asked for by so*

many employers that it is hard to get by without membership so on several occasions I have thought about joining just to add it to my CV! **(Respondent 62)**

It seems to me that there are so many moaners digging on the archaeology circuit who spend most of their time complaining instead of actually doing the work they are paid for (albeit badly). People who are not in it for the archaeology and just see it as a job should do everyone who loves the job a favour by getting out of archaeology. **(Respondent 68)**

I'm glad someone has decided to get the 'word in the field'. There are many different opinions as to the problems inherent in the current commercial archaeology system and many different solutions. The main problem I see is apathy; archaeologists are not the most 'go-getting' bunch of people. They complain, a lot, but no one seems to do anything. A complete lack of organised rebellion has led to the continuing poor pay and conditions. Many archaeologists I speak to do not join the IFA or union because they say what good do they do for the

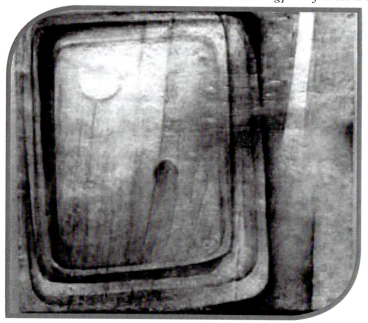

Figure 41: Philip Barker
UNTITLED *c* 1985.

money. Neither organisation has any real authority to make change. The only factor to influence companies, as this is a commercial activity, is money. Archaeology is not suited to a profit making process due to the nature of the work. It cannot be neatly slotted into the planning process like a contract plumber or electrician can on a building job. **(Respondent 55)**

It is clear to see once more how fiercely polarised opinions are within the profession. The respondents often expressed very strong views suggesting that more people should join the IFA, a union or any other body that could improve conditions within the profession. These people tend to bemoan the lack of organisation that has seen little or no action taken to demand improvements in pay and conditions. On the other hand are those who are just as vehement that nothing will change even if they were to join the IFA, or a union. They often refuse to even countenance paying any money to the IFA, believing that it merely represents the employers to the disadvantage of site staff. Of course, one has to point out that the IFA merely represents its membership and to refuse to join on the grounds that it does not represent you is a circular argument.

Competitive tendering and the post–PPG16 world

As expressed above, a large number of commercial archaeologists believe that it is competitive tendering that is directly responsible for the perceived problems with their jobs. This is, however, hotly debated. There is a strong counter argument, already expressed in an excerpt above, that the sheer number of jobs, the pay, and the conditions of employment have never been better than they are today.

What is unclear, however, is whether more substantial improvements could have been made under a non-competitive system. Beyond the immediate issues of employment it is also beyond question that the advent of competitive tendering in the mid to late 1980s, and then the publication of PPG16 in 1990, irrevocably altered the practice of developer-led archaeology. The following excerpts refer specifically to some of these changes:

Everything today is small scale watching briefs or office based assessments. I chiefly joined for the working outside, social life and camaraderie bit, sadly those days are long gone. (**Respondent 5**)

The system obviously has its problems at the moment, but all in all it could be worse. For example, read about the Cape Town 'Prestwich Burial Site' that has been in the South African news recently. The total lack of planning infrastructure here left authorities completely unable to cope with the surprise discovery of a mass burial site during development. (**Respondent 10**)

It's fast becoming a parody of itself. I feel we are reaching a stage when the skills needed to close a project quickly and profitably are far more important than the ability to excavate and record a site properly. (**Respondent 57**)

And what do I hate most about commercial archaeology: the fact that prices in competitive tendering are pared down to such a degree that it is impossible to do a decent job on the archaeology without putting in unpaid time (something I do frequently) and that there is no-one who ensures good standards are maintained. And the fact that so many managers appear to have no idea what an excavation involves and have no interest in the archaeology. (**Respondent 117**)

The quality of curators is highly variable- from the excellent to the frankly piss poor. Planning archaeologists should be recruited on the basis of their comprehension of archaeological practice, rather than the capacity to administer local authority paperwork. (**Respondent 119**)

Figure 42: Philip Barker UNTITLED *c* 1997.

These excerpts illustrate the often contradictory opinions regarding the effects of competitive tendering and PPG16 since the late 1980s and 1990 respectively. The broad consensus appears to be that there has been an improvement and that at least the introduction of PPG16 provided a system that has seen archaeological remains recorded rather than simply destroyed. However, it is also clear from the submissions as a whole that there is a feeling that PPG16 should have been a starting point for a more visceral reorganisation of the profession, and that competitive tendering should have achieved far more in the area of pay and conditions of employment. A large number of respondents question whether archaeology, as an essentially academic discipline, really belongs in the market-place to that extent, but the majority seem to accept that it is currently the only workable system. There is an overwhelming sense, when reading the submissions, of a prevailing romantic attachment to archaeology that is often anti-establishment

Figure 43: A rural site. © *Vicki Herring*

and at times even revels in the difficult working conditions as something akin to rites of passage. There seems to be a paradox that half of the profession want to be treated as professionals, while the other half enjoy the somewhat 'liminal' status that archaeology has within society. However, the frustration of all the respondents who feel that they are not able to do their best because of conditions imposed on them by clients, employers or even staff, is palpable and seems, in a number of cases, to be the final straw that drives them out of the profession.

Creative writing

The romance of archaeology, tinged somewhat with a darkly humorous appreciation of its associated difficulties, is often expressed creatively. It is far from universal, but many sites inspire diggers to produce written work which records their experiences in a more lasting way than the ubiquitous oral testimonies of staff who worked on famous, infamous or challenging sites and which become incorporated into a kind of folklore. The following pieces of poetry, prose and song are good examples of creative material generated by archaeologists and help to augment the picture of the profession as it is seen from within. Of particular interest is this first piece, which recalls many years of change within the profession from its research-led days while still retaining an almost wide-eyed enthusiasm and love for archaeology.

"I REMEMBER...." by Redwald

(Previously printed in the Royal Photographic Society 'Archaeology and Heritage Group' Newsletter, Autumn 2003)

I remember a time before 'contexts' were invented. When stratification was far more important than any other aspect of the dig, even the plans. I remember when we did not do risk assessments before each campaign, before flash-jackets and helmets became de rigeur, and when we dug skeletons without benefit of masks and gloves.

I remember when ablutions meant standing in a washing-up bowl in a damp tent trying to remove the sweat. We grovelled before local volunteers, especially those with luxurious bathrooms, hoping for an invitation 'to coffee'. If the invitation was not forthcoming there was always Army Stores saltwater soap on a shingle beach or mud spit, if we were digging a coastal site.

I remember a time after wartime powdered milk was discontinued, but before the modern variety came on to the market in the mid-sixties. This was also before coolboxes, so someone with transport was always deputed to go and collect the milk for tea breaks. I remember collecting water from a clear stream, and making tea with it. Days later, we walked upstream and discovered its source in a cess-pit. Nobody died.

I remember Elsans. The worst thing about them was the fact that they had to be regularly emptied, usually by someone on the most ignored duty list on the site. I remember the uncomfortable realisation (always in the dark!!) that the last person on this duty had 'forgotten.' The popular story then current, of someone retching and siphoning out the Elsan is probably apocryphal! As a supervisor I remember the free drinks arriving on my table in the pub when I was trying to compile the duty rota, and how nice everyone could be until they saw their names on the list.

I remember digging down eighteen feet (six metres) without shoring, helmets etc., with barrow-runs on the three foot baulks all around. On one occasion, a loaded barrow fell on to a volunteer below, gouging a deep cut diagonally across his back; luckily this was his only injury, and after stitching in the local infirmary he was back on site later the same day. I remember digging out medieval drains towards a beck which was known to be polluted; I spent six weeks in isolation, nearly died, and did not sue anyone! How naïve were we then?

I remember digging a medieval plague-pit without gloves or mask. Lunch was Marmite sandwiches, eaten in the pit to save time. There were no hand-washing facilities. On the same site a colleague and I emptied a lead coffin; we ended up plastered with whitish oxide, which we washed off in the disgusting urban beck nearby. I see him regularly still, and neither of us is the worse for our experience.

I remember piling seven or eight people into one car each morning, and the smell on the return trip! Younger volunteers lived on baked beans, so it was probably a good job that most people smoked, or the site hut would have quickly become uninhabitable! In those days the smokers stayed inside.

I remember camping in the corner of a Northamptonshire potato field; idyllic until the farmer sprayed the crop and the spiders all took refuge in the tent with us. The same farmer asked us to fumigate his storage silos. I remember being the last down, behind someone who was scared of ladders, and consequently very slow moving! I choked for days, but it cured my cold. One evening in the pub near the latter site, (Or perhaps another nearby – it's a long time ago!) we met the real Mr J.C. Bamford, the man who invented the famous yellow workhorse. Speaking of personalities, I remember digging with the person who really did sit on a metal grid-peg and ended up in hospital with a punctured colon, so that one at least is not apocryphal.

I remember meeting Basil Brown, the man who discovered that ship; my over-riding impression was of how short and slight he was. I also met Charles Phillips who dug the same ship so masterly, and he was a really big man. I remember too,

HERITAGE RESEARCH SERIES No. 1

Paul Johnstone, who invented television archaeology. He died shortly after I met him, and archaeology lost one of its best publicisers. I remember too, Honey, the famous archaeological cat, who was immortalised in poetry.

I remember living on a council tip in Suffolk. One morning, hearing a rustle inside the tent awning I peeped out and saw a bambi with its snout in our rubbish box. The following morning, hearing the same rustling I woke my wife, who peered out and found an army of rats all over the awning! I remember one evening when the zip failed on the same tent, fastening my long-suffering wife inside. It was our anniversary, and we had a table booked at a restaurant in Ipswich; we were late, and the tent never fastened properly again.

I remember seeing a (new) volunteer accidentally fall into a recently-excavated grave; he ended up lying alongside a long-dead monk, and when he realised this he demolished the skeleton in his haste to escape. We never saw him again!

Unfortunately, I also remember other things like the friend who was killed when a JCB passed too close to the deep trench he was working in. I remember too the girl who died; one summer she was on site with us, the next she was gone. Did her fondness for walking around in bare feet and ignoring rain, even in city streets, contribute to her demise, we wondered?

I wonder just how many of our later ailments were the delayed result of those risks? Is my asthma at least partially a consequence of the fungicide exposure in that grain silo? I am pretty certain that my creaky knees are the result of kneeling and trowelling without a padded kneeler, and my hearing was undoubtedly damaged by sticking my unprotected head out of an aeroplane in company with Derrick Riley in the seventies. Knowing that, I would do it again for the experience of flying with one of the 'greats.'

No, I never scoff at risk-assessments, masks and gloves, flash jackets and helmets. Yes, it's great to remember the early, naïve, days of our calling, but we must be mature enough to realise that taking risks is foolish, and accidents are largely avoidable. Archaeology, like most professions, has matured and there is no place left for the risk-taker. This applies even more so to the voluntary sector.

"But, in spite of everything, didn't we enjoy ourselves?"

Honey the archaeological cat, referred to in the above piece, has herself entered archaeological folklore. Although her story dates from before commercial archaeology she is not the only pet to have become associated with certain sites or excavators. This poem recalls the days of nomadism when archaeological sites were home for several months a year and Honey famously adapted to her changing surroundings.

"AN ARCHAEOLOGICAL CAT"
by Kenneth Wilson

Our Honey was no common farmyard cat.

She qualified as an aristocrat.

A cat most proud, and beautiful to see,

And so well trained in archaeology.

She never mixed potsherds on a tray,

Or sat on baulks to bar a barrow's way;

And if she saw a mouse so fat and big,

It was taboo to chase it round the dig.

In tent or caravan she was at home,

And round the fields at night she used to roam,

But with the dawn outside the tent she'd sit

And for her breakfast wait, when stove was lit.

On to the dig her way she would make,

To tell us when it was time to break

And make the tea, or stop work for a meal;

And when dusk came she to the site would steal

To warn us that the working day was done,

The time had come to play with Honey Bun.

Alas, at Silbury Hill she met her end,

No more our tent from farm dogs to defend.

Around the land she travelled far and wide;

Now peacefully she lies, well stratified.

The following pieces are all site songs adapted from existing lyrics to suit the particular circumstances. Site songs are quite common, though far from ubiquitous, and are a wonderful summary of people's attitudes, behaviour and the conditions on site at the time. The first song, "Diggers' Lament", captures a period of time when people were abandoning the 'circuit' in favour of the more stable, long-term work provided by developer-led projects. The subsequent songs are all from the 1990s and illustrate the day-to-day difficulties faced by many archaeologists on sites across the country, both from the weather, the management, and the regional curators.

"DIGGERS LAMENT"
by Laura Templeton and Robin Jackson

To the tune of 'And the Band Played Waltzing Matilda'. Written for the Newsletter produced at the end of the Deansway Project in Worcester in 1989.

When I was a young man I carried my trowel,

And lived the life of a digger;

From Durham's Green Basin to the Stanwick Outback,

Letting my beard grow bigger.

Then in May '88, Charles Mundy said son

It's time to stop rambling, there's work to be done,

So they gave me a hard hat and they promised me fun,

And sent me away to Worcester.

And the band played "Stairway to Heaven",

As they dragged us away from our tents,

And amid all the tears and the shouts and the fears

We began to pay something called rent.

How well I remember that terrible day

With the mud stains the sand and the gravel.

And how in that place that they called Deansway

We set up the Visitors Centre.

Joe Public was ready – Malc primed them all well,

They rained us with insults and questions as well,

And in five minutes flat – a site tour to hell,

Try explaining those pits to Phil Barker.

And the band played "Stairway to Heaven"

As we slipped off to bury our stash,

We buried ours while site one smoked theirs;

Not even paid weekly in cash.

Now those that were digging did their best to survive,

In a mad world of bluebags and thinking;

And for ten weary months I kept myself alive,

Sustained by copious drinking.

Then a large pint of best knocked me arse over tit,

And when I came to I felt a right twit,

Learnt it was my round and decided to split

Never knew there were worse things than Pat Kearney.

And the band played "Stairway to Heaven",

I gave up the circuit so dear,

For to hang tents and pegs a man needs two legs

And I'd just drunk far too much beer.

So they picked up the diggers, the warped and insane,

And shipped them back to the section.

The harmless, the legless the blindly inane

All under Mundy's direction.

As the van drew into the section drive,

I looked at the place where my trowel used to be,

And thanked Christ there was nothing there waiting for me

To sort and to draw and to sieve.

And the band played "Stairway to Heaven"

As we unloaded the bags from the van

We piled them up here and we piled them up there,

They'll sieve them as fast as they can.

And now every summer I sit in my tent

With the public appointments before me,

Remembering the comrades, now aged and spent

At Raunds and at Thwing and at Stanwick.

Some still work the circuit, all bent all stiff and all white

The forgotten heroes of unpublished sites

And the young people ask "Are their minds still alright?"

And I ask myself the same question.

And the band played "Stairway to Heaven",

And the diggers still answer the call,

And year after year their numbers get fewer,

Soon no-one will dig there at all.

"ERMINE STREET" by Rachel Gardner, 1991
(The Glentham – Welton Pipeline Song) - To the tune of 'Baker Street' by Gerry Rafferty.

Finding you way down on Ermine Street,

Mud in your hair and dead on your feet:

Well, another winter day, now you'll drink the night away and forget about
    everything.

This shitty weather makes you feel so cold;

You've got two feet of water in your favourite hole,

And it hasn't taken long to find out you were wrong when you thought
    digging could be fun.

You used to think it was romantic –

Hot sun, lost cities, it's so romantic –

But you're freezing; you're freezing now.

Three more weeks and it'll be over –

You know you'll miss it when it's all over –

But it's snowing; it's snowing now.

Way down the site there's an Iron Age pit:

Pump out the water and then bale it a bit.

Put the kettle on for tea, and go back again to see that the water is three feet deep.

The snow is falling as you set up your plan –

Pick up the pencil, but you can't feel your hands,

And the puddles start to freeze as you get down on your knees, and the snow
    drifts across the street.

You know you've got to keep digging –

You know the pipeline never stops digging,

And it's moving; it's moving on.

Then you turn up: it's a new morning –

Two feet of snow to shovel this morning –

You're digging; you're digging on.

"A WAY OUT OF LONDON" by Rachel Gardner, 1998
(The Parsonage Farm Christmas Carol) — To the tune of 'Away in a Manger'

A way out of London, no warmth and no charm,

No sense and no parking at Parsonage Farm

The clouds in the grey sky roll down from the West:

We're cold and bewildered, bogged down and depressed.

The rainwater's flowing, it silts up our holes;

The mud's getting deeper, our barrows won't roll.

We watch the sun sinking at quarter to three,

And half-section post-holes it's too dark to see.

With two months' extension and there days to go,

There must be some work on, but where, we don't know.

There's only one thing that we all know full well:

We're damned all this winter to CTRL.

"STRIP AND RECORD" by Rachel Gardner, 1998
To the tune of 'Cockles and Mussels'

Outside London city, it's all fairly shitty,

As the world-famous MoLAS's cool starts to go:

They're not very hot on Northumberland's Bottom,

Saying "Strip it, record it, backfill, backfill O!"

Backfill, backfill O, backfill, backfill O,

Saying "Strip it, record it, backfill, backfill O!"

The whole Kentish region was under the Legion:

If Claudius Caesar slept here, we don't know,

But the Evaluator said "Nothing's that great here,

So strip it, record it, backfill, backfill O!"

We've got Samian collections from ditch intersections –

Though no-one likes Romans, we don't let it show –

But the London Museum, when they come to see them,

Say "Strip it, record it, backfill, backfill O!"

We've got old watercourses, and very dead horses,

And a huge beehive oven, but we've got to go:

The people who pay us don't like burnt flint layers –

They say "Strip it, record it, backfill, backfill O!"

We think that we've finished: our team has diminished,

But Kent County Council is telling us "No,

Your sections are shitty, your spoilheaps aren't pretty,

And you strip it, record it, backfill, backfill O!"

It's not very funny: we've got no more money,

The only things grinning round here are the bones.

With too much to do, we're three weeks overdue:

We just strip it, record it, backfill, backfill O!

"A SITE CALLED WATTLE SYKE" by Rachel Gardner, 1990
(The Wattle Syke Song) – To the tune of 'House of the Rising Sun' by The Animals

There is a site in West Yorkshire:

They call it Wattle Syke.

It's been the ruin of many a poor digger:

I know just what it's like.
Well, Wakefield District Council
Don't seem to know we're here;
Our director ain't a digging man,
Down in West Yorkshire.

Now the only things a digger needs
Are a shovel and a spade,
And a floor to spread his sleeping bag,
Because he's not been paid.

Professor, tell you students
Not to do what I have done:
To spend their days in dust and poverty
By the side of the A1.

One foot's on the platform,
The other's on the train:
I've had enough of Wattle Syke –
I'm going home again.

There is a site in West Yorkshire:
They call it Wattle Syke.
It's been the ruin of many a poor digger.
I know just what it's like.

Figure 44: Under pressure. © *Vicki Herring*

"THE RAMSGATE DOUBLE DITCH SONG" by Rachel Gardner, 1999

(The First Ramsgate Harbour Song) – To the tune of 'The Drover's Dream'

I've been in this ditch all day, trowelling off the yellow-grey
From the greyish-yellow silting on the floor,
Then the sun moves overhead, all my yellow turns to red:
O, I don't believe in natural any more.

Now it's twenty-five past ten, and I've cleaned it up again,
But I shan't be out of here till ten to four,
'Cos the yellow's breaking grey, and my edge has gone away:
O, I don't believe in natural any more.

When the blue sky turns to grey, all the shadows go away,
And I've found the recut edge this time for sure,
But my work was all in vain as the sun comes out again:
O, I don't believe in natural any more.

Now I'm tearing out my hair, 'cos there's yellow everywhere,
And it really looks like what I'm looking for,
But I have to take the hint, when I find that retouched flint:
O, I don't believe in natural any more.

After two days in the sun, you can't see what I have done,
So I needn't stay and do it any more,
But I know that life's a bitch, as I start the other ditch:
O, I don't believe in natural any more.

Figure 45: A rural site II. © *Vicki Herring*

The creative writing presented here is interesting for a number of reasons. Firstly it can not go unnoticed that they rarely refer to the process of excavation or archaeological remains, with the exception of the last site song which is wholly concerned with the difficulties sometimes associated with identifying subtle changes in soil. Instead the main sources of the material are the on-site relationships, the nature of 'the job' and the often challenging weather conditions faced by staff. In fact many of the site songs from the 1990s appear to have been written in the extremes of winter or summer when archaeologists are faced with cold and wet, or hot and dusty conditions. Secondly, this material documents aspects of commercial archaeology that might otherwise be overlooked and represents a rather unique site archive of the kind that might be utilised in a reflexive methodology (Hodder 2000). Thirdly, the creative work gives the kind of detailed, site-specific information that is often lacking from the 'factual' submissions in which archaeologists provide a commentary on the commercial sector as a whole. The two sources of written data, when combined, create for the reader a more comprehensive picture that deals with specifics and generalities, and allows for a far greater understanding of all of the issues than would otherwise be possible.

CHAPTER FIVE:
The Interviews – Part one: career paths

Figure 46: Conversation at the Christmas meal. © *Jon Hall*

In this chapter the interview data is used to examine the many and varied routes by which commercial archaeologists became interested in archaeology; pursued qualifications, experience and employment; and succeeded or otherwise within the profession. This chapter will demonstrate the current challenges of employment within commercial archaeology.

Methodology

This study is not the first to use the interviewing of archaeologists as a tool of data collection. It is, however, the first to use extensive, qualitative interviews with British commercial archaeologists. The Institute of Field Archaeology's Equal Opportunities Working Party (Morris 1992) conducted a small number of interviews during the preparation of their report. Having intended to interview 30 archaeologists from all sectors of the discipline, they later decided that it would be too time-consuming and expensive and subsequently conducted only seven interviews (Morris 1992: 9-10). The working party utilised a 'structured' interview technique, making notes against a guide questionnaire and found that "the range of topics discussed demonstrated the limitations of using the questionnaire method alone to gather information, and hinted at the existence of some serious underlying problems" (Morris 1992: 10).

Moser (1995) used 'semi-structured' interviewing as a tool in her research into the formation of Australian archaeology. Starting with a set of themes she allowed the dialogue with her participants to govern the content of the interview. This allowed her access to 'less official' views of the discipline as a whole, but also provided specific information regarding "the features that characterised people's training in archaeology and their subsequent careers in the profession" (Moser 1995:57). Given the Australian context the professionals in Moser's study were limited to academic or museum-based archaeologists, but she was able to conduct over 50 detailed interviews with those involved in "either teaching, researching or learning the subject" (Moser 1995: 57).

Edgeworth (2003) conducted interviews with British commercial archaeologists, but his methodology and intent were quite different from those employed here. During his research into the Ethnography of Archaeological Practice he recorded a number of on-site observations in November and December 1989, which were intended to illuminate the archaeological process as practiced by the individuals with whom he worked. Edgeworth's observations come from his own role as participant in the excavation, as well as the interviews conducted with other site staff. These interviews were loosely structured and involved him leaving the feature he was engaged with and walking to another part of the site to

> Ask the digger(s) working there to tell me about the material field they were working upon, the nature of their task in excavating it, the way in which it had been tackled so far, the problems encountered, the plans for further excavation, and so on. Each interview was different, since the questions and answers related specifically to the unique configuration of material evidence directly in view, but the general idea was to gather information about 1. the history, 2. the present circumstances, and 3. the future orientation of the excavation of that part of the site. An interview could last anything from ten minutes to half an hour, after which I drew a sketch of the material field – with particular emphasis on the features or patterns which had figured in our conversation. (Edgeworth 2003: 22)

Edgeworth's interviews are more like the conversations recalled in the analysis of the participant observation study (Chapter Six) than the 'semi-structured' (sometimes called 'unstructured') sociological interviewing technique employed by Moser and subsequently selected for use in the collection of data for this study.

It is important to clarify the nature of the interview process, conducted as part of this research process, as the term 'interview' perhaps creates an illusion of rigid data gathering. Because of the nature of the topic it was decided that the best way of approaching the many issues faced by commercial archaeologists was to assign them some authority in determining the course of the interview. For instance, a fixed set of questions tends to force the interviewees to respond to the issues that the interviewer deems important. This 'Structured' or 'Survey' form of interviewing is "presented as a data collection device involving situations where the interviewer merely poses questions and records answers in a set pattern" (Burgess 1984: 101). This is undoubtedly useful if one is undertaking an opinion poll on a single issue, or a narrow range of issues, which can be encompassed by concise questioning. However, it was not felt to be useful simply to ask people whether they thought that, for example, commercial archaeology was in crisis or not. The most important aspect of this component of the research was to find out, to continue the example, why people thought that commercial archaeology was in crisis, what their personal experiences could tell us about the crisis and how the often marginalized, junior site staff were treated as a result of that crisis. A concern of this research was to give a voice to the large numbers of commercial archaeologists who felt that they were not being listened to by professional governing bodies (eg the IFA) or national and local government.

For these reasons, the 'Unstructured' or 'Informal' Interview technique as described by Breakwell (1990), Burgess (1982,1984), Mason (1996, 2002), Fetterman (1998) and others was adopted for this analysis. Burgess (1984: 102) states that "there is a long tradition in social science research where interviews have been perceived as 'conversations with a purpose'". Most of the sources cited above agreed broadly on the nature of an unstructured, qualitative interview, but some also highlight potential pitfalls. Fetterman (1998), for example, warns that an informal interview technique will lead inevitably to a "contamination" in which the natural, relaxed tone leads the interviewer to ask leading questions. He also warns of the importance of sensitivity and timing during interviews.

> *The chance to ask a gang member about illegal activities might be lost if during the interview that individual receives a phone call from another gang member warning about an unidentified informer in the community. That moment, however, might be the best time to ask about informants and the pressures of community life. An ethnographer must learn to be attentive to a person's shifts in tone because these changes are important cues to attitudes and feelings. An elderly woman's shift from soft, eloquent speech to frightened, quivering whispers when she mentions the death of her spouse is a cue that the questioner should proceed delicately.*
> **(Fetterman 1998: 39)**

Breakwell (1990) also gives useful guidelines for the formulation of questions. These guidelines are largely designed to avoid confusion, both during the interview and in the subsequent analysis. They include not using 'double barrelled' questions – effectively two separate questions – in which a single response can create uncertainty, avoiding complex phrases or jargon and not using double negatives. These guidelines are, as are Fetterman's, good rules for everyday conversation, which are perhaps not actively considered until one enters an interview setting. However, the informal, conversational nature of the interview does sometimes lead to mistakes being made by the interviewer. It is important to be aware of these guidelines so that one can clarify the precise question being asked in order to avoid confusion.

As per standard methodology each interview was begun with a pre-conceived set of themes that needed to be addressed in greater or lesser detail. Beyond these the course and nature of the interview was determined by the active dialogue between the participant(s) and myself, as the interviewer. The six basic themes were the following –

1   A brief work/life history of the participant.

2   How they felt about the job they were doing.

3   Perceptions of the job they do, including, for example:

   i How their perceptions about it have changed.

   ii Public/non-archaeologist perceptions of it.

4   The current situation in the profession.
       This theme included issues such as:
              i   Pay, contracts, promotion etc.
              ii   Quality of the work.
              iii Competitive Tendering.
              iv   PPG16.
              v   IFA.
              vi   Prospect.

5   The future of the profession, eg
              i   How did they imagine it would change?
              ii   How would they LIKE it to change?

6   Any questions or comments they would like to raise.

The order or exact content of the dialogue was entirely flexible. These themes were used merely as a guide, and occasionally as a reminder of fresh directions if the interview seemed to be drying up.

It is also important to clarify the terminology that was applied to the process. There has been some debate about the correct way to refer to the interviewees and this depends to some extent on the type of interview technique applied. I am firmly of the opinion, however, that in this case the archaeologists with whom I recorded interviews were actually 'participants' in my research – actively contributing to the creation of the 'data' and causing me to adjust my opinions and approach to the subject. Mason supports this approach when she writes that unstructured interviewing is not the 'excavation of knowledge', ie that it is something that can be revealed through appropriate questioning. Instead the interview is "a site of knowledge construction, and the interviewee and interviewer [are] co-participants in the process" (Mason 2002: 227).

It was felt that the best way of opening the conversation with the participant was to reassure them that it was an informal conversation; that their anonymity would be secure; and that the taped record of our 'interview' would be for my use only. A number of people made it clear that they would be happy to have their identities known, and that they were glad to be part of something that they hoped might improve the working conditions of commercial archaeologists. Others were a little more wary and would only participate with guarantees of anonymity. Because of this, and because I was predictably working largely in the city and environs of Southampton, it was decided that it would be best to apply anonymity to all interviews so that those with concerns could not be identified if key information was given by their colleagues in other interviews.

It was found that beginning the interviews with a question about the archaeological background of the participant was a useful way of breaking the ice. In most cases it was not necessary at this stage to ask many questions to draw information out of the respondent, but it established some key areas that I could move on to. It also seemed to help people to relax somewhat, rather than starting by asking them for detailed perceptions of the archaeological profession. It was my intention to establish a rapport with the participant and to create a conversational rather than a cold, interrogative atmosphere. I wanted an open dialogue in which interviewer and interviewee were equal participants in the process. It is interesting and important to note, however, that the quality of the interviews did improve significantly with experience. This was only really evident when listening to them all again once the 28 interviews had been conducted. I found that my interviewing technique was, initially, rather less natural than it was to become and this produced interviews that sometimes sounded a little stilted. Despite producing some good data the first few interviews seemed less naturally conversational than I had hoped, but a significant improvement can be seen from the interviews with Participant 3 and Participants 4 and 5 onwards. The quality of the data obtained also improved as I became more comfortable with the process.

A prime example of a good interview amidst a challenging environment is the one held with Participant 19. Having spent the previous two weeks working with this individual, discussing aspects of my project and generally becoming friends, we were finally able to record an interview on the floor of the transit lounge at Vienna Airport. Despite occasional outbursts from the PA system and the ebb and flow of passengers catching connecting flights, the quality of the recording was very good. Furthermore the participant required very little encouragement or steering from me to discuss his background and perspectives and the majority of my themes were covered in a very natural manner. This was helped largely by the fact that his interests coincided with many of mine and that he had therefore considered many of the themes addressed in this study long before we met. Having chatted briefly beforehand I turned the tape recorder on and the interview began:

P19:	*Would you like a sound level check?*
Me:	[laughs] *Testing, testing.*
P19:	*Hello, hello…*
Me:	*So, you're 39?*
P19:	*38, but 39 in… too damn soon…*
Me:	[laughs] *and you've been digging since…?*
P19:	*Professionally since 17, so that's nigh on 22 years.*
Me:	*So – if you can remember! – Can you just give me a brief background; how you got into archaeology, your motivations. You know, just a bit of bio.*
P19:	*Bio. Right. Starting at the age of three with the excavation of a budgie skeleton… do you mind if I get comfortable?*
Me:	*No, no.*
P19:	*Thank you.* [pause] *Age of 3 excavated a budgie skeleton with my mother's best fish knives and then laid out the skeleton on the table.*
Me:	*Fantastic.*
P19:	*And then got into Dinosaurs, of course. Bit of Geology. By the time I was 10 I was a member of a local society – the [City] Archaeological Field Society. Age of 13 I answered an advert in Popular Archaeology magazine and went to live in a cave down in the Wye Valley with the remarkable [name].*
Me:	*Was that the King Arthur's…?*

P19:	*No, this was cave 5615.*
Me:	*Oh… [sarcastically] that one…*
P19:	*Above Symonds Yat.*
Me:	*Ah, okay.*
P19:	*Very famous for its cider, as I discovered. I went there for, four weeks I lived in that cave and it was hard. Hard going. My mother decided that it would either make me or break me in archaeology. I absolutely loved it. So by next year I had gone to Dordogne with [name] again…*

[PA Calls out gate number for the next flight to board]

Me:	*Keep going, it's okay.*

[PA Stops]

P19:	[To PA] *Thank you.*
[Continuing]	*Went to Dordogne with [name] and became an altar boy as well as an archaeologist.*

[The Airport clock chimes electronically over the PA, sounding rather like a church bell]

P19:	*How apt*
Me:	[laughs]

I discovered fairly early on that another effective method was to interview archaeologists in pairs. This not only helped participants relax, especially if they did not know me, but off-set the feeling that they were in some way being judged and interrogated. On the contrary it sometimes put me more under the spotlight and in a position of 'weakness'. The dialogue developed a life of its own as often one of the pair would respond to something their partner had said with a question or comment of their own. Choosing the right pair did have its own difficulties however. For instance, it was important that both complemented each other. There would be no point having one very vocal participant and the other happy to sit back and listen without taking part. Equally there would be little point having one Manager and one Site Assistant as it could potentially prejudice the dialogue and make it impossible for either to speak freely. Choosing the right pair was also not always possible if I had no previous knowledge of the people involved, though if I was interviewing new people I tried to encourage them to bring a friend who they were comfortable with. This not only helped me in providing more participants, but helped create a more relaxed setting.

Choosing the location of the interviews was more opportunistic. In general it could be described as one of two options – at work, or out of work. I undertook some interviews in lunch breaks on site if it was possible to find somewhere private to talk. At other times I visited unit offices and arranged times to interview staff that was convenient to them and acceptable to their employers. A good, open relationship with unit managers proved to be invaluable, for without this my approaches were viewed with wariness and sometimes suspicion. It was important that everyone understood what I was aiming to do and that my presence was not going to undermine the unit management, but was intended to allow every member of staff to comment openly. I found that if site supervisors or managers were not keen to participate this trickled down and meant it was difficult to find anyone who would freely volunteer. In contrast, the units in which the management were very supportive of my research were very productive and the majority of staff were keen to get involved.

When interviewing staff at the unit office we either found somewhere private to talk where we would not be disturbed within the office, or left and found a different setting. Depending on the time of the day a nearby, quiet pub was a productive location not least because they are comfortable, relaxing settings in which to discuss many pertinent issues. The choice of location was also partially dependant on whether I already knew the participant(s) as it was not always appropriate to retire to a pub with archaeologists that I was not familiar with, or, more pertinently, did not know me and perhaps needed reassuring that my research was professional and potentially valuable.

Each interview lasted, on average, between 45 minutes to an hour and was recorded, initially on an Olympus Pearlcorder J300 Microcassette Recorder and subsequently, after that became faulty, on a Sony Microcassette-corder M-450. At the analytical stage each interview was listened to a number of times to identify key themes, many of which had already been raised during the written submissions to the online survey and would recur within the 'participant observation' analysis. Excerpts from a number of interviews were then transcribed which best reflected the variety of opinions within those themes. The anonymity of participants has been protected throughout as some of the comments may prejudice their ability to retain or to find work. For this reason it was decided not to include complete transcripts of all the interviews as an appendix, as to do so while protecting the anonymity of the participants would have required substantial editing. This would, in many respects, have negated the value of the complete transcripts. Excerpts were chosen in which the names of units and individuals could be concealed – for legal and ethical reasons – without undermining the quality of the personal narrative contained within the excerpt. In contrast to the 'participant observation' analysis in Chapter Six it was decided to number the participants in the interviews (see the Appendix for the complete list of participants) as their names do not figure as part of a narrative description and their words alone are enough to humanise the issues. In order to allow the reader to better understand the position of the participants, the first occurrence of this code in the transcripts not only includes their identifying participant number, ie P1, but also their gender, M or F for Male or Female, and their age. Because participants often refer to the number of years they have been working in commercial archaeology, or when they graduated etc, I also include the month and year of the interview. The final code will therefore take the form of, for example, P1-F23-04/2003. This may seem somewhat unwieldy, but it allows the reader to draw wider and more meaningful conclusions from the statements made by the participants. It was only deemed necessary, however, to use this full code in the first instance of each excerpt. Where names, units or places are referred to I have blanked them out in cases where they might identify the participant rather than trying to change them. In this way the words that appear in the transcribed excerpts – apart from where I indicate non-verbal interactions, the cutting of parts of the interview or the removal of the names of people, places and units – are exactly as they were spoken by the participant. This includes, in some cases, swearing and colloquialisms.

In this chapter the focus will be on the career paths taken by the participants, from their earliest expressions of interest, through their university years, their first experiences of commercial archaeology and the subsequent development of their careers. Their perceptions of the job, including pay, conditions and representation within professional bodies and Trade Unions, will be dealt with separately in Chapter Seven.

Thematic analysis

Born or converted archaeologists

The interviews give a definite sense that the participants fall into one of two camps. By this I mean those that had a very early interest in archaeology, perhaps even before they really understood what archaeology was, and those that became archaeologists as a result of enjoying the degree course that they had chosen simply because it looked interesting, or, perhaps, through the Manpower Services Commission. A common story amongst 'born' archaeologists was of early forays into excavation and experiencing the thrill of discovery at an early age. Equally, a number cite frequent family trips to famous archaeological sites, or media coverage of archaeology as early factors in their interest.

Me:	*…If you can give me a background. How you got into archaeology; Where the interest came from. Just general biographical info.*
P21-F26-12/2004:	*Are we going back to being three years old, digging in the garden here or are we…?* [laughs] *I excavated my dead Guinea Pigs when I was about 10, so… I did the typical 'I want to do archaeology' because my parents took me round Roman villas when I was a kid and I was absolutely fascinated by it all. So I always had this fascination with archaeology. Went through GCSEs and A-Level, not really thinking about it as a viable option really, but then, when I was doing my A-Levels I decided that was what I was going to do at university.*

Other participants even stated that they 'knew' they were going to be an archaeologist and seem to have undertaken quite ambitious excavations in their parents' back gardens or locally.

P12-M25-02/2004:	*I was always digging holes in the back garden, trying to find stuff. From a very early age. And that just developed into an interest in history and then archaeology … My parents wanted me to be an engineer, but* [laughs] *it's natural really. I knew very early really. I didn't even know what an archaeologist was. It was nothing to do with 'Time Team' or any of the other… it was a love of discovery… it developed from there really…*
P13-M25-02/2004:	*Same sort of thing really… As a kid… I found a lovely little arrowhead when I was about seven or eight years old… From then on I thought 'Wow. This is incredible' and I was digging holes… I found a dead… pig cemetery in the village… probably wasn't very old at all… and I dug all that up and took it into school…*
P12:	[laughs]
P13:	*… thought I'd find a dinosaur or something but oh, no…*

Some even explored this early interest by taking part in training excavations as young as 13, such as P19. Having already excavated a budgie skeleton at a very young age he then answered an advert in an archaeological magazine for a training dig in England and subsequently went abroad to continue his training. It is very interesting to note, however, that the training was not just in fieldwork methods, but also included lessons in what the Site Director thought it meant to 'be' an archaeologist. Throughout this interview P19 frequently made very 'masculine' comments regarding the nature of archaeology and these opinions were clearly learnt early in his career. Although he would be appalled to be considered sexist it is often hard to see how women fit into his perception of archaeology, and there has to be a suspicion that many, otherwise liberal-minded, male archaeologists harbour similar views.

P19-M38-08/2004:   *I went back to France when I was 15 as well and realised that I really was an archaeologist, that it was part of my... I don't know if there's such a thing as a natural archaeologist, but I just knew I was. Turned out that [name] wasn't actually a Doctor in archaeology, but that he was modern dance from Toronto University, nicked 30 quid of mine and buggered off and became a monk in Switzerland, but that's another story.*

Me: *How bizarre.*

P19:   *He taught me several things. He taught me that to be an archaeologist you have to drink, smoke and whore and that also to be an archaeologist you had to believe what you've found, to believe all your theories, but be absolutely prepared to change them if they were wrong.*

Me: *Okay.*

P19:   *So, an example of the first one was the use of copper in the Palaeolithic period – find lots of copper nodules on the ground surface, dating 30,000BP – so he made me write a paper about why copper was used by Palaeolithic people and then destroyed it completely and showed me that you have to be tough, you have to accept... he helped me actually write it and made me, my thought processes, work out why it was a viable possibility, how to structure it how to work out, this is at the age of 14, and then during one incredibly drunken night in France ripped it to pieces and thus showed me that every theory has a hole in it so to come up with an airtight one is almost impossible, but you have to be able to defend what you believe in. If you can't defend it, then be prepared to change your mind.*

Most participants with an early interest in the discipline followed much more conventional routes into archaeology. A common way is to gain experience as a volunteer with units working locally. P20 and P28 both did just that, though the former started before his A-Levels while the latter took a year out between A-Levels and University.

P20-M38-10/2004:   *I think I mainly got into archaeology because, when I was a kid, we used to do family holidays up*

	north in Wales and we used to go and look round castles and that sort of thing. Also, particularly in the area I come from in [county], round [town], there were a lot of excavations going on in the area when I was at school. So, the first project I went to see was at primary school. We went to see the Roman baths in [town] which were being excavated by the Central Excavation Unit. They were fantastic. Massive buildings. They're stuck under a car park now.
Me:	*Nice.*
P20:	*[laughs] Yeah so, basically got into it. I think it was more going to see the excavations that fired my interest and when I was at Secondary School there was a lot of development going on around [town], including the bypass, and there was a big research project at [monument] in the mid 80s, which English Heritage funded, and they were all done by [unit]. I did a bit of digging at [site], where the big Waitrose store is now in [town], in the middle of the Roman town where they've got roads and stuff and then they found a huge Neolithic monument underneath it as well.*
Me:	*When was that?*
P20:	*1982, or 3.*
Me:	*How old were you?*
P20:	*About 16. So, yeah, I got into it that way and did A-Levels at school and applied for Archaeology at University.*

In comparison with P20, P28 actually took a whole year before starting his degree to work with a local council unit, but now feels that this may have been a mistake. His motives at the time were based on an admirable understanding of the importance of fieldwork, combined with youthful exuberance.

P28–M34–08/2005:	*I kind of, I was already crossing over from one world to the other, because my interest in archaeology was academic to begin with and I decided that, as an academic, I decided quite early that I would never understand it unless I'd done it properly, so that's why I got the experience. And also I wanted to have fun. I was 18 and there was a bunch of hardcore, drug-addled f★★kwits [laughs] digging archaeology near me so I decided to get in on the scene.*

However, earlier in the interview P28 suggested that he felt he should have either completed his academic education, or stayed in field archaeology long enough to complete his 'on site' education, but instead ended up with something in the middle that was far less effective.

P28–M34–08/2005:	*I started getting interested in archaeology when I was at school… Left school with the requisite A-Levels and a deferred place at [university] to study Ancient History and Archaeology. Took a gap year and went to work with the [County] Council Field Archaeology Unit, as it was then…*

In hindsight I should either have stayed working as an archaeologist for three or four years and then done a degree or I should have gone straight from school and done the degree first, because I ended up with a botched bag of knowledge and a reasonable amount of knowledge of the methodologies of excavation, but with enough... I was cocky enough to think I knew quite a bit, and not clever enough to realise that I could do a lot better. I really could have done a lot better. I think that tempered my.... I started to find university a bit boring to some extent because I was interested in excavation... Having done a degree on Ancient History and Archaeology really I honed down onto British archaeology which I could probably have done more effectively at a different university, if I'd thought about it, but I didn't particularly at the time.

Me: *I don't suppose you really have the information to hand at that point of your life to really pick and choose do you?*

P28: *No. I didn't know really what I was doing. As I said if I'd stayed in archaeology for three or four years I would have known and I would have had a far more effective academic foundation. I would have worked a damn site harder as well. [laughs]*

The difficulties of university study when one already has a large amount of fieldwork experience are discussed in more detail below, but it seems that a large number of participants chose a degree in archaeology because of an already flourishing interest in the discipline. However, the interview with P3 provides an interesting, alternative insight. Despite all the early interest expressed in the following excerpt, fired as it was largely by media coverage of archaeology, he did not initially pursue archaeology as a degree subject. Opting instead for an engineering career, it was not until his late twenties that he retrained as an archaeologist and built upon the interest he had had as a child.

P3-M40-04/2003: *I'd always wanted to do it. Since I was a little kid. I was about seven years old. I remember I was seven or eight and we went on a school trip to Portchester Castle and Fishbourne Palace and around that time there was also a Tutankhamen exhibition at the BM, came over in 71 when I was eight years old. I just dreamt of... when I saw it, and TV programmes I just thought 'Wow, that'd be brilliant to be an archaeologist'. And it sounds cheesy ... but when I was a kid I used to think it was like time travel being an archaeologist.*

Me: *A foot in the past?*

P3: *Yeah, when you, you know... I suppose I must have seen something about Howard Carter opening up the tomb and things like that and you just think you're the first person to expose something to the open air that maybe had been hidden for thousands of years I just thought that was mind boggling thing to be able to do for a* *living. I just thought 'God, how do people get to do that?', but when I got to my teenage years... I always had an interest in it, but the sort of school I went to the Careers Officer wouldn't even have known how to spell archaeology, let alone point me in the right direction.*

In that excerpt P3 indicates that he felt limited in his options at school and perhaps blames the Careers Officer for not being more receptive to non-mainstream careers. For P3 and others – those one might consider 'converted' archaeologists – often the interest was there, but it was not really fully expressed until during their degree courses. However, for many, the degree was not initially planned as a route into an archaeological career.

P26–M25–12/2004: *If I'm honest I have no idea. I grew up in [county] and my family would often take us to [monument] or wherever, so I guess I had an interest from there, but when it came to... in the Sixth Form, choosing... I definitely wanted to go to university, but I needed to know what. I'd never thought about doing archaeology, but there it was, so I looked more into it and just became really excited by the prospect of doing it so got into [university], loved my time there, but when I came out the job prospects were sort of... I guess it hadn't really crossed my mind, because I was there to do a degree and I thought if I can't get a job in archaeology then I have a degree to prove that I have some sort of intelligence.*

Some participants did not even seem to have given archaeology any thought at all prior to choosing their degree course.

Me: *Okay cool. I don't suppose you remember, way back when, what it was that kind of attracted you to archaeology before you went to university?*

P1–F23–04/2003: *Before I went to university?*

Me: *Yeah.*

P1: *Erm. I had History and Geography as my A-Levels and I looked through the prospectuses for courses involving History and Geography and there was one at [university] that was Geography and Archaeology which I thought sounded jolly interesting and so I decided to apply for the hell of it!*

Me: *You hadn't been on any training digs or anything like that?*

P1: *Nope. I had not planned a career in archaeology at all.*

Me: *Okay.*

P1: *It was quite haphazard.*

For a number of those who came into archaeology by virtue of a university course, it seems to have been the excavation experience that really confirmed their interest in the subject. In the following excerpt P4 seems to have drifted into archaeology and been converted by the fieldwork during her course – she even goes so far as to describe it herself as 'changing her' – while P5 took advantage of a council training excavation immediately prior to university.

Me:	*Going back to how you got into archaeology what was your initial, what was your motivation? Did you do a degree and drift into it or was it something that you thought....?*
P4–F26–02/2004:	*I did the degree and then I thought 'I can't do anything else'* [laughs]
Me:	*Really?*
P4:	*Pretty much. I'd never done, I'd never worked before I did my degree so I'd never seen any other, kind of, vocation type thing, really, nothing I had experience in and I figured you get a degree that's what you're doing it for, it's your career and I figured that's the only thing I can do, but within that there's a whole range. That's the beauty of archaeology.*
P5–M24–02/2004:	*That's true. Yeah I was the same really. Well, I wanted to do archaeology before I started my degree, because I went digging before I started my degree. I went for a, you know you go on, when you do the A-Levels you go on random trips round universities. I was bored for an hour, I had an hour free on a trip to UCL and then there was a tour going round the archaeology department and I thought 'Oh, I'll have a look round there.' Looked round and I thought 'This looks like quite good fun.' [laughs] And I thought 'Oh, I'll go on a dig to see if I actually like it' and went on a…*
P4:	*That's what changed me, going on a dig*
P5:	*So, yeah, went on a dig. It was like a little county council training thing. It wasn't… a lot there, but it was quite good fun and I thought 'I quite like doing this.'*

In the early years of their flourishing interest in archaeology very few participants seem to have established commercial archaeology in preference to an academic career, though many share a real passion for fieldwork and it might be this that was to become the main consideration later in life when balanced against the largely office-based work of an academic. It is reasonable to suppose, therefore, that these early experiences are common to all archaeologists and it is interesting to note the prevalence, amongst the reflections of those who were already becoming involved in fieldwork, of the apparently masculine nature of their experiences. Commercial archaeology is largely seen as a bastion of liberal-mindedness and acceptance of lifestyles that might otherwise be considered 'alternative', particularly amongst younger staff. It seems incongruous to many that it might also harbour implicit sexism. However, Lucas gives an important reminder that explicit sexism was present in archaeology until fairly recently.

Digging is, after all, a masculine occupation, and while more women than men are likely to do well in the pot-washing shed or in the laboratory, shovel-wielding females are not everyday sights in Western society. If they are to be useful on site (and the right women can be splendid excavators), they must be prepared to be accepted as men, eschewing the traditional rights of their sex. It is vastly time-consuming for men working in one area to be constantly hopping up and down to push barrows for women working in another. **(Noel Hume 1969: 60 as quoted in Lucas 2001b: 8)**

In light of this it is less surprising that P19 was taught that "to be an archaeologist you have to drink, smoke and whore" and that P28 was attracted by an apparently masculine 'scene' that combined hard, physical work with a thriving drugs culture. However, regardless of the individual interpretation of what it meant 'to be' an archaeologist, it is clear that all of the participants developed a passion for the subject, and often this was based in the enjoyment of fieldwork.

University years

By dividing the participants into 'born' and 'converted' archaeologists in the previous section it was not the intention to be divisive, nor or is it to imply that one is better than the other. However, it does illustrate the two main paths taken by archaeologists and the different ways their interest expressed itself in their youth. It is interesting to see that those who had done quite a lot of excavation prior to starting their university courses felt either unchallenged by the course or that it did not address specific areas of interest that had already begun to form. P19's relationship with his university course was so bad that he never actually finished his degree, despite trying a number of times.

P19–M38–08/2004:	*By the end of the second year, halfway through the second year at university, I thought what a bunch of wankers and I buggered off to [city].*
Me:	*The [unit]?*
P19:	*Yep.*
Me:	*So what year is that?*
P19:	*That is 1983. Is it 83 or 84? Oh god knows, it's all so long ago now...*
P19:	*Started on a site called [site]. Turned up at the gates... it was £60 a week... lot of money [laughs] ...*
P19:	*So I turned up at the gates on the Friday afternoon and said to the director 'right, where do I live?' and he said 'I don't know. I'll see you on Monday. 9 o'clock sharp.'. So I went to a pub and met, what normally happens in my life from now onwards, met some females and they looked after me for the next year. Which was nice. Was very handy. Me and my rat...*
P19:	*Within, I'd say about three months of working there, I'd ripped all the lumbar muscles by not learning how to use a shovel properly. So a brief point in time when I'm lying on my back doing nothing. I eventually get back, with no sick pay... my mother sending cash down to keep me alive... went back to work and [name] put me in to being a draughtsman. So I picked up a pencil, which of course is very good for the back*

*as well, and I began drawing the abbey at [site],
which I found I had a real aptitude for and I
became the site draughtsman.*

...

P19:

*Went back to university where I lasted precisely
a month before I fell out with the lecturers again,
so I returned to [city]. I then sort of wandered
around northern England doing a bit of this and a
bit of that and, believe it or not, a year later I went
back to university again where this time I think I
only made it two weeks.*

P19 clearly felt he was going to learn a lot more by working in archaeology
than he would at university. In contrast, other participants saw university as an
opportunity to gain valuable fieldwork experience so that they would have a
greater chance of employment after graduation.

P20-M38-10/2004:

*...Did it at [university], 1986–1989, and did
as many fieldwork projects as I could find that
were going in the department. If anybody said
they needed any help, I used to volunteer to help
them out to try to get more field experience.*

Me:

*What was the minimum fieldwork requirement
then? Was there one?*

P20:

*Yeah, there was. It was six weeks. Three weeks
abroad and three weeks on the departmental
training excavation. A compulsory six weeks. I
went to [country] in the first year. I did field
walking near [city] and then in my last year I
worked on the departmental project in [different
country]. When I left college I was going to
join the army. Was going to go into the Royal
Artillery, but I thought I'd give archaeology a try
instead, because I'd made various friends at [unit]
from working in [town]. A couple of friends who
graduated the year before I did went to work for
[unit] as well. When I graduated I spent about
two months on the dole and then got my first job,
just as a Site Assistant, at [unit] in 1990. And
then spent about a year digging and then I did
six months working on the Monument Protection
programme, down in [county] when that was
going on.*

Participant 2, despite not having any fieldwork experience before his university
course, also took the opportunity to gain as much as possible. The attitude towards
fieldwork expressed by P20 and P2 seem to be what sets future field archaeologists
apart from the majority of students on a degree course. P2 also seems to have
benefited from switching from one university to another half way through his
course, which gave him more opportunities to participate in fieldwork.

Me:

*So do you remember, like... presumably you did
your... you did two years at [university] and
then another two years at [university] so how
many months training digs did you do?*

P2-M24-04/2003:

*At [the former] I did six weeks and at [the
latter] I did two months – which was more than
they were asking for it was purely...*

Me:	*That's three and a half months in total!*
P2:	*Yeah sure…* [the former] *were asking for two weeks and* [the latter] *were asking for two weeks per year so I just kept on going really.*
Me:	*That's a lot more than most universities, so presumably you were at quite an advantage when you came out with your experience.*
P2:	*Erm… If you look at students in general coming out of university I suppose yeah, but the people who are going into commercial archaeology are generally the ones like myself who do that bit extra while they're at university. That extra couple of weeks here and there just because they enjoyed it and they're the fellas that you now see in commercial archaeology rather than the ones who only did the two weeks per year – the minimum they had to do – have now gone onto different things.*

Other universities are particularly renowned for offering a course that is weighted towards the practical side of archaeology. P4 and P5 both attended the same university and found that their fieldwork requirement was well above the average. It is particularly interesting to note, however, that despite this P5 later expanded on P4's assertion that 'you don't need a degree to be a digger' by saying that it should be based on apprenticeships (see the section on 'On the Job Training' below).

Me:	*What was the fieldwork component like on your course?*
P4–F26-02/2004:	*We go…*
P5–M24-02/2004:	*16 weeks minimum…*
P4:	*Yeah, 16 weeks minimum and then you split between time on site and museum type experience. They encourage that. Or you can do all on site, or all in museums.*
Me:	*That's well above average isn't it?*
P5:	*It is, it is, I think…*
P4:	*That's the thing about it, it produces much more 'ready' students than other places.*
	…
Me:	*Where do you think the emphasis lies in terms of training? Because a lot of people say that universities should be producing field archaeologists…*
P4:	*I think it depends on the degree though as well. If they classify it as an 'arts' degree then you assume then it's going to be a lot more practical than 'science'… no, no, 'science' is going to be a lot more practical and 'arts' is going to be theoretical and you assume from that…*
P5:	*Yeah, what…* [university] *is a 'science' one and…*
P4:	*You wouldn't know before you went into it I don't think.*

P5:	*... they can dig. You might not be too good at it, but you know the basics, but if you come out of [university] or [university] with a BA then you could tell me everything I want to know about Human Evolution or the theory aspect, but they couldn't tell you about PPG16 or how to draw a section or anything like that... but I don't think you need a degree to be a digger.*
Me:	*No?*
P4:	*No, not really.*

...

Me:	*So it sounds like there's quite a division between fieldwork based degrees and theoretical, classroom based ones, do you think there should be more... not advertising, but they should be sold as such..?*
P4:	*So people know what they're going into?*
Me:	*Yeah.*
P5:	*Yeah.*
P4:	*Yeah. And because of the two weeks experience thing [prior to starting the course at University] you knew that you would need a practical knowledge base before you even got there. You knew that.*

A number of participants, even those with a reasonable fieldwork component to their course, felt that their time on university training digs did not prepare them in the slightest for their future careers in commercial archaeology. It is very interesting indeed that P1 uses the term 'real' archaeology to differentiate between contract work and the academic environment. This was not the only occasion or the only participant to use 'real' archaeology, or 'real' world, to identify commercial archaeology in opposition to the perceived unreality of academia. This perhaps highlights the inadequacy of the training received or, alternatively, the perception that there is unlimited time and money for research, in contrast to commercial archaeology.

Me:	*...and you did, presumably, what was it? A two month training dig?*
P1-F23-04/2003:	*Yes.*
Me:	*... So you started work with [unit] in the summer of 2000 [having just graduated]?*
P1:	*Yep.*
Me:	*So presumably that was your first experience of any kind of....*
P1:	*'Real' archaeology?*
Me:	*'Real' archaeology yeah. So how did that compare to the training digs?*
P1:	*A world apart from training digs! You used mattocks rather than trowels for a start! It was all much more time pressured and a different way of recording, less... not necessarily less accurate, but less faffy.*

Me:	*Yeah sure.*
P1:	*'Get on with it, get it done, get it out the way, get onto the next thing'*
Me:	*And erm… how did you feel? I mean did you feel prepared by the training digs you'd done? Did you feel they'd prepared you for…*
P1:	*Not at all, not at all. Digging at university is nothing like going into the real world of archaeology. Total and utter shock in a kind of dive in… dive in headfirst… The thing with university digging is they want to make their digs last you know? If they can get five years out of a site that's fantastic for them.*
Me:	*Yeah sure.*
P1:	*Of course they want everyone to turn up and trowel it for weeks because it lasts longer. It's not the same rushed pace, hack it through that construction is.*
Me:	*Although I guess academics would say in their defence that it's about being ultra-detailed isn't it and getting that extra detail in the excavation?*
P1:	*It is, but to be honest, if you're a good field archaeologist and you work in the construction industry, you can get just as much information in three days with a mattock as you can in three months with a trowel.*
Me:	*Yeah sure.*
P1:	*No reason why you can't get the same information. Maybe not exactly the same meticulous quality, but the end result and the information you gain I don't think you lose anything by doing it faster.*

A common theme amongst those participants who studied for a degree before starting their archaeological careers, was the expressed desire to gain as much fieldwork experience as they could in those years. There is an awareness that a degree in itself is not going to set one job applicant apart from another, and that fieldwork, being the bedrock of commercial archaeology, was as important a commodity as academic prowess, if not more so. It is interesting to note that the participants who appear to have benefited least from their time at university were those who had already accrued substantial fieldwork experience. There is a real sense that youthful exuberance, combined with an over-confidence borne of months already spent in the field, made them difficult students to teach and P19 appears to remain dismissive of the relevance of university courses. A number of participants also highlighted the difference between academic fieldwork and 'real' (ie commercial) fieldwork, perceiving university excavations as slightly ponderous in comparison. During the course of the interviews many participants expressed a sense of pride that they were able to excavate archaeological features very quickly, whilst still recovering and recording the important information. Commercial pressures have made this an invaluable skill, but there is also an inherent desire to be seen as a hard worker.

The MSC

Not all archaeologists came through the routes outlined above and, as previously discussed in Chapter One, the Manpower Services Commission (MSC) schemes provided highly sought-after funding for archaeology in Britain as well as a large number of jobs for the long term unemployed. In many respects the MSC is considered a great success, despite only running for a few years and often being thought controversial at the time. Staff still employed in commercial archaeology who can trace their roots back to an MSC placement are often imbued with a certain amount of kudos, based on the widely held belief that the sort of apprenticeship-style training they received often far exceeded that currently available. That particular issue will be dealt with in more detail in the chapter which analyses the perceptions of commercial archaeologists, as expressed through the interviews, but P7 described how he came to archaeology through an MSC placement in 1987. Despite already having a passing interest in archaeology it was the MSC that actually brought him into the profession and he describes the training he received in his first job.

P7-M55-02/2004:	*...I've always liked archaeology from a distance. At least when I was younger. I remember Mortimer Wheeler's programs on the television and... I can remember when they did [site] in the 1970s... I remember driving past on the bus and thinking 'I'd like to go and volunteer and do that', but I was much shyer in those days than I am now so I never did. So, I actually got physically into it the same way [P6] did... through the Manpower Services Scheme. I went for an interview with [unit] in November... 87... and they took me on to do work in the SMR... and digging... so I did a bit of both there... you got good training at [unit], they were very good, but that lasted until the council got short of money and decided to cut back, that was in 92, so they got rid of quite a lot people. There weren't many left.*

P10 and P11 similarly came into the profession through the MSC, both being considered long term unemployed in the 1980s. They both already had degrees in unrelated subjects before being given an MSC placement, though it is interesting to note that P11 nearly had studied archaeology at university but had ruled it out because of a disability.

Me:	*First of all I just want to get an idea of your backgrounds in archaeology. Your work histories I suppose ... How and why you got into archaeology...*
P10-M50-02/2004:	*We were both at Manpower...*
P11-F50-02/2004:	*That's right.*
P10:	*So we were long-term unemployed in the... 80s.*
P11:	*80s... yep... yeah, it had to be nine months. You had to have been unemployed for at least nine months.*
P10:	*No it was six months for me...*
P11:	*Was it?*

P10:	*Yeah it counted even if you were just doing casual work through an agency.*
P11:	*I finished my degree and, I think it was about nine months, and then I started at [unit], at the MSC scheme up there, and I was there for a year and then I went to [unit]…*
Me:	*So you did your degree before you were on Manpower Services?*
P11:	*Yes. Yeah…*
Me:	*Was that in archaeology?*
P11:	*No it wasn't. It was actually History and English. So nothing to do with archaeology. I nearly did do archaeology, but I didn't in the end, because of the physical limitations that I have… cos I've got [a condition] I can't actually crouch on the ground and so I've never dug. In all the years I've worked in archaeology I've never actually dug [laughs] I've always worked indoors on the finds. That's what I did in [unit]. We were doing post-ex on a site up there…*
Me:	*Did you both start on the scheme at the same time?*
P10:	*No, [P11] was there before I was…*
P11:	*Yeah. I wasn't on the scheme when I went to [unit]. Just [the first unit]. That's what got me started. … And your degree's not in archaeology either is it?*
P10:	*No, I'm a Biologist.*
Me:	*Was that before or after you did the scheme?*
P10:	*No, that was well before.*

The Manpower Services Commission brought in a large number of staff into the fledgling profession during the years it operated. Despite some concerns at the time, particularly that a large number of MSC staff were simply not interested in archaeology and that site supervisors were kept busy 'policing' their excavations (Crump 1987), those who remained in the profession are often highly thought of today. They benefited not only from extensive, on the job training, but also because a number of them were able to maintain extended periods of employment that allowed them to develop their skills though years of on-site experience.

First job and first impressions

It is clear that, for many of the participants who had only experienced university training or research digs, their first job in commercial archaeology was often something of a culture shock. Many of them described how they sent their CV out to lots of different units before getting their first chance to get invaluable commercial site experience. For P3, however, graduating in 1990 – when the profession was still run in some areas much as it was during the Manpower Services era - meant that his degree qualified him straight away for a Supervisory role with a local unit. Despite that it did not guarantee him a long-term position.

P3-M40-04/2003:	*I graduated in 1990 and I've been digging since then.*

Me:	*Ah okay. So how did your career pan out then?*
P3:	*I started off, the first job I got was with [unit], running a small excavation in [town]. I can't actually remember how I heard about the job. I think I just phoned them up out the blue. It's such a long time ago I can't remember, but I think I phoned them up out of the blue and sort of said 'Have you got any work going?' and they said 'Oh, you know, send us your CV.' So I sent them my CV and within a few weeks of graduating they had me supervising… I mean it was only a funny little site. I suppose it was about… all in all, it was a funny L-shaped area…but it was only about a 60 by 60 or 80 by 80 area in [town]… right opposite the museum. And [name] was already working there and even then he was a very competent digger, but [name] who used to run [unit] at the time was really into people having a degree and so, even though experience-wise after I graduated, with volunteering and that, I probably had about 6 months experience … So I was absolutely bricking it to be honest. Even though I was only supervising [name] to start with and in the end I had a team of about six*
Me:	*In at the deep end then!*
P3:	*But, I really did feel like 'f★★king hell, getting me to supervise' and when I first, the first couple of days [name] had his nose put out of joint – that's not being funny to [name] – but, he was quite a competent digger. He didn't need me to be honest. He was more competent than I was at that time, easy, but cos I had a degree they thought, the person who was the hire and fire person at [unit] as well as [name] thought having a degree was 'oh yeah he must be okay' … so I worked for them for six months, then I got a job back with [unit] for about a year.*
Me:	*Was that supervising as well?*
P3:	*No, no it wasn't.. Just digging. And then I went, in the 90's I went [abroad] quite a few times and when I came back I used to basically work for [unit] on and off or [unit]. And when I couldn't get work with them I used to, what I call 'chimpo' agency work, which is where you just go, I don't know why, I suppose I just wanted to work outdoors but I didn't want to do indoors agency work where you work in an office, but the external work that you do is generally low paid…*
Me:	*Labouring stuff?*
P3:	*Yeah, labouring, van driving, warehouse work.*

By contrast P20 had a reasonably stable first three years in the profession, but did not become a supervisor for about two and a half years. After 1993 he spent increasing amounts of time working on training digs for friends and for the local university, returning for short spells with the same commercial unit in between.

Me:	So you started working for [unit] in 1990 and you were there right the way through until you came here?
P20-M38-10/2004:	No, not really. I did a year there and then I did this thing down in [county] which was with [county] Council and then I went back with [unit] for... that would be the end of 1991 and then worked right the way through 92 to the beginning of 93. A friend of mine at [unit] did a lot of work in Jordan, and Iraq as well, and he was working on a project where they wanted experienced supervisors to teach students on a training excavation on a big Tel site in the Jordan valley, so he asked me if I'd like to do that so I said 'yeah' ... so I went off to Jordan then for about two months in 1993. And then came back and worked for [unit] again for about two months and then did a [university] training dig down in [town], supervising on that as well.
Me:	Was that [name]'s site?
P20:	Yeah. It was actually run by [name] and [name], but [name] was working on it.
Me:	Oh, right.
P20:	They decided to bring in professionals from [unit] to run it and most of the people who worked on it were ex-[university] students. So it was just, overall, more professional. I think. But that was just a month and then I did three or four months working with [unit] and then I went out to the Middle East again in 1994. Did a 2nd century monument on the same project in Jordan and then two months up in Syria. It was two different projects but that was just... the project that was running after the one we did in Jordan and the director said 'Do you fancy coming up to Syria' so I said 'Okay!'
Me:	[laughs]
P20:	So yeah. I did that and then... after that it was back to... [unit] again. Supervising.

For P19, having never finished his degree, the story was rather different. In the mid to late 80s he was essentially completing his training, on-site and off-site. For him, it seems, 'being' an archaeologist was about more than just the job you did and this assessment of the profession at that time was repeated in a number of other interviews. The contempt he had for those he did not consider 'tough diggers' at this time is plain in this excerpt and again highlights his perception of the masculinity of the profession.

| P19-M38-08/2004: | Back to [city] and thus began a love-hate relationship with [unit] which taught me a lot about how to dig a site, metres of sites, how to be tough, how to drink, how to be part of a group, wandering about.... Being one of the big units of the time they were sort of... you were either with [unit] or [unit] that was it... It was all cutting edge stuff at the time. |

Me: *So we're now up to mid to late 80's?*

P19:   *About 88. 87 or 88. Went up to... where did I go then? Where the hell did I go? Oh, I went up to the amazing site of [site], Scotland, which was an entire Roman fort which we excavated. 70 archaeologists in one place. We were trouble. I mean we were just a vicious drunken rabble with loins attached. I then met my first wife and we then, she was still at [university] so I continued wandering about and going to [city] and we went across to the [unit] when it was still [part of the] university, did some stuff at [town], anywhere that would have us. You're still on contracts that were a decent amount of time – three months here, four months there,*

Me: *So you can actually get somewhere to live for a bit?*

P19:   *Yeah. I mean I lived in some terrible places. In [town] I supplemented my meagre wage by giving talks at the weekend, wandering around in a cloak, pretending to be a Celtic merchant. I also sold off bits of the stairs as genuine Roman tent-pegs [laughs] a pound a shot. Everyone was happy. Then we decided there was a chance to go abroad, so she needed to go abroad to [country] so using my experience we blagged our way onto this American site, which was great until we got there... cos they used the British diggers as people who knew how to dig...*

Me: *Using a different system?*

P19:   *With a different system and they just, they were people who wore kneeling pads and gloves and stuff like this, they were not rough-tough diggers. I mean, by that time I was about 20, 21, and thought I was tough as anything. Had a good time there... [laughs] ... So I got in this habit now of work in Britain half the year and go abroad the other half of the year.*

P28 spent the first two years following his graduation in around 1993 moving around like many others, but it is particularly interesting to note in the following excerpt that, when offered a supervisory post, he turned it down. Instead he opted to move to a different unit at which he felt he could better broaden his field experience. He puts this decision down to a realisation that his mixed bag of experience and an unrewarding time at university had left him without the skills that he had previously thought he had. Both P19, above, and P28 paint a picture of an archaeologist being forged rather than taught.

P28-M34-08/2005:   *So I worked at [unit] for six or seven months, maybe even less... and got laid off from there, just before the [site] Project. Was offered a job back on the [site] Project, but wisely I think, in hindsight, decided to go to work for a new unit just starting in [county] which was a private thing called the [unit]. They used to be the North [county] District Council Unit and they were basically shuffled off by the council and turned*

	into a private unit and sold on for I think £5, including all the equipment and everything else.
Me:	*Just to offload them?*
P28:	*Just to offload. And work was taken up by [name] – who I will say for the record is a fine gentleman – and he gave me lots of opportunities that I wouldn't have otherwise had in a larger unit. So that was quite a wise choice. I was there for 18 months digging a Romano-British graveyard largely. All cut into chalk. Very nice and generally mucking about. At the end of a year and a half I was offered a supervisory position, but at the same time [unit] were looking for staff and I wanted to get some more experience. Particularly to get experience of deep strat sites, and I wanted to work in [city].*
Me:	*So you'd been digging for about two years since university at this point?*
P28:	*Yeah. I guess about two years and I was just beginning to realise that I didn't know what I was doing. I knew I could probably bodge it, but I decided to head off to [city], like many before me, to really get hammered in the ways of the archaeological world. And I spent 18 months with [unit] on some of the best sites I think they did. [site]. Big Roman waterfront site. Waterlogged. Absolutely lovely. … Various others. I don't… well, I say I don't think I did a bad day's archaeology… I mean I don't think I had a bad day's worth of archaeology to dig, as opposed to digging it badly [laughs].*

A decade later the situation for new graduates was broadly similar though perhaps not as colourful. P21 actually volunteered to be interviewed precisely because she felt that her career path was so straight forward that it was worth documenting.

P21-F26-12/2004:	*…Left [university], sent my CV out to a few places…*
Me:	*When was this?*
P21:	*I graduated in 2000. So 97 to 2000 … So sent my CV out to the field companies and [unit] phoned me up and offered me a job…*
Me:	*Nice. Straight into it then?*
P21:	*I think I've got quite an unusual route through the whole thing really. That's why I thought it'd be interesting to talk to you, because, I mean, obviously, in the past it's been very much a sort of… people working here and there and here and there and all over the place and getting one contract, then another contract with another company… whereas I always seemed to… I've only ever worked for [unit].*

Similarly, P4 and P5, working for a different unit to P21, found stable work after an initial period of uncertainty and were still with that company a couple of years later. Being a small unit they had found it fairly easy to gain extra experience and responsibility and by the time of the interview both of them were supervisors. It is interesting to note, however, that both P4 and P5 got their first chances to show off their specialisms by taking the workload off busy senior staff. This does highlight the need for junior staff to be prepared to put themselves forward when opportunities like this arise.

Me:	*You finished when you were 21, at [university]?*
P4-F26-2/2004:	*Yeah, 99 I finished.*
Me:	*Did you go straight into digging?*
P4:	*I went straight into looking for digging jobs … but I signed on, got bit work with [unit] and every now and then I'd get a contract from them for one or two weeks and then, three months was the longest I got from them in one stint. That was off and on for about a year and a half. I also worked for a castle…*
Me:	*Was that National Trust?*
P4:	*It wasn't National Trust no, it's owned by the council and run as a wedding type place. More heritage than archaeology … So yeah, it was just bit work for a year and a half, two years and then I started with [unit].*
Me:	*Have you been full time ever since?*
P4:	*Yeah. I got a two week contract with them initially and then got laid off, because of work not being definite, the next contract, and then they called me up for the [site]…*
Me:	*And you're now a supervisor?*
P4:	*Yeah, I went pretty quickly because I, after [site], because [name] was pregnant I got the opportunity to take over Finds more and more which helped her out and then I did the whole, well a few sites, processing the finds and writing the reports. I've done about three or four sites now. So that was purely luck, because [name] happened to be pregnant when I got the job [laughs] So I was quite lucky in that respect and then I stuck with that basically. Then they put me on [site]… as a supervisor.*
Me:	*And that's not long after you started?*
P4:	*About a year after I started. I think it was. Yeah I must have been there about a year and then [site] came along … So I was already a Finds Supervisor, but that was purely in the office and Site Supervisor came with [site].*
Me:	*So that worked out quite well.*
P4:	*Yes. Definitely. [laughs]*
Me:	*What about you [P5]?*
P5-M24-02/2004:	*Hmmm? [laughs]*
Me:	*When did you… you graduated at the same time didn't you?*

P5:	*No, I was in the year below…*
P4:	*Yeah, the year below.*
P5:	*…so I'm 24 at the moment. So yeah, I graduated, when did I graduate? 2000 I graduated from my degree and then I went on to do a Masters in Osteo.*
Me:	*Right.*
P5:	*Graduated from that at the end of 2001. And then, basically, spent about three weeks unemployed and then they said 'Oh, we need someone for the [site] evaluation.' … and I got a two week contract on [that] and then I was laid off for about three weeks?*
P4:	*Yeah.*
P5:	*Yeah, it wasn't long really and then they needed me for a site of [name]'s in [city] and I've been employed ever since. Because it was after that they needed someone to do all the washing and post-ex and then…*
P4:	*That wasn't very long was it? Your bone specialism was…*
P5:	*It took about a year.*
P4:	*Yeah.*
P5:	*Yeah.*
Me:	*Is that mostly what you do now?*
P5:	*It's what I do now, yeah really.*
Me:	*A full time thing.*
P5:	*Yeah I started as a Site Assistant and the first year I spent as a Site Assistant and general in the office odd jobs, wash finds … and then it was [name]'s [city] site I first did the bones for, because he needed the report doing really quickly and [name] was busy … and I said 'I can do bones. I've got my Masters' and … they said 'Ok, you can do them' and then I did them and they were happy with the report…*

For P26, having received little or no practical training at university, his first experiences of commercial archaeology seem to have been quite a shock to the system. One can only assume that it was his proximity to the site that played a large factor in him getting the job with so little field experience, though it might indicate the low esteem that university training excavations are held in if it was not deemed an important consideration. P26 himself seems to have been surprised by this. It is also very interesting to note that, in the absence of adequate university training P26 found himself subject to the kind of apprenticeship–style, on the job training that had been so prevalent a decade or more earlier. It also seems to have been a 'make or break' moment in his career as he was starting in late Autumn/ early Winter and the weather was not very good at all, yet, by the time that stint finished, and particularly when he returned to that unit the following summer, he was clearly enjoying the experience.

P26-M25-12/2004:   *...and... so that was 2000...*

Me: *That's when you graduated?*

P26:   *Yeah, and I applied to 30 or 40... same as everyone else really... applied to everybody, getting tonnes of letters back saying 'no, but we'll keep you on file'. I actually went in for a small operation which I needed to do, but I thought it would be a good time to do it, and just as I was recovering from that I got a phone call from [unit] to say that they had a job in [town]... [university] had no practical at all so I had done barely any practical, digging... site work at all. So I okayed that with them... 'Having seen my CV you do realise..?' So I went down there and worked for three months until Christmas on the Roman site down there which was amazing. And it was really good... a really good crew who helped me out and showed me the ropes. Then, I didn't have my contract renewed until the following summer... In between I worked for [unit] for two weeks... and two weeks only [laughs] ... it was actually only eight days because it was over Easter, but it was up in [city] and my then girlfriend lived near... and I was working for Asda at the time anyway so I needed to get outside again.... And I phoned up [unit] and they said 'Yeah, start next Monday... up in [county]' and I've been with them ever since.*

Me: *And that was?*

P26:   *That was 2001. So a little bit in 2000 and then 2001 onwards.*

...

Me: *So when you started on site... I mean... you said you'd cleared it with people so you...*

P26:   *I was with very experienced diggers... old school diggers... whole group of them who lived down in [town]. They all took me under their wings and showed me all sorts of things... planning and whatever ... literally absolutely everything. From the first day I think I was trowelling back and someone showed me how to clean back and then someone showed me how to plan, to draw sections, set up dumpy levels, things like that.*

Me: *Did you, when you started did you start on a normal digger's rate, or did they have a special training rate? How did that work?*

P26:   *I've no idea. It was a week contract, or a fortnightly contract, but then the second day I was there they extended it to the end of Christmas. I guess I was another number, but ... it was a sharp learning curve.*

Me: *Yeah, absolutely. I think if you've got the old lags taking you under their wing then you probably end up...*

P26:	*You know more. That was the thing. It was them training me. Nothing from… no-one actually came over and said, or sat me down… I had to ask. But I guess, you turn up on site half way through someone else's site, they're not really going to stop what they're doing to…*
Me:	*You must have felt a bit intimidated I guess, or did you not really think about it?*
P26:	*I guess not no. A lot of the time it was chucking it down with rain and we were squelching around in mud and… A couple of days… Like the first couple of weeks were quite hard because I was thinking 'Is this really what I want to do?' You know, getting up at five every morning, getting the train down just to stand in rain and the freezing cold. But then, by the end of it, I really enjoyed it and when I went back in the summer it was just like the best time I've ever had.*

The situation for recent graduates starting in commercial archaeology in the UK has changed somewhat over the last 15 years, and no longer would a degree instantly qualify staff for supervisory roles. However, in many respects much has not changed. Often graduates are slightly overwhelmed by the pace, the noise and the expectations of colleagues, supervisors and managers on commercial sites, being a far cry from their university training digs. Many feel totally unprepared and there is a sense, among some of the participants, that only those who are able to adapt quickly to the new order will rediscover their enjoyment of fieldwork and survive in the profession.

On the job Training

As many graduate archaeologists quickly realise, when starting work for the first time with a commercial unit, there is still an awful lot to learn even if their course had a large practical element to it. P26, above, was very lucky in that the deficiencies of his university training were soon put straight by the experienced archaeologists on his first site. Not everyone will be as lucky as P26 and the provision of standardised, on the job, training is rarely a consideration of a commercial unit. The debate between the units and the universities rages fiercely, with both claiming that it is the other's role to train site staff. This debate is reflected in the interviews. Site staff, however, seem largely to be of the opinion that the answer is actually somewhere in the middle – ie that universities should better prepare their students for a career in archaeology, and that units should accept the burden of providing continuing professional development to ensure that their staff can expand their skill base. P1, like P26 was largely dependant on training from her first supervisor when she started work for a commercial unit.

Me:	*So how long would you say, when you started digging with* [unit], *how long would you say it took you before you felt confident on site?*
P1–F23–04/2003:	*Properly confident, probably about six months.*
Me:	*Right.*
P1:	*I would say.*
Me:	*Cool. And… erm… presumably in that time you had a supervisor or something take you under*

	their wing, or was it just general people that worked with you?
P1:	*I was actually very lucky I worked with a man called [P3] who believes in training all his new staff to do things exactly how he likes which is the proper way, so I was one of the fortunate ones. Many people start off and aren't given any instruction at all.*
Me:	*Yeah*
P1:	*But [P3] was very good and told me how things should be done and what was expected and looked at my paperwork and told me if my stratigraphic matrices were right or wrong and things like that.*
Me:	*Okay, cool.*
P1:	*Very good really.*
Me:	*Yeah.*
P1:	*[laughing] I owe the man a lot.*

Clearly, despite having two months of training excavations under her belt when she left university, P1 had very little confidence in her abilities when she started working professionally and was trained by her supervisor. P11, like a number of participants, actually suggests that degree courses should be clearly divided into those that cater for students with academic inclinations and those who want to develop practical skills so that they are better prepared when starting work.

P11-F50-02/2004:	*Archaeology is something that you can't learn about in a book. You've actually got to go and dig. Because you have to be there, and you have to…*
Me:	*Get the feel of it?*
P11:	*And sometimes it's very hard to see things and that comes with experience. Unless you're out doing that you're not going to be able to do it. So, I think doing a degree gives you something obviously, it's very useful, but I think the training… you actually need that as well, and that's equally useful…*
Me:	*Do you think universities should have a higher fieldwork component then?*
P11:	*Yeah. I think if people want to be field archaeologists then yes. I mean you can have those who just want to be academic archaeologists, but you can select your courses a bit more. I mean, even now there are some universities where you know you're going to do more actual practical archaeology.*

P4 and P5 go even further than this and suggest that perhaps a degree should not be a prerequisite for archaeological employment, apart from more senior posts. They, like a number of others, prefer the idea of site-based apprenticeships (there is currently a move in the IFA towards establishing an NVQ in practical archaeology). It might be a divisive step to further separate site staff and managers in this way, but it would certainly guarantee a level of practical expertise from the beginning.

Me:	It's difficult to know whether… the units say the universities should train diggers, and the universities say that units should train diggers…
P4-F26-02/2004:	It's always one or other isn't it? I don't think it would cost much for units to give a basic training, but they should have basic knowledge before they get in… whatever course they did in archaeology…
P5-M24-02/2004:	Well, you've always got to do a bit of basic stuff on context sheets…
Me:	An 'orientation'..?
P5:	But the problem is when you've got to train people about actually how you use a context sheet or a…
P4:	Yeah, or how to use a mattock and… It gets a bit tedious…
P5:	Yeah, I suppose I think digging should be apprenticeships. You shouldn't have to have a degree to be a digger, it should be apprenticeships. I think a degree should be more if you want to go to a higher level, like Project Manager…

P28 is clear in his belief that it is the commercial pressures placed on site supervisors that are responsible for inadequate training of new staff. He is equally clear, however, that, in his opinion, the current situation is driving down standards to a dangerous level given that fieldwork famously represents an 'unrepeatable experiment'.

| Me: | But you think the quality of work, it's still possible to produce that quality of work with the staff that are available, it's just not being… |
| P28-M34-08/2005: | Ah, no. I think there needs to be far more training as well. I think part of the reason there isn't the training there used to be is because the supervisors don't have time to train people up. There's a lot of people, failing field workers, field archaeologists, who, but for the want of twenty minutes a day of the supervisor's time could make f**king good archaeologists, but they're not getting it and they're… I couldn't believe that I still find, as you know I try to train people on site, always have done. I try to share information, share methodology and share… the way of doing stuff, as according to the lore… l-o-r-e and not necessarily l-a-w…. and it's simply not happening. I've had to explain to people who have been working for the [unit] for two years exactly what it is they're planning and how to plan. They have no, they still have no idea and they've worked in commercial archaeology for two years. Somebody showed them how to do it once at university and they've been doing it wrong ever since and nobody's bothered to correct them. Context sheets with three words on them. For Christ's sake you can't do…you know, words fail me, these people have been allowed to continue working because they shift large amounts of soil, but what they're producing is… |

Me:	*Shoddy?*
P28:	*Shoddy. And archaeology is total destruction and what you leave behind is your records and that's it, so…*

The contrast to this is the experience of P26, not only to be trained by experienced site staff when he first started work, but also later in his career when he was offered the kind of on the job training that is very rarely encountered in the profession. This was only possible because he was working for a very large unit on a large, well-funded project. Although initiatives such as this are clearly admirable (the IFA is currently trying to encourage similar training programmes) it is doubtful whether smaller units could afford to follow suit.

P26-M25-12/2004:	*I was given the opportunity… Because I was there… there were 37 people or something who started the first day, and we'd spent a couple of weeks sorting everything out, setting it up, and they went round with a list of names and said 'Right, what are you interested in?' because they've got this theory on working on site and gathering new skills and all things like that, so I think it was environmental, CAD, surveying and finds and I just said 'Yeah, put my name down for everything' and the following day I was told I was going to be doing CAD, so I thought 'Oh, that's quite cool' because I've always wanted to do that and I did it for 18 months which is quite cool.*
Me:	*Oh wow.*
P26:	*It took us like four months… I thought we were going to rotate round, but it took about four months to train us up to do the job we were doing…*
Me:	*Ok. From what you were saying I thought it'd be a day off site going 'Alright, this is how you do it, blah blah blah.' You know, like a grounding, but that sounds fantastic.*
P26:	*Yeah, there was one PO [Project Officer], well a supervisor at the time, she's now a PO, from [unit], who had done it before and they took two… myself and a girl from [unit]… to train us up completely. It took four months to train us properly, while [name] was doing her job. We were doing digitising and things like that and after four months we were doing her job for her so then she became PO and went out and did other things and we were just running the office. Which is quite cool, because I got to learn so many different things and now, as it stands, if [that site] comes up I'm one of the first names on the list. It's really good for me, because I'm always being called back in to do post-ex work things like that. Which is fantastic for me.*

A concern expressed by some units is that such high quality training could inevitably lead to staff taking their new skills elsewhere, to the financial detriment of those who trained them and possibly to the benefit of their competition. P26 states quite clearly that he would not be averse to using his CAD training to earn more money with a different company – probably outside of commercial archaeology. However, he is also very clear that he would prefer to remain with his current employers. The onus, it seems, is on the units themselves to reward extra skills and training so that those staff who do want to expand their skill base do not find themselves forced to leave commercial archaeology in order to benefit from them.

P26-M25-12/2004: *…I mean I would like to stay here. I really would. But I know that it might get to the point where I just can't do it… I've actually gone a good stage further with the CAD from what I've been taught. I've been using it a lot here. I mean, at the moment we're doing a lot of work for the [site]… a lot of desk-based stuff… … so I'm using the CAD there, and then I'm trying to wangle it with [name] that [unit] will pay for me to do a City and Guilds in CAD. That starts in January. … I'll just go down there every Thursday night. I know how to use the program, I just want some sort of certification to show that… rather than just turning up and saying "I can do this, this and this.." …You see, if you look through the papers, the jobs you see, CAD jobs, in there…. I mean, one of my friends when we were at [site], she had this piece of paper, a job advert, stuck on her computer, and it was basically exactly the same job as she was doing, if not simpler, just using CAD, and it was something like 25 grand, 26 grand, something like that and every day she'd come in and say 'Why am I here…? Why am I doing this…?'*

The provision of practical training varies massively between university courses and between units. Some, like P26, are lucky enough to encounter workplace training opportunities that allow them to move into whole new areas of expertise. By far the greater number leave university with inadequate, compulsory practical training bolstered by time spent volunteering on other projects. Of those, some are taken under the wing of experienced commercial staff to complete their basic training, whilst many more are expected to pick it up as they go along. A number of participants express a profound concern that, unless this training gap is bridged, professional standards will continue to decline.

Supervising/managing

For many site staff the promotion to supervisor is an unclear process that often means spending a few months effectively working as a supervisor before actually being given the job title and, more importantly, the appropriate remuneration. Some units are much better and have clearly defined systems for promotion and career development, but broadly speaking the experiences of P28 reflect the more common pattern of drifting toward greater responsibility (eg P3, P4, P5, P12, P14, P21, P22, P23, P24, P26).

P28-M34-08/2005: *About 97. Summer of 97… no it was Christmas 97–98. Spent three months on the dole and then got a job with [unit] doing what I thought was probably the worst archaeology I've ever done at a big site in [town] at the, Christ what was it* *called..? The* [site]. ... [unit] *had done a ropey job tendering and there wasn't enough money. Wasn't enough time. We were moving off areas before the archaeology had been properly assessed even, not even excavated. It was not a good time. Having worked for the* [previous unit] *to a certain standard, having to really botch stuff and for the management to care very much less about getting the archaeology done than bringing in the money and keeping the developers happy, that gave me a rather sour taste in the mouth really. I didn't feel like working for much longer so I worked for five months and then went back to the, ah, went up to* [city] *and worked for the County Council for three or four months. And this is when there wasn't much work about and we were working one month contracts. Same as usual really. One month contracts. Couple of week contracts. And we got peremptorily laid off from them with a day's notice I think it was. The day before the contract was due to be renewed. They just phoned up, they phoned up site and said 'Don't bother coming in next week.' That's not a good way of treating excavators really. I remember it was a bit of a f★★ker because we'd just... I was with a mate. We'd moved up together to* [city] *from* [city] *and we were trying to put a deposit down on a flat. We'd got all that organised and stuff and we had to pull out at the last minute. It was just a pain. You know how these things are. So then I went back to* [unit] *for six or seven months as a supervisor. Started doing my own evaluations.*

Me: *Was that your first supervising job?*

P28:   *I was supposed to be an Assistant Supervisor at* [the post-Christmas 98 unit], *but effectively I seemed to be paid as a digger, used as Supervisor and I had a title that was somewhere between the two.*

Me: [laughs]

P28:   *I was supervising about five or six other guys on an area, so yeah I guess I should have been a supervisor, but I had quite a lot more responsibility than that implies. I was putting together... I was working site matrices up to be useable, which they weren't particularly, and trying to cobble together the information that was being lost rapidly. God knows what that turned out like eventually. No doubt it's languishing, the report's languishing on the developer's shelves gathering dust.*

Similarly P20 had spells supervising sites after about three years experience, in around 1994, and it seems clear that this did not lead to increased stability in his employment. In actual fact it might even be the case that, with the extra responsibility under his belt (and on his CV) he was able to move around much more freely and work wherever he wanted, though by the time he left commercial archaeology he was clearly looking for something more stable.

Me: *How long had you been at [unit] before you were supervising?*

P20-M38-10/2004: *Actively for three years, but... apart from this thing I did on the Monument Protection programme for six months I'd just been digging solidly for two... two and a half years of solid field archaeology before I'd been asked to supervise... And then, yeah, I worked all through 94, 95... 95 I spent most of the year doing post-excavation for the project in Jordan [poor sound quality for a few seconds] and a couple of [university] training digs as well. And then I stayed up there... no, I came back down here and then, about six months later I went back up there and did another training dig for [university] and stayed up there for about a year working for people like [unit] and [unit], [university] unit and just, yeah, just working my way around there... on sites all over the north of England... I went out to Jordan again in 97 which was to do another post-excavation project on a site I hadn't worked on, but it was a big Byzantine cemetery down in the south. I did some of the post-ex for that for about six months and then came back to Britain... I can't really remember that... I might have gone back to [unit]... oh, I did yeah, did some big road schemes for [unit] ...And that would have been about a year and a half there and I went out to Jordan again for three months in 2000, doing a survey looking for Roman military sites...*

Me: *This was all part of the same project in Jordan was it?*

P20: *No. This was a different project. It was a friend of mine's PhD. ... It wasn't paid or anything, but I got my airfare ... And I did that and I came back again and finally decided that I was... Did a couple of jobs with [unit] and they were increasingly being jobs in... big construction jobs places like [site] ... and the [road scheme] and I decided I was paying for a house in [town] and I was hardly ever staying there... because of that and because of the fact that I thought the standard of person doing field archaeology had dropped considerably since I started...*

Me: *Really?*

P20: *Yeah, I decided to try and do something else so I worked for about nine months in 2000 doing jobs for friends basically. I put up fences, did furniture removal and things like that, and then I saw this job advertised at [university] and I thought this would be more stable... it would be the first permanent job I'd ever had!*

Me: *And that was 2001?*

P20: *2001 yeah. Beginning of.*

For some archaeologists the best way to ensure some stability and control over their career is to establish their own company. P11 and P10 decided to form a unit with a few colleagues after being made redundant in 1992. They wanted it to be run as a 'co-operative' and is currently one of only two or three such units in the UK. It is interesting to note that this was their first experience of management, having previously been 'junior' staff.

P11-F50-02/2004: *…when we actually left [unit], because of the way it happened we were all quite bitter and we had all decided definitely we did not want to be in a position where there was somebody else who had that kind of control over us again, that we couldn't do anything about it, so they can turn round and say 'We've decided that we're going to get rid of you' with… nothing you can do about it… and that's one of the reasons we set up a co-op rather than anything else, because we wanted all to be equal, and all to be in control of it. We felt quite strongly about that, and I think we still do don't we? We feel like that…*

P10-M50-02/2004: *Absolutely.*

…

Me: *In terms of the structure of [unit], do you think it causes any friction with other units, or is not an issue?*

P10: *Other units seem to accept it readily enough, although because we… the way we formed we work the way we work… sometimes they don't take us seriously. But that's okay. That's an advantage sometimes. People don't take you seriously and then suddenly 'Oh dear, look, we've got more work than you have'…*

P11: *I think it pales over the years. I think certainly in the early days, because we came from a hierarchical unit where we weren't particularly high… one of our original members was a Project Officer there so they all assumed that she was the boss. They couldn't quite get their heads around the fact that we were all equal.*

P19 had also set up his own company, but purely as a way of maintaining a self-employed status. He did, however, also become a Project Manager in a more conventional sense and described in his interview how he considers that one site in particular was his finest moment as he was forced to act quickly and improvise in order to record an important building. Clearly it was the making, but, very nearly, also the breaking of him.

P19-M38-08/2004: *So by 2002, December, [Building's] on fire and bizarrely enough I find myself called in with* [two national bodies and the City Council], *a couple of architects and the Fire Brigade and, I find myself in the fabulous position now where we're all gabbling away in the* [city offices] *and I take control and I went, right, lets number the buildings I want the floor levels that, this building's number one, number two, number three. We all know what we're talking about then. I'll be on site on… tomorrow morning… what time* do you start? Demolition was saying right we can get down there for then. What's the building that's most under threat? …That was a real tough one because all eyes were on me to be able to produce the goods and I had three historians trying, I mean you're talking about a site where normally you would learn a bit about the site first, work out what you were doing, come up with a scheme, in you go. But here we had no idea what we were going to find … I had a fixed budget of twenty grand. Twenty grand!

Me: For a year?

P19:   For the whole caboodle… and to produce a report. I managed to squeeze it up to twenty five grand, which was still a bag of shite.

Me: Surely that's virtually impossible isn't it?

P19:   That's what it was, it was virtually impossible, but I was not going to be beaten. We took nearly 2,800 photographs.

Me: Wow!

P19:   Sometimes dangling from fireman's ladders sometimes dangling from demolition… We were able to help the demolition guys out, like we'd say if you take down that wall there's this going to happen, I mean one of the fabulous times, there's one of the walls, in 1929 the architect had replaced the entire inside of the [name] building with a steel girder frame and replaced the entire frontage with wood, made to look like steel, very convincing. The surprise that the demolition guys had when they first whacked it, cos they wouldn't believe it and then they whacked it and it was like 'f**king hell'. Arches that shouldn't have stayed up, they couldn't understand why they were staying up. Walls that were going to be, oh there was one disaster. The walls weren't tied in because they'd been done at different times and the entire frontage of [the building] collapsed. Nobody was hurt, but we had prepared people for it. We knew what to expect. … After four months most of the site was down. I saved what I could. And then began the process of reconstructing the entire site on computer from the photographs, using new technology. Once we'd done that we had a two-dimensional model we were able to trace dimensions and elevations of the site, ground plans, tie ground plans with historical maps, documents, photographs, cartographic. So a year later, bizarrely enough, we produced a report which was, are you ready? 173 illustrations; 500 pages of text and an appendix which ran to − including all the context registers and photographics − 700 pages. … By that time I had gone absolutely barking mad. The pressure was appalling, because I wasn't just doing [that site] I'm running three or four other sites at the same time… and making sure people are getting paid and running big sites… cemetery sites and a couple of others.

Later in the interview P19 went on to describe his feeling that site staff simply do not understand the work of Project Managers, but that, in many respects, greater communication is required to resolve this particular issue.

P19-M38-08/2004:   *I think the 'unrealistic expectations' thing is quite accurate. 'Oh, I could do the management.' I mean the number of people that I hear say 'Oh, but a Project Manager just sits, just sits in the office all day, smoking fags, drinking coffee and ordering up the odd portaloo.' And as I say I have this breadth of knowledge now where if only it was so easy. Whole loads of things. You don't stop. You know, it can be seven days a week making sure that it all runs smoothly. They'd certainly whinge if it didn't run smoothly.*

Me: *yeah, yeah.*

P19:   *Cos there's a hundred and one things to do. If you're properly organised you can get it all done, but in a way I think there has to be a bit more of an understanding between management above supervisor level and the lower ranks.*

Me: *Yeah, sure. It should be in both directions.*

P19:   *Absolutely.*

The overwhelming sense from the interviews was that the hierarchies of units, and in particular the step from digger to supervisor, were blurred and unclear. There often appeared to be some frustration regarding the absence of clearly defined roles or pay scales and the route through which one might achieve promotion. This theme was also often expressed in the written submissions, with a number of embittered respondents citing incidents of 'cronyism' in the promotion of staff. At management level there is a feeling that junior staff often do not fully appreciate the complexities involved in running projects and units. The reader is left with an impression of poor communication between staff of all levels and an ad hoc, and somewhat unprofessional, approach to grading, promotion and career advancement.

'County mountie'

P19 was the most advanced, career-wise, of all the participants and provided an amazing insight into the archaeological process. Not only did he have experience of Project Management, but a few months before the interview he had successfully applied for a job as a County Archaeologist. This is often referred to within the profession as a 'County Mountie', and is a curatorial post within the council's planning department that sets and monitors the archaeological conditions imposed on developers. City councils often have their own curatorial post which is referred to as a 'City Archaeologist' within the profession. There is a widely-held opinion that County and City Archaeologists should have much more power to force developers and units to work to a certain standard, though there is an equally strong opinion that the quality of County and City Archaeologists is hugely variable. In areas where the curatorial archaeologist is weak, and/or inexperienced, the quality of the archaeological work that is undertaken is also often considered to be of dubious quality. P19's account of his work in this role gives a unique, and slightly startling, view of the profession.

P19-M38-08/2004: *Three weeks later, after I'd resigned, as if by magic an advert went up on BAJR 'Wanted: Assistant Archaeologist for [county] for duties as the [county] archaeologist'. So I apply. I buy a suit. I prepare to take it back. I have no degree. I have no idea what planning is all about. I'd always been fighting it. I'm the poacher. I go into the interview. … A week later I get a phone call 'You've got the job'. Hells teeth I've become a County Mountie. 22 years later. That was this year. It was a six month contract. I started and I thought I actually really care and I felt I could make a difference now because for once there was a person in the position who knew everything I had done in the past to, sort of, beat the system. I knew how to put out a tender on a contract to win a tender. I knew how to, the one difference was as a unit manager, a unit director, I still cared about the archaeology. That for me was the most important thing. To lose archaeology… I was prepared to say 'there's archaeology there, let's find a way round it.' I was prepared to do that, but I was not prepared to compromise archaeology. Ever. I would like that on the record please [laughs] but when I actually then joined up with them [county] had never had an archaeologist before, so until that time only the planners themselves had dealt with the archaeology on the few occasions that they felt it was necessary which was basically, you know, it had to be some sort of f★★k-off big castle nearby, or a scheduled monument, before they'd go 'Hmm'…*

Me: *Right.*

P19: *And I was appalled at the practices of the other units. And I came down on them like a tonne of bricks and they did not like it, but they weedled and wiggled and attempted to say 'Oh, that's quite right, we wanted it' and I'm now getting this back that we wanted a strong 'county' to tell us to do these things. I felt that's a bit of cop-out as a unit should be doing that themselves… should be self-policing.*

Me: *But I suppose the units aren't going to take a lead on that because they lose… an 'edge'.*

P19: *They lose the contract to someone else, but I think you have to have a fairer, more level playing field. They have that now with us. … We call up archaeologists and say 'what's this? Do you call this a tender?' I think the more that we do that and the more the clients… I mean I've sent back stuff three or four times 'Inadequate, again, inadequate, again'. Before I came here I changed [archaeological] conditions from one 50m trench to over 20km of trenching.*

Me: *Jesus.*

P19: *The client's going to pay for that. They're going to remember that. If units want to piss about they're* *not going to do it in [county]. … I go out in the field and it's strange because all these diggers are scared of me and I say 'Don't be scared' you know 'I want you to use your initiative. Why aren't you putting trenches through the field boundaries here?' 'Well, we didn't feel…' 'But the whole f**king thing is going to be under eight and a half thousand houses. Now, what are these field boundaries going to tell you?' 'Well, I don't know.' 'Think. Think what they're going to tell you. It's got an up cast, has it got a ditch?' 'No, no, there's no ditch.' 'Well, how did they make that bank? And if there's no ditch where did the earth come from to make the bank?' 'Oh, I don't know' 'Well find out. Ask the questions. I want a story I don't want you coming up to me and going 'context a, context b'. Use your imagination. Give me the story.'*

…

P19:   *I made another company, I mean apart from the fact that [developer] had trashed an entire half kilometre. I then sent them out to do a watching brief, this archaeology company. I go out at the end of the day and go up to the site and f**k me if they're not using toothed buckets on an enormous open cast mining machine…*

Me: *A Box…*

P19:   *…and box-scrapers, and they say 'We can't find… we'll never see the archaeology in this.' 'Well why haven't you phoned me?' 'Oh, er..' 'Right I'm going to stop this site anyway' and went straight down to the site manager and said to him 'I have good news and bad news' and he was going 'Oh, what's the good news?' so I said 'Sorry it's just bad news. I'm closing down your site.' And he went 'You can't do that.' And I went 'You've breached your conditions twice now. I want all these men stopped now.' I thought I was going to be beaten to death by them, but yeah he had to stop. They're learning, both the units and the contractors – the clients, you know – that you abide by the conditions. You're not going to get away with it. …*

Conclusion

During this chapter excerpts from a number of interviews were used to illustrate the varied career paths taken by the participants in my study. This analysis has demonstrated that, although there is a great variety of backgrounds and experiences, there is, broadly speaking, also often great similarity in the ways in which commercial archaeologists pursue their interests, qualifications and, subsequently, their careers in a broadly masculinised environment. The over-riding impression is that commercial staff often have to make a number of sacrifices in order to further their archaeological careers, but that P19 is right in his assessment that "if you're lucky and really want to be an archaeologist for the rest of your life then you'll make it." The sense that success in pursuing a career requires luck, hard work, but above all dedication and often also self-sacrifice undoubtedly contributes to the appeal of the job. The unwritten code that only those who really want to succeed, therefore the best and most dedicated, will do so generates a greater professional status than membership of the Institute of Field Archaeologists could ever achieve. In actual fact this might go some way towards an understanding of some of the scepticism directed at the IFA, for someone can achieve the highest level of membership without necessarily suffering for their 'art' in the commercial sector. It also explains some of the contempt for those regarded as poor fieldworkers, managers or curators because of the sense that they are some how undermining the 'code'. Equally those who work in consultancy are perceived as having turned 'to the dark side' because they have put money ahead of a passion for excavation and have therefore not been prepared to make that sacrifice. As P19 states, "you're not going to get rich as an archaeologist. It's a lifestyle choice."

CHAPTER SIX:
...It's about taking part

Figure 47: Trowelling in ice cubes. © *Jon Hall*

Introduction

An important aspect of this research has been to place the written submissions of archaeologists, the interviews with archaeologists and the results of the online survey into the context of contemporary 'commercial' archaeology. By doing this it is possible to demonstrate how interpersonal relationships, working conditions, site hierarchies and day-to-day activities are all central to the experience of 'being' a commercial archaeologist. It is important to understand, when reading the comments of site staff, managers or specialists, how the profession evolved and the stages through which it has passed in a relatively short period of time. In fact, far from being a static state of affairs, or a slowly evolving process, it is the constant flux in the professional realm of commercial archaeology that has seen a wide variety of different types of people drawn to this area in recent years. For these reasons, the image that 'commercial' archaeology conjures in the minds of those who remain external to it – including the majority of academic archaeologists – is often based on hearsay and speculation dating from the largely volunteer 'rescue' work of the 1960s and 1970s, the Manpower Services funded projects of the 1980s, or the early post-PPG16 years.

The first chapter of this book outlined the historiography of contract archaeology to provide a background from which some of the themes intrinsic to this research could be examined. This chapter will draw upon an extended

'Participant Observation' study which was undertaken during a two-month period of employment with an archaeological unit during the winter of 2004–5. By virtue of the nature of the research methodology, it is not appropriate for me to use a third person writing style when discussing data of this type, as this separates me, as the author, from the research that was undertaken. Qualitative research is often concerned with thematic, narrative analysis, but its most fundamental tenant is that the thoughts and perceptions of individuals are of paramount importance and this must also include the author who can not be, in any meaningful sense, completely objective. To conceal my own participation in the data collection and analysis seems, therefore, incongruous to this aim.

I begin by discussing the nature of the project and the hierarchy of staff employed on the site and then turn to an analysis of the ways in which my perceptions of these changed. This process of interpretation began before I started work on the project, when I heard rumours of problems with it, and continued for the entire duration of my participant observation as I continued to piece together an understanding of the site hierarchy. Secondly, I discuss my relationship with the other 'diggers' on the project, beginning from the first day I began work on site expecting to know no-one through to the end of site party when I had made a number of established relationships. This section is divided into the first phase – which constitutes my first impressions – followed by a discussion of my relationship with the archaeologists in the area to which I was assigned for the first month, before moving on to consider the wider site. The third section considers the conditions of employment, principally the nature of our contracts and issues arising from our pay and financial concerns, before moving on to discuss the physical concerns in the fourth section – namely the effects on our bodies of working on a large, high-pressure urban site in the middle of winter. Having established the role of fatigue in the errors of judgement that lead to accidents on site, the fifth section is a detailed analysis of an accident I had myself and its repercussions – both on my fitness and ability to perform my role, and on my relationship with my supervisors and peers. The value of this component of the research is that it provides a more nuanced account of the nature in which commercial archaeology is practiced. It is valuable because it provides insights into the complexities that structure working on contract projects – especially working conditions.

Methodology

Participant Observation is rooted in the concept that the

> *Social world is not objective but involves subjective meanings and experiences that are constructed by participants in social situations. Accordingly, it is the task of the social scientist to interpret the meanings and experiences of social actors, a task that can only be achieved through participation with the individuals involved.*
> **(Burgess 1984: 78)**

Therefore this body of data takes the form of a daily diary of events on site, from the first day when I arrived to work for a unit that I had not previously worked for, right through to the end of site party. It was only by utilising this data collection method that I would be able to observe and document some of the unique and subjective experiences of commercial archaeologists in situ.

I became aware during the course of this period of data collection that the topics I was choosing to highlight each day changed focus – from initial thoughts on meeting new people and attempting to assess them as potential friends and workmates right through to discussions about the site with people that had by then become good friends. I also became aware for the first time, having had no reason to give it much thought previously, of the social dynamics of introducing new people to an established group of commercial archaeologists. Of course I was very aware of this when I was the new person gradually feeling my way in, working out where to sit at break time and who was most welcoming, but for the first time I recognised the point at which I became one of the old, established crew for a new intake of diggers later on. I vividly remember, though I did not think to record it at the time, how I had spent each break time on the first day with a different group of people. Initially in the smoking room because that's where I had put my bag during our site induction, but I soon got the impression that it was mostly the supervisors who used this room (and besides which I was trying to give up smoking). I then moved to the main room for lunch where I realised that everyone had their own seats next to their friends and there wasn't really room, so I had spent the afternoon break in the specifically non-smoking room where I had managed to find a chair and joined in a very open conversation. I assumed at the time that the people were just more welcoming in that room, but I eventually discovered that everyone there was fairly new to the unit (by which I mean a month or less) and had just gravitated towards each other, as I had, almost without realising it and were consequently also more open to new people.

During the period over which I made my observations I adopted the position that Gold (1958) first describes as a 'complete participant'. This is one of four main roles adopted by observers since the 1950s (Burgess 1984; Gerson and Horowitz 2002), which extend from the 'complete observer' – in which capacity the researcher is not able to engage with the participants in a meaningful way and merely documents activity from a distance – through to the more productive (and more often used) 'complete participant'. In practice this meant that I worked as a full-time Project Assistant within the organisation and never let my observer role interfere with my work or, for that matter, become known. Instead, having returned home in the evening, I wrote a detailed account of the day's activities. The aspects of the day that were recorded in this way were those which had been significant enough to make an impression and this was, in effect, the only practical methodology under the circumstances. What has become interesting to me subsequently, however, is the thought that in attempting to observe the people and situations around me this study has, by its nature, almost become about my perceptions and myself. Rather than being an objective observer, I became the medium, the "main instrument" (Burgess 1984: 79), through which other people were described and events reported. In this instance, where the 'complete participant' is also an experienced archaeologist, it still nevertheless provides valid qualitative data and sets a stage upon which the experiences of others can be discussed. In fact I was able to completely immerse myself in the environment and the relationships I was forming by virtue of being willing and able to fit in. I felt that this gave me a distinct advantage as "the social characteristics of the observer are often too different to offer any chance to disguise one's status or purposes" (Gerson and Horowitz 2002: 212). There are, of course, obvious advantages to being seen as an 'outsider', in the sense that the observer is able to ask apparently naïve questions to draw out answers from the individuals that they are studying, but to some extent I was both an 'insider' and an 'outsider'. I was an 'insider' in the sense of being an archaeologist, but I was also new to the company within which I had found employment and I was situated very firmly outside of the already established relationships.

A risk associated with assuming the role of 'complete participant' is that the observer might become too involved with the subjects of the study because there is no separation or distance. This ultimately interferes with the research process (Burgess 1984; Gerson and Horowitz 2002). It is something that I did become aware of in my own work, in the sense that my observations regarding people who had become friends were perhaps coloured by my feelings for them. It was also apparent to me in writing the analysis, during which it was often difficult to maintain a distance and be critical of those friends if it were required. Despite these issues, the observations represent a fair portrayal of life on a large urban, archaeological site and the fact that I was able to immerse myself, and forge friendships, is actually a strength in this research.

Finally, before discussing any of the issues raised in the 'participant observation' analysis, it is important to note that I have had to change the names of the individuals, companies and places referred to where these might compromise the anonymity of individuals and, in some instances, for legal reasons. Rather than using a system such as that adopted by Edgeworth (2003), in which letters are used to represent individuals, I opted instead to change the names. I feel that this particular research tool is about revealing the lives of real people and that by reducing them to a code or number within the text it becomes harder to relate to them and the situations they find themselves in.

The project and site hierarchy

Before I started work the unit had already been on site for about a month so many relationships and routines had already been established. The archaeological work was taking place ahead of a large development in an historic town and as such was a high profile site. Yet right from the beginning of my involvement, even before I was given the job, I was becoming aware that there were some contentious issues behind the scenes:

> *Talking to Ed Carver in the pub I heard an interesting story about the Marlow site. He heard from some of his old friends from Aston Archaeology that this site had originally been theirs, contracted to them by Barwicks… Barwicks had done the initial evaluation some time ago and informed their client that there was 1 metre of stratigraphy to excavate and Aston subsequently won the tender. Having taken on extra staff they quickly realised that someone at Barwicks had made an error with the levels they had taken and there was actually TWO metres of stratigraphy.*
> **(Diary entry: Monday 29th November 2004)**

This error had led to the work needing to be reassessed. It would be no surprise if it had gone back out to tender at this stage, but it seemed that instead the job had been taken off Aston and handed to Highfield, their main competitor for large projects. This in turn had resulted in the extra staff that had been taken on for this project being laid off, though a number moved straight over to Highfield. During the period I worked on this site I heard a number of variations on this story, though I couldn't say with any certainty which was the accurate version.

Billy was telling me that Barwicks are up against it with this site. In another version of the saga it seems that it wasn't the amount of stratigraphy that was the problem, but its depth below the foundation of the building that's going up. The archaeology below a certain [depth] is being left for the future as it won't be directly impacted upon by the building (although of course no-one really knows what effect the weight of a building has on the stratigraphy...). Either way though, Barwicks were under the impression that there was about a metre less excavation required and because the mistake was theirs and they are the agents for the developers apparently they are having to cover the cost.
(Diary entry: Wednesday 15th December 2004)

Talking to the Highfield Project officer some time later in the project I heard yet another view of the situation.

He's [Ed, the Highfield Project Officer] *beginning to show the strain of the 22nd Jan deadline. I asked if it was because of the mistake that Barwicks made with the levels that meant we would be hard-pushed to finish on time. This had been my assumption. Ed told me that an error had crept into the evaluation reports when Barwicks and Patera Archaeology had used different TBM values. This hadn't been spotted at any stage until Aston began the excavation (it should have been picked up at any one of a number of desk-based stages by all units involved) and although Ed wasn't sure if the original mistake had been Barwicks or Patera Archaeology, when Aston pointed it out Barwicks had taken offence. The rest was more or less what I'd heard elsewhere. Interestingly though Ed joked that Highfield were the only unit to have done nothing wrong and were saddled with an unachievable target (though someone else told me that the tender had effectively assumed everyone doing every hour of overtime available which is crazy).*
(Diary entry: Thursday 13th January 2005)

This issue of overtime became a serious issue of discontent early in my time on the site. This was due, I suspect, to the initial uncertainty surrounding the number or hours we were required to work each day, but also because of a suspicion that this pressure was the result of someone else's mistake.

Clive [the Project Manager] *announced that he wanted us to work overtime until 7pm. According to him it was the only way of achieving the necessary deadlines. I suspect these are so difficult because of the problems that Barwicks have created for themselves and I noted with interest that there was sympathy for Aston and antipathy for Barwicks amongst anyone who expressed an opinion on the recent events. I also heard that Aston is suing Barwicks over the mistake that cost them the site, but this is an unconfirmed rumour at the moment.*
(Diary entry: Monday 13th December 2004)

The exact timetable for the working day remained unclear for a few days until the managers decided it was time to clarify the situation. Unfortunately, by this stage, the universal confusion had evolved into a sense of irritation and discontent amongst some of the site staff who had begun to feel that they had no say whatsoever in the hours they were being asked to work. Personally speaking, I had been used to working 8am to 4pm days, or thereabouts, and the current arrangement felt like a long day – even without the overtime on top. Having said that, I was all too aware that my time with this unit was about collecting data for my research and earning money and as such I did not want to rock the boat. However, things on site came to a head in the middle of my first week.

The issue of the working day was still rumbling on this afternoon. Final clarification of the 8am till 5pm hours was handed down from the main office by Clive, who had come to site today. I thought it had all been made clear the other day, but there's been some uncertainty. Clive's announcement of the hours during afternoon tea-break was a little bluntly delivered and one or two people were antagonised by it. Lloyd in particular was really aggravated and started asking about the unit's position on the European working week legislation. It seems odd to me. We are contractually expected to work from 8am till 5pm, yet apparently we are being paid overtime from 4:30pm. The only reason I can see for this is to get round any problem of the compulsory working day, by claiming that the final half hour is overtime… even though it's compulsory… Anyway, Lloyd's state of frustration combined with the stress already on Clive resulted in an incredible scene in the site hut. Both of them were yelling at each other and then that became a poke in the chest, which became a face pressed up close to the other and then Clive's hand came up and cuffed the digger round the side of the head. It was a half punch, half slap. It was like something from a pub car park. I'm not sure anyone could believe it. Within seconds a few of the other diggers and supervisors had stepped in to make sure it didn't escalate further and it was diffused. Both of them left the site hut to get some fresh air and calm down, leaving the rest of us slightly bemused.
(Diary entry: Wednesday 15th December 2004)

I had never witnessed anything like that in all my time on commercial projects. I'm convinced that neither Lloyd nor Clive is violent or confrontational, yet it is a testimony to the stress that people were beginning to feel that led to this temporary breakdown of the hierarchy. Fortunately they were able to resolve their differences that afternoon and there were no repercussions from that incident. It was interesting in the following days, however, that it had divided opinion on site. Some, notably the newer staff, felt that Lloyd had been right to raise the issue – though were quick to distance themselves from the confrontation itself. Their opinion seemed to be that you need people like Lloyd to keep the management 'honest'. Some of the staff that had been with Highfield for a while had a different perspective.

A number of people were quick to defend Clive. Those that had worked with him before were in no doubt that he was one of the good guys. A sound archaeologist and a rare breed of manager who was able to run a safe and happy site and still get it done to deadlines.

This point was reinforced when the heavens opened about mid-morning and those of us outside the covered area found ourselves trudging and slipping about next to some very deep pits. Clive came over and told us to stop for safety reasons. Many managers I've worked for would have considered it dereliction of duty for us to suggest that it wasn't safe without the evidence of a broken body at the base of a Roman well. My opinion of him rose suitably.
(Diary entry: Thursday 16th December 2004)

Although Clive was clearly the senior Highfield archaeologist on site I believed, initially, that he was the Project Officer – a site-management position that is often quite hands on – rather than a more senior Project Manager who tends to be far more office-based and, from experience, less well thought of. It's interesting in hindsight how long it took me to establish the exact structure of the site hierarchy, which was never made overtly clear. On my first day Clive had given me the site induction, yet prior to starting I had been told by the office to report to Steve Cooper – who I later discovered was one of the Area Supervisors. Ed Everett's exact role had also been a bit of a mystery for quite a while and there seemed to be no clue in the work he was undertaking.

> *This Ed is the Site Supervisor or Assistant Project Officer (I'm*
> *not entirely clear what his role is but he seemed to spend most of*
> *today dealing with administration so he could easily be either).*
> **(Diary entry: Monday 13th December 2004)**

It wasn't until Tuesday 18th January, during a chat with Ed Twist – another of the Area Supervisors – that I finally had confirmation of the structure.

> *Talking to Ed Twist later on I finally managed to clarify the site*
> *hierarchy. From what he was saying Clive is the Project Manager,*
> *not Project Officer. Ed Everett is, as I suspected, a junior Project*
> *Officer. Beneath Ed Everett the Area Supervisors – Ed Twist,*
> *Steve, Colin and Tom – have broadly similar status, but Ed Twist*
> *does seem to be the one who runs the show in Ed Everett's absence.*
> **(Diary entry: Tuesday 18th January 2005)**

At the senior level the hierarchy had little impact on my working day, yet this lack of clarity was present right the way through the structure of the unit meaning that new staff were often unsure who to go to if they had questions. On my first days in the Area to which I had been assigned I think it was only my experience on site that helped identify the structure. This was partly confused by the fact that Colin, the Area Supervisor was away that day, but I had the idea that people were deferring to one young man in particular.

> *...another young-ish guy called Dave who seems to be an Assistant*
> *Supervisor. He may be a full Supervisor, but he seems a little young*
> *(24 or 25) and quite quiet.*
> **(Diary entry: Monday 13th December 2004)**

I had been familiar with the concept of Assistant Supervisor from other units with which I had worked. Generally it was a token promotion that recognised ability and loyalty, but with only minor extra responsibilities and barely any financial reward – a kind of stepping stone position that earmarked people for future promotion. What was interesting at this unit was that they appeared to ask more from their Assistant Supervisors and gave them designated roles.

> *The Highfield unit have an unusual system – or at least it is unusual*
> *to me – which means that whenever I want a level or a co-ordinate*
> *I have to ask Dave, as he is the designated EDM/ Total Station*
> *operator. I'm not sure who else is trained in its use, but it seems to*
> *be an established system to have one person you can call upon to do*
> *it. I also had to ask someone from an entirely different area to come*
> *over and take a digital photograph of the feature I was excavating...*
> *It seems odd to me, but maybe the others find it perfectly normal.*
> **(Diary entry: Tuesday 14th December 2004)**

It wasn't really until during overtime on the first Saturday that I had the chance to get to know Colin, my first Area Supervisor. He seemed a little unsure of himself at times, but we did become good friends and I had a lot of respect for him.

> *Colin is … 34 and has been working in commercial archaeology for about 8 years… He was saying it was quite a challenge to be on this site because all of his time with Highfield was spent on the big [rural] projects… which use different recording systems. Having been put on this site he faced the interesting situation of having to work out the methodology and then persuade the others that he knew what he was doing! I also noticed that he referred to some of the others as the 'Highfield lot'. I suspect he was mostly referring to those who actually live up there, but there aren't many of them on this site and it was almost as if, after five years on large, almost autonomous projects, he didn't feel part of the unit.*
> **(Diary entry: Saturday 18th December 2004)**

These reflections on the hierarchical structure of the project highlight a number of key themes relating to employment and management practices currently prevalent in commercial archaeology. The very nature of the way in which Highfield Archaeology won the contract for the project seems to suggest unprofessional practice. A serious error had occurred during an early phase, which had not been picked up until much later. It was only when Aston Archaeology had begun to work on the site that a Project Officer had noticed the error and, realising that it would mean thousands of pounds of extra work, had reported it to the consultancy, Barwicks. It was not perfectly clear what had happened next, but the indication, from a number of sources, was that rather than put the work out to tender again, this time for the correct depth of stratigraphy, Barwicks had simply taken the site away from Aston and handed it to Highfield. If this is true it seems to suggest petulance of an extreme nature, which had cost a number of diggers their jobs with Aston (having been hired specifically for this project). The sympathy that many staff had for the situation that Aston Archaeology found themselves in stemmed largely from the redundancies that had been forced upon them. It was not felt to be a fair outcome, despite the fact that some staff had been hired by Highfield purely because of this extra work. A number of locally-based staff had managed to move from Aston to Highfield and remained on the Marlow site, but the feeling was largely that Barwicks had behaved very badly over the whole affair and that it was the diggers who were ultimately suffering, both through the redundancies at Aston and the extra pressure now on Highfield to complete the work to an accelerated timetable. Other issues were more indicative of general trends within the profession. For example, the poor communication between management and site staff which resulted in the uncertainty and, ultimately, a physical confrontation resulting from the stress surrounding the issue of the working day. This could have been resolved much earlier, had the management been more sympathetic to the needs of some site staff and made the position clear from the very outset. There was a real sense of disenfranchisement amongst some of the diggers that decisions were being made that affected them without any consultation or consideration. This served only to highlight their status as temporary staff in the most dismissive of ways. Equally no effort was made to make the site hierarchy clear to new members of staff. In terms of day to day work the impact may have been negligible as we all knew who our 'area supervisor' was, but it did exacerbate the feeling of being an outsider and there was a tangible social division between those who had been at the unit for some time, and therefore 'knew the score', and those of us who were newcomers. This division only began to break down towards the end of the project and, no doubt, the newcomers who remained with the unit and moved onto a new site would have become 'established staff' in the eyes of a new intake of diggers.

The diggers

It is hard, in some respects, to try and analyse the relationships I formed on this site. Even having given new names to the individuals, I feel that I am in some way betraying the friendships that we had by discussing them as objects of my observations. However, it was my belief from the outset that this could not be undertaken as a 'scientific' process. It was for this very reason that I chose not to 'code' the individuals, but to rename them. My aim was always to observe the 'peopling' of an archaeological site and to record not only the management of the site, but the interpersonal relationships. I have always found that the relationships on site, and particularly the vibrant sense of camaraderie, are an important part of any project and it is in this context that I feel able to discuss those with which I shared the experience.

On this particular site there were approximately 30 junior site staff plus five or six supervisors and above. My time amongst these people was limited by the duration of the project to about two months. Despite becoming friends with many of the people on site I realise in hindsight that the number I can discuss in any detail is limited to only a handful. This is perhaps natural given the way in which we form relationships in the workplace, but means that – although a large number of people are mentioned with some regularity in my notes – I only feel able to discuss my closest colleagues.

Establishing links

It was particularly interesting how much time in the first few days was spent establishing backgrounds and links to people. In commercial archaeology the vast majority of the workforce is young, making it easier to form friendships (which are often nurtured in the nearest pub, especially if there is only a Bed and Breakfast to call home during the working week), but they are also quite mobile and consequently it is often the case that you will find yourself working with the same people at different units. The first phase is often spent reacquainting yourself with these people. The second phase normally occurs sometime later, when you have made new friends and begin to talk about previous employers. With staff in commercial archaeology numbering only about 2,100 at the time it is common that you will find yourself working with people with whom you have mutual friends.

> I was pleased to find that I had ended up with a nice bunch of diggers. In fact most of the crew seemed really nice. I already knew one girl that I had worked with previously, one guy who had done his Masters at Southampton last year and one guy who I was convinced I knew from working in London four years ago. He recognised me too, but we compared units that we had worked for and who we knew, but kept drawing blanks. I am sure it was London, but it may well be that it was actually in the pub with a mutual archaeological friend rather on site. There's a couple of other names and faces that look vaguely familiar, but I don't have the faintest idea what the link is there. Maybe it will come to me.
> **(Diary entry: Monday 13th December 2004)**

I finally managed to place a couple of other faces. Ed, the site supervisor, was on the same site as me in Ireland in 2000. I had to really rack my brains for that one. The other one was the guy, Kevin, who I thought I knew from London. We were both absolutely stumped again and had more or less decided it must have been at a pub with a mutual friend. From that we established that an old housemate of mine from when I was digging in London was someone that Kevin had worked with on a foreign dig. He asked if I had done any foreign digs and when I told him I had worked in Molvania for a few summers he said that he had worked with a guy doing a PhD who had worked there. I knew one of my friends had previously worked for Highfield so I assumed it was him. No, said Kevin, the guy he worked with was when he was at another unit, working in Southampton. And that guy was working on the 'Invisible Diggers Project'....

It might seem odd to devote so much time to the various connections with my new colleagues, but it always happens when you start a new site. If you don't have direct links, or if you're newer to the job, you will probably have the "Which unit have you come from?" conversation. This invariably leads to "Oh, I used to work there. Do you know so-and-so, or so-and-so?" It's the way it works. It's the way that you establish someone's credentials and demonstrate yours, but I think most importantly it means that it never really feels like starting work for a new unit. Of course fundamentally it's just because archaeology is such a small profession.

(Diary entry: Tuesday 14th December 2004)

The size of the archaeological profession creates a rather strong feeling of community that undoubtedly adds to its perceived charm. The importance of shared experiences, particularly amongst the younger and more mobile members of staff, binds the 'diggers' together in a way that transcends any loyalty to individual employers. It might even be true that this unity of experience is the root of that feeling of community. Unit managers and directors are perceived as being tied to one unit or region. They belong to a loose community of archaeologists that includes the entire discipline. In contrast, the community of 'diggers', particularly amongst those who have substantial field experience and have worked for a number of employers, is a far stronger bond that has been forged over a number of years, tested by adversity, but strengthened by shared experiences and camaraderie.

Area five

When I was first sent to work on Area five I had been told that Colin was the Area Supervisor, and as such I had instantly made assumptions about him and his level of experience. With the 'diggers' though it takes a little more time before you can fully understand how you fit into the group dynamic. It is an important part of the process to establish the experience of the archaeologists with whom you find yourself working, so that you are aware to whom you should defer and whom you might reasonably offer advice. It is merely about finding your level in the 'team', but often archaeologists make initial assumptions about each other based on brief conversations and throw-away comments. Edgeworth (2003) records a number of conversations that took place during his research on a commercial archaeological site in 1989. During one, in which he was attempting to draw out a description of the process by which archaeologists recognise finds as they work, he notes the exasperation which his necessarily faux naïve questioning produced in his colleague.

Q.   *"Is it like driving a car, say, where you can talk and daydream while driving at the same time?"*

A.   *"A bit like that… the only thing I can't do at the same time as trowelling is talk, because I like to look at someone while I'm talking to them."*

Q.   *"So you need to use your eyes for trowelling then?"*

A.   *"Yes, obviously."*

Q.   *"But some skills, like playing a guitar for instance, can be performed blindfolded. Why can't trowelling?"*

A.   *"Because the guitar is always there… it doesn't change while you're playing it…"*

Q.   *"…but the ground you're trowelling does?"*

A.   *"Yes."*

(Edgeworth 2003: 54)

It may sound a very 'political' way of describing the formation of relationships, but as an experienced archaeologist you do not want to be underestimated, nor do you want to be guilty of patronising people through making obvious comments. You are also, on a thoroughly human level, attempting to establish which of your new colleagues you can form friendships with. I did not realise at the time I started on Area five, but it was only really Colin the Supervisor and Dave the Assistant Supervisor who had been with the unit for any length of time. However, having worked for units that had been good for keeping staff on for long periods, my assumption was that they were all 'old hands'. The exception to this though was Sam. He had started the same day as me and even during the induction we had I was making assumptions about him.

> *Sam seemed to be quite a bit younger. My impression was that he was in his early twenties and keen to impress with his enthusiasm – though it might just as easily be the contrary, ie that myself, Karl and Kathy were just much more blasé about being on a big urban site.*
> **(Diary entry: Monday 13th December 2004)**

I assumed, based on his age and his manner, that Sam was not particularly experienced on site. It transpired that in this instance I was correct, as he had only been working for about three months when he started on this site. This is not to say that he was a bad archaeologist. Far from it. He had the blend of enthusiasm, common sense and an ability to shift lots of dirt that managers love to see. When I say that I judged him on his 'manner' I really mean that I got the impression that he was at times unfamiliar with life as a commercial archaeologist.

> *Went to the Crown with Sam after work – we couldn't persuade Laura and Linn to come out – and we chatted about archaeology. He's blaming his recent split with his girlfriend on the instability of the job, but I told him that this is probably as good it gets! I think he should gamble on a long-term job with Highfield and move out of his parent's place. His ex works in the Midlands and they clearly adore each other. If it was*

me I'd move up there and gamble on digging work (and temp. if there wasn't anyway). I hear that a unit up there is looking for people so I suggested that he try them. At the end of the day he's only 23 and time is on his side. **(Diary entry: Tuesday 8th February 2005)**

An interesting contrast to Sam was Bill. He had been in Area 5 for some time when I started and I assumed that he had been with the unit for a while. I hadn't been able to talk to Bill on the first day and had merely lumped him together with some of the others.

There's also a trio of older diggers (mid to late 30s). They seem much less interested in the greasy pole than they are in enjoying what they do. It seems that all of them have been around the circuit and worked all over, moving from London, for example, when they got bored and on to a new challenge. **(Diary entry: Monday 13th December 2004)**

Despite the fact that I had begun to sit with Bill, Sam and a few others at break-time all I really learned about him in the first few days was that he played in a punk band. It wasn't until we both did overtime on the first Saturday that we got to talk properly.

Today was also an opportunity to learn more about the other guys. It turns out that Bill is 34 and spent a number of years working in the building trade. Eventually, having become a building site manager, he decided that the stress of the job wasn't worth it and left to go to university to study archaeology. He graduated this summer and has only been digging for a few months, but he's clearly enjoying it despite earning less than half what he was on a few years ago. He did say that he only intends to stay in the field for another year or two. **(Diary entry: Saturday 18th December 2004)**

Ironically, therefore, Bill and Sam had almost exactly the same experience on site. In fact they had both worked for Aston before being made redundant when they lost this site and had both moved straight over to Highfield. It was Bill's manner and his age that had led me to make the wrong assumption about him. In hindsight I suspect that it was his apparent familiarity with being on a building site, but also the knowledgeable way he discussed the work at hand. I discovered that his degree had been a very practical one and as such he had acquired a number of skills that most recent graduates do not have. Perhaps it was also something to do with the fact that, being a bit older and more thoughtful, he was less inclined to make throwaway comments that betrayed his relative lack of experience, unlike Sam whose youthful exuberance sometimes made it a little more obvious. Bill and I became very good friends over the course of the project, having a similar sense of humour and being of roughly the same age and attitude to the job.

Returning to work today [after a spell off, recovering from an injury] *I wasn't really sure what to expect. I bumped into Bill on the train to Marlow – his car had died while I'd been away – and told him what I'd been told. In return he brought me up to date with the site goings-on, though admittedly much of that was reduced to one phrase. "Same old, same old" he said and we both nodded knowingly.* **(Diary entry: Monday 31st January 2005)**

And despite my initial concerns about returning to work I soon settled back into it

It was really good to be back on site and to feel like part of the team again. Much as I love the archaeology it's the camaraderie that really makes or breaks even the best sites. This site has a really great crew and at the end of the day I popped to the Crown for a quick pint with Bill.
(Diary entry: Monday 31st January 2005)

Because I had started my time on site working in Area five, my best friends throughout this project were those that I had met in the first few days. Joe was another of the 'trio of older diggers' from that area. He was a very interesting character, but only once came to the pub after work and that was the night of the end of site meal. I had assumed that he, along with Bill, had a number of years experience, but when I discovered that he was currently working on a PhD I became unsure of exactly how much field experience he had. Joe was quite mysterious throughout this project and our conversations on site and at break time were almost invariably superficial or humorous by nature. I came to like Joe a lot, but never felt that I knew him particularly well. Occasionally he would make a passing reference to something in his past that would shed more light on his background and he had clearly lived an interesting life. It also became increasingly clear that he was very experienced on site, and I discovered towards the end of the project that he had worked for some years in Rome. Despite this he clearly never felt the need to pass comment on the site, or how it was being run, or even talk about the archaeology much at all. As such this made him something of a peculiarity. However, it was Joe who had first pointed out the apparent distinction in where people sat – at a stage when I was probably too new myself to notice.

Had an interesting discussion about site politics over lunch. We were talking about the hierarchy within the 'archaeologist' grade site staff on the project and Joe pointed out the differentiation between the two parts of the site hut – two portacabins linked together. In our section a dozen people regularly sat and chatted – predominantly myself, Bill, Joe, Sam, Laura, Karl, Kathy and Roberta. Of these the majority were on fixed term contracts until mid-January – effectively the duration of this project – and had been taken on specifically for it, or shortly before. In the other half of the cabin 20 or so diggers sat and by far the majority of these were people who had been with the unit for some time and probably saw a long-term future with them. It sounds far more sinister than it really is. Of course the people who have been with the unit for longer already have established friendships and relationships and they sit with their friends at break-time so it's not a conscious exclusion of new or temporary people.
(Diary entry: Thursday 16th December 2004)

Yet again the theme of camaraderie features strongly in my diary accounts. Throughout the process of forging new friendships on site there is an awareness that one may need to rely on these people in the future. My friendship with Bill was based on his steady nature and the attitudes, opinions and humour that we shared. There is an implicit suggestion in the diary that Sam, on the other hand, was someone who needed a little advice and guidance in order to adjust to life as a commercial archaeologist. Despite having the same archaeological experience as Sam, Bill was a few years older and benefited both from his previous work on building sites and an explicitly practical degree course. The camaraderie I had with Bill and several others did become particularly important when I returned to work following time off after an injury. I was somewhat concerned about the reaction I would get from my colleagues and Bill was the first to put me at ease. His reply of "same old, same old" when I was asking him about work on the train in the morning, might easily be seen as dismissive, but in actual fact I took it to mean that nothing had changed and that, therefore, my reintegration into the 'team' would require little effort. It is also interesting to note that, even after Area five was finished and handed over to the developers, the friendships I made there in the first few weeks were the ones that lasted throughout the project, despite getting to know more people on other areas.

The wider site

As well as making friends in Area five it is of course natural that over time one makes friends with whom the contact is outside of normal site activities. The first person to really put me at ease on the first day, and someone who was to become a very good friend, was Laura.

> The fact that I hadn't taken my own old and battered PPE [Personal Protective Equipment including 'hardhat', 'steelies' – steel toed boots – and 'hi vis' / 'flash' gear – high visibility, fluorescent clothing] and that the new kit hadn't arrived as promised meant that I was not able to work on site… not an auspicious start to my first day. In the end I was asked to catalogue the finds that were stored in one of the back rooms. I was shown what to do by Ed Twist, who is either a long-term digger or a supervisor I'm not sure, but either I didn't listen or he didn't explain properly and I was getting a little fraught with it all and feeling very much like the 'new kid'. Laura – an experienced digger in her late twenties judging from her manner – was apparently doing the same job yesterday so when she passed by she took pity on me and showed me the right way of doing it. She was very welcoming and I felt much more at ease afterwards. Despite my previous experience I felt very isolated and unsure in this role and was really grateful for her help.
> **(Diary entry: Monday 13th December 2004)**

Although I never worked on site with Laura, despite both being on Area one for a time after Christmas, our friendship was mostly based on conversations in the tea hut at break time – during which I most often sat with her, Bill, Sam, Joe and Roberta. When I had started on site we used an old building for our office and welfare space, but during my first week we moved into a conjoined pair of huts so that the building could be demolished. Collecting our bags and moving to the huts I had gone through the first hut into the far one and dumped my stuff on a chair in the corner along with Bill, Sam and Joe, with whom I'd been working on Area 5. Kevin had joined us occasionally for the first few days and, presumably because he and Laura knew each other well from a previous unit, Laura also started to sit with us. Laura and Roberta had become friends and ultimately the latter also joined us. From Wednesday 15th December when we moved into the huts, to the end of site in mid-February, we established a regular seating pattern – almost to the extent of having our own chairs. New people starting on site only occasionally affected this, though we quickly adapted to include them in our circle.

Consequently there are very few references to Laura in terms of work on site and even a few weeks into the project I was still a little unclear about her professional background. This was highlighted when I was starting to excavate a feature that had initially been assumed by Steve to be Roman. I had found a few sherds of pottery and a cock-spur and I was reassessing this provisional dating.

Judging from the colour of the glaze and the quality of the fabric I guessed it might be mid to late medieval, and somewhere in the back of my mind I thought I remembered being told that chickens were introduced into Britain after the Romans... or perhaps that was Turkeys. I asked Laura as I was under the impression that she was a finds person. She wasn't as it turned out but she said she was pretty sure there were chickens in the Iron Age. As soon as she said that I remembered some theory about hollows by roundhouses being caused by chickens scratching...
(Diary entry: Wednesday 5th January 2005)

Along with Bill and Sam, Laura was one of the people I spoke to in the pub after work. It provided an interesting opportunity to talk about the site, but also her experiences at other units including one particularly bad time not too long ago.

It was interesting to hear her views on how the site was being run. She felt that the level of communication was very poor, citing the example of how the weekly extensions to the site deadlines were often not announced but trickled round site in word of mouth fashion. Still, it sounds better than her last unit – she had been off sick for some time, but had been reassured that it wouldn't affect her contract as she had been with them for some time. The unit even encouraged her to extend the lease on her house only to fail to renew her contract a short time later – despite keeping on all the other diggers, including some that had only been with them a short time. She was still very bitter about it. She said that she half expected to be sacked for being off sick for so long, but the worst thing was to be reassured that it was okay beforehand!
(Diary entry: Tuesday 1st February 2005)

Of the three of my best friends on site, Laura had the most experience and was someone with whom I could discuss a number of the wider issues of working in 'commercial' archaeology, from contracts, pay and management right through to the quality of site huts and Bed and Breakfast accommodation on projects.

Conditions of employment

A concern of site staff, one that is often at the forefront of their minds, is the general conditions of employment that prevail in commercial archaeology. As in the case referred to above, site staff often find that not only are their interests given a very low priority by unit management, but also in some cases it can seem that no thought whatsoever is given to the well being of the more junior staff.

My initial contract with this unit was a fairly standard one and was essentially project-specific. The first fixed-term contract ran from 11th December 2004 to the 14th January 2005. Shortly after New Year most of us received a letter extending our fixed-term contracts to the 18th February, though none of us paid much attention as we all knew that we could be laid off with a week's notice. We merely trusted that we would remain on this site until it was finished. I had been assured from the start that the project could well run until the end of January, and the deadline was eventually extended from the 22nd to the 29th January and then finally to the 11th February. Final confirmation of the end of the site and the plans for next week did not actually materialise until the penultimate day, however, leaving little time for us to make decisions.

Crunch Day. Clive brought news of the plans for next week... Most of us had become convinced that a small team would remain here to finish up and those of us based locally seemed strong candidates. The

"Small Team" was a lot smaller than we had anticipated though and suddenly nearly all of us who had been taken on for this project found ourselves on the "available" section of the [unit's] deployment list. A note was pinned up on the wall to the effect that "those not deployed here next week will probably end up on a rural 'away' dig. Let Clive know if you want to hand your notice in."

I had to remind myself that I hadn't taken this job for the long haul, but I was actually surprised how annoyed I was initially by the apparent rejection! Bill was asked back for the watching brief next week, and while that was occurring the area supervisors plus about four assistant supervisors and diggers would be involved in the finishing up of the main areas. **(Diary entry: Thursday 10th February 2005)**

Of the remaining staff the majority ended up being posted to the rural site, though a number did hand their notice in – which had to be backdated to the previous Friday to comply with the unit's policy of a full week's notice. Of those that I know did hand their notice in Joe and I had PhDs to return to (and, although I would have stayed on for any further local work, by this point I had a back injury – see below), Laura wanted some time off to recover and Bill said he would leave after the watching brief as he had some other work to do. A couple of others did not want to be sent on an 'away' project and also handed their notice in.

During this project I was paid marginally above the average for a 'project assistant'/'site assistant'/'archaeologist' – my basic weekly pay being £255.84. With the compulsory half an hour overtime per day on top, and after Tax and National Insurance deductions, I was taking home about £220 per week. Relative to other junior positions in commercial archaeology this represents a good wage, yet it still only works out at £13,303.68 a year for a post that required a degree and experience in the field (compared to the 2004 national average earnings, as calculated by the Office of National Statistics, of £22,248). It is easy to see how the issue of pay has become such a pivotal one in archaeological labour-relations, yet I have previously found that site staff are realistic and far from greedy and this was reinforced during my observations on this project.

We agreed that the pay isn't ideal, but in every other aspect it can be a really great job. It's not even as though we wanted much more money, but we both agreed that an extra £3,000 a year – roughly what you'd get for London weighting – would make all the difference if you're working anywhere in the south of England. **(Diary entry: Thursday 18th January 2005)**

When I started on the site I found the first two weeks something of a struggle, as most archaeologists do after a period of unemployment. With limited earning potential it is rare that junior staff have sufficient savings to make the period up to the first payday a comfortable one. Thankfully most units pay on a weekly basis, but this still means two working weeks from the day you start with a new unit to that first wage slip.

Money is an issue at the moment. Being paid a week in arrears I had to borrow some money from my brother so that I could afford to buy food last week and with two working days left [till pay day] I am having to put things on cheque and save the £5 remaining in my wallet for other stuff. [The woman in the unit office] *misinformed*

me about when I was due to be paid, though I suspected it was because she hadn't been paid weekly herself and didn't understand the system!
(Diary entry: Tuesday 21st December 2004)

There is also, as previously mentioned, a feeling that unit managers have no respect for their junior staff. This may or may not be the case, but it is never so keenly felt as when experts or dignitaries visit the site and those who have become intimately familiar with their features and the surrounding area are almost invariably overlooked or invisible.

The morning saw a delegation from Barwicks and the City Council getting a site tour. There seemed to be a mixture of interested faces and those who were more concerned whether we'd get finished in time, chatting quietly and nervously amongst themselves. Of course none of them showed the slightest interest in interacting with those of us on site and even our own management happily discussed the archaeology despite only visiting the site intermittently. Of course they are paid to know what's going on (or to at least SOUND like they know), but it is one of the big gripes that no-one ever seems to ask us!
(Diary entry: Wednesday 15th December 2004)

Professor Nicholas Clump visited us today. He was the man who more or less defined urban archaeology for most people and knows Marlow's archaeology better than nearly anyone. I wasn't clear whether he had been invited, or had invited himself, but he certainly got the red carpet treatment from Barwicks, Highfield and the Council archaeologists. This also meant that contact with diggers was kept to an absolute minimum and the tour was given over lunch-break.
(Diary entry: Wednesday 5th January 2005)

This perceived lack of respect, whether intentional or not, has important implications for the relationship between the administrators and managers of archaeological units and the junior staff that are employed by units. Clearly this relationship can become strained and at times malice can be perceived where it is not present.

Someone who was not having a good day was Simon. He's one of the younger diggers with only a few months experience and he showed his age a bit today. Although today was technically payday – the money is normally transferred electronically straight into our accounts every Friday morning – his bank had told him that his pay hadn't gone in. The unit office was adamant that it had left their account as normal. It sounded like one of those irritating glitches that sometimes occur with banks, but I imagined the money would arrive eventually. Simon however adopted, for a time, an approach of 'no pay no work' and sat around. He said to me "Why should I work for no pay?" My suggestion was that he wasn't being robbed, that he would be paid, and that it was almost certainly a banking issue, but he was very close to walking off site in a mini-strike. I tried to dissuade him from this. Although I am in favour of taking action when necessary I felt that he was misdirecting his anger and was only likely to succeed in getting himself sacked. He didn't help his situation when Ed Everett tried to speak to him and recommend people to speak to in the office.

At that point apparently Simon had a go at Ed. I could understand his frustration but he clearly couldn't see where the problem lay.
(Diary entry: Friday 14th January 2005)

In this instance it transpired that it was merely a banking error and Simon's pay did appear in his account during Friday evening. However, this incident is interesting because it highlights the poor relationship many site staff have with their managers. Simon was undoubtedly rather naïve in his reaction to the problem, firstly in assuming that it was a deliberate and malicious act and, secondly, in believing that threatening to walk off site would solve the problem. His youth and inexperience, combined with an apparent 'expectation' that the unit management would take advantage of him, were clearly at the root of his reaction. What is more interesting, however, is that he appears not to have discussed the problem with someone who could reassure him, ie someone with more experience, and it fell to me to try, despite not knowing him very well. In hindsight it seems that the most interesting aspect of this event is that it appears to represent a failure of the 'support network' that diggers provide for each other, which should have persuaded Simon that there was no need to overreact.

Physiological reactions

During the first few days of my time on this project I decided that it would be valuable to record my body's reaction to being out on site as a measure of the effects of this kind of work – an element often overlooked when considering the physical experience of fieldwork. Initially I expressed a concern that this would make me sound like a hypochondriac. I suspect this is perhaps a specifically male fear when faced with something that could be taken as a weakness, though many women I have worked with are even less willing to show any vulnerability – perhaps for fear of being labelled as weaker than the men. It is worth mentioning, however, that many archaeologists who have only experienced academic, research or training digs will probably have very little idea of the sheer hard work and technique employed by a skilled commercial field archaeologist. Many archaeologists pride themselves on this ability yet it is massively under-appreciated and rarely seen as a skill. We often joked that we would like to get some academic archaeologists down to site and see how long they lasted, though of course to begin with I was myself quite out of practice. It did provide an interesting opportunity, however, to document all the physiological stresses from the first days on site. Archaeological excavation, by its very nature, is a physically demanding process. The archaeologist's relationship with the site (or feature) upon which he or she works goes beyond merely the removal of soil and engagement with the physical, archaeological remains, but also includes other aspects, such as the weather. As others have already discussed (Moser 1995,1998; Lucas 2001a; Yarrow 2003) the physical relationship between archaeologists and archaeology is central to the experience of – and production of knowledge through – fieldwork. Furthermore, the often adverse nature of the physical conditions serve to strengthen the bonds between archaeologists, both in the immediate experiencing and in the re-telling in a social environment. Moser (1998: 24) states that "one of the major 'shared experiences' associated with fieldwork is the enduring of hardships and ordeals that go hand in hand with working outdoors. Surviving the difficulties associated with fieldwork is a fundamental rite of passage in archaeology and serves to unite us." There is often even a masculine perception that a truly 'hardcore' archaeologist will seek to compound the difficulties of fieldwork through the self-inflicted adversity that follows a night in the pub.

I have also noticed my physiological reaction to being back on site after a break of about two months (and my first commercial site for about six)... Mostly I've noticed how incredibly tired I am after only two days on site. It's a slightly longer day than I used to do, but I also used to go to the pub most nights after leaving site and I currently have no idea how I managed that. My fingers, hands and wrists are also incredibly stiff and crackly after two days of actually fairly light mattocking and shovelling, but I think the main root of that is the hard and fast trowel work on some very compact clay deposits – I reached that conclusion because my right hand feels slightly bruised where the butt of the trowel has jabbed into it repeatedly. I've also noticed that the skin on my fingers is drying out rapidly and there's already traces of ground-in dirt that seems impossible to wash off. This sounds like a really odd observation, but at this time of the year the combination of cold [wet] air and certain soil types (from memory I think clay is the worst) can sometimes cause the skin of your fingers to dry out and crack, creating unpleasant sores.
(Diary entry: Tuesday 14th December 2004)

Amusingly, in hindsight, I was very quick to reassure the reader that I was not being a hypochondriac and that all of these minor complaints were just 'part of the job'.

Despite this peculiar list of ailments there is nothing that I haven't had before and nothing that causes me any concern. It is just that my body needs to readjust to being on site and most of them will fade in a few days as the skin toughens up again, calluses replace blisters and the muscles remember what they're supposed to do.
(Diary entry: Tuesday 14th December 2004)

I have always found that urban archaeological sites are harder physically than rural ones. This is probably because of the sheer quantity of soil that has to be removed when large occupation layers cover the site plus the higher incidence of deep wells and rubbish pits. We also have to adjust the way we work and find efficient and practical ways of mattocking in confined spaces and removing the spoil from deep holes to shovelling boards that may be above our heads.

It was a hard afternoon's work. I really felt the aches in the evening, having forgotten how out of practice I was. I noticed particularly a nasty crick in my neck from shovelling spoil slightly behind me – you have a tendency to turn your head as you do so and it can cause you some gip. I'd forgotten that particular advice.
(Diary entry: Thursday 16th December 2004)

I'm certainly noticing some major stiffness in my neck at the moment. I have decided it is because of the type of shovelling we have to do on crowded urban sites, which means you are often twisting and throwing the spoil behind you. I think it might be something to do with turning your head, while your shoulders are fully tensed, to make sure it actually goes in the barrow. I know a few people have mentioned the same thing.
(Diary entry: Friday 17th December 2004)

There are also, of course the effects of working in winter, which places extra strains on the body.

HERITAGE RESEARCH SERIES No. 1

The Shortest Day and the coldest so far. Kneeling next to the posthole
I was excavating my knees went numb with the cold and popped and
crackled noisily when I stood up.
(Diary entry: Tuesday 21st December 2004)

I still remember my first winter as a digger out on site. I wasn't even vaguely prepared for the cold and a line of us, who were supposed to be trowelling the site, knelt huddled tightly over, trying to get as close to the ground as we could so that the icy wind would pass over us and watching the small amount of warmth from our knees slowly ebbing into the icy ground, which gradually melted. All this time we were trying to trowel and still keep our arm in close to our body to help us keep warm. It was thoroughly miserable and shortly after that I began to give my kit a bit more consideration so that in the future I was far better prepared.

It was very cold today and the top inch or so of the ground was
frozen. Pieces of ice from broken puddles remained scattered on the
surface of the site like shards of glass throughout the day. Despite
this the weather has actually been very mild thus far. My normal
winter work clothes consist of full-legged thermal long johns under
combat trousers; thick boot socks and normal socks; one long-sleeved
t-shirt, under a short sleeved t-shirt, with an optional thin woollen
jumper. Depending on whether I'm working manually or recording
a feature I either wear a hi-vis vest or a full, quilted hi-vis jacket.
Generally I wear the vest underneath my jacket so that I can easily
swap between the two as required, without having to return to the
site hut to do so. Similarly there are times when it is necessary to
wear a woollen hat underneath the hard hat, though it doesn't take
much physical activity before that becomes uncomfortably warm.
(Diary entry: Monday 20th December 2004)

It is very interesting to note that the general tone of the observations changes after the Christmas break – which amounted to seven days holiday. Aside from a brief reference to the fact that we all appear to have put on weight and got out of the habit of getting up early, the nature of the physiological effects appears to change. For one thing I suddenly start going to the pub after work with a number of people from site – something I would not even have considered in the first two weeks due to the fatigue I was feeling. I also do not seem to be recording the daily effects of the work, either because my body had by then adjusted to it or because it no longer seemed noteworthy. The one factor that is referred to is the problems we were all having with painful, cracked skin.

The seemingly permanent cold and damp seems to be causing a few of
us problems with the skin on our hands. Laura and Roberta share some
bizarre, perfumed herbal moisturiser over lunch break. Bill occasionally
pulls out an old Salsa tub with vegan moisturiser in it. I wait until I
have got home and had a shower before I use Neutrogena. It's the only
moisturiser I've ever found that stops my hands from cracking in these
conditions. **(Diary entry: Tuesday 11th January 2005)**

Towards the end of the project, however, I again make a reference to the physical condition of people on site. By this time I seem fairly certain what the root cause is and it goes beyond the daily aches and pains that were discussed previously.

Seems like there's a few of us who are 'broken' at the moment.
Laura has a problem with her feet that means she's limping around

site and Nat apparently fell down the stairs and broke her Coccyx. Bill put his back out the other week, but seems better now and Ed Twist is recovering from a gastro-enteritis kind of thing. Kevin D. had his hand bandaged after slicing into his knuckle on a sharp piece of flint earlier. Judging from the amount of blood he should probably have had stitches, but has carried on. It seems almost like everyone is getting tired and careless, or rundown and susceptible to illness. I'd estimate that at least half of the original crew are mildly ill or injured.
(Diary entry: Tuesday 8th February 2005)

[2084] makes an impression

It was not just other people who seemed to have become 'tired and careless'. I was to miss a number of days on site because of an injury following a fall. I had been excavating an interesting late medieval feature, cut [2084]. It had appeared to have some kind of light-industrial function – being composed initially of very compact deposits of burnt clay and charcoal over what appeared to be a chalk surface, or a cap. There were also voids around the edge that seemed to represent a rotted timber lining. As I had excavated further into this circular feature it began to look like an earlier well had been deliberately backfilled and reused. Underneath one solid layer of burnt clay – including pieces of what appeared to be clay lining that had presumably covered the timber – was a thick layer of large flint nodules. These stones were perfectly sealed by the clay and no soil had found its way in to this layer even after 500 years.

I gave up trying to bottom pit [2084] because it was getting too constricted. As a compromise I stopped at another burnt clay deposit 1.2m from the chalk surface, cleaned up the whole section (which was tricky because of the very loose flint cobbles which were inclined to drop out of the section at the slightest provocation) and photographed it with the black and white and colour SLR and the digital camera and then drew it. The next stage will be to take out the second half down to the same burnt clay deposit, and then continue removing the first half.
(Diary entry: Tuesday 11th January 2005)

I had become aware that the impression of the timber lining was still present even at this depth, which made me a little less certain about the sequence I had imagined – I had assumed the timber lining was part of the later reuse of the well, but it now appeared that it was perhaps one of the original structural elements. Intrigued by this I had used a road-iron to see if the voids went much deeper and had established that I was still quite some distance from the bottom of the feature. I measured and drew a quick sketch plan to show that the timber lining was continuing at this level and then, having taken the other half out by context, I began to remove the burnt clay layer.

Once I started excavating the burnt clay layer at the bottom of the pit the whole nature of the feature changed. I stuck the shovel in and heard an odd hollow sound. Next time the shovel broke clean through and opened a void beneath me – much to my surprise! I clambered out of the pit and fetched a road iron and soon established that the void was limited and didn't present an immediate danger to me so I decided that I was still safe to work in the pit... It seemed to me that the clay was capping an organic fill, and once that had rotted and

reduced it had left this void. Very interesting. I made sure that I had taken a lot of measurements in case it collapsed before I was able to properly draw the section and climbed back in… The organic fill was quite easy to dig, though I was aware that the hollow sound was still there. It seemed to be getting softer and I kept the road-iron at hand to check for voids. When I picked it up and with minimal effort slid it a metre through the deposit with no resistance I decided that it was probably time to get out. I would not be in the least surprised to find the fill collapsed into a 10m deep well by the time I get to work tomorrow! At least I was able to record and draw everything first.
(Diary entry: Thursday 13th January 2005)

Despite taking these precautions and being aware that I was now well over the recommended safe depth – another reason to stop digging – there was an ironic turn of events still to come. In the afternoon I was merely intending to tidy up the artificial base of the feature (ie the point at which I had stopped) so that it could be photographed and planned. I had even found a ladder so that I didn't have to mountaineer my way in and out of the well.

It has been a very satisfying feature to work on, but [2084] had an opportunity to make a mark on me in another way. When I was climbing in this afternoon, shortly after lunch, I was holding the shovel in one hand as I went down the ladder. The ladder twisted underneath me and I fell backwards into the well. It was an odd moment as I fell, half expecting the whole thing to open up beneath me when I landed, but a stone sticking out of the side jabbed me painfully between the shoulder blades, knocking the wind out of my lungs, before I landed awkwardly and twisted to the left… When I climbed out and was able to breath properly again I began to feel sick, and when that passed it was replaced with a stabbing, restrictive pain in my back. For a while I was concerned that I had done something quite serious, but I took some Ibuprofen and completed an Accident Report…
(Diary entry: Thursday 13th January 2005)

I went into work the next day, but was only able to do paperwork. My back was becoming increasingly painful and everyone was advising me to go to the doctor. Since Christmas I had been working on Area 1 under the supervision of Steve Cooper. He was particularly understanding and even phoned the office for me to double-check that I was eligible for sick pay, which it turned out I was. On the following Monday I visited my GP who suggested that I had an injury to the thoracic ligaments and muscles and advised against heavy work for two weeks. Returning to work the next day I found that even 'light duties' – which predominantly meant cleaning the site hut and taking over the tea-making duties – were painful. It is interesting in hindsight to read my account at the time, in which I appear particularly concerned that people might think I was exaggerating the injury or avoiding work.

When [Clive] arrived I was still in the site hut and I was slightly apprehensive that he might think I was just swinging the lead. It instantly became clear that he was quite well informed about my injury though, as he started by saying that he'd heard I was on "light duties" and then asking how my back was. With pleasantries out of the way he looked me straight in the eyes and asked, "Was there something

we [the unit/ supervisors] *could have done to prevent the accident in the first place?" I imagine any company would be terrified of an employee suffering an accident in the workplace these days, as it seems common for people to abdicate all personal responsibility and sue for a quick profit. I was happy to tell him that it was my own fault. I hadn't checked that the ladder was footed properly and I had a shovel in one hand. I wasn't concentrating and really should know better. He agreed that 'these things happen' but added that he was keen that everyone learnt from it. Yet again I was impressed by Clive's approach to his staff.*
(Diary entry: Tuesday 18th January 2005)

The next day I returned to the GP and explained the situation and he certified me unfit for work for two weeks. At about this time I also began a course of treatment with a chiropractor who felt that I had jarred some of the thoracic vertebrae. She also expressed a concern that I could have a small compression fracture – though this was finally ruled out when my GP referred me for an x-ray on the 2nd March, by which time I was still suffering some discomfort. However, in terms of my work on the site, I returned to it at the end of January.

When [I] got to site Linn and Laura fussed over me – which was nice – and then when it was time to go out on site I chatted to Clive and Ed Twist about the state of my back. Ed suggested I carry on taking working shots on the digi, but Clive was keen for me to be a little more productive than that. He suggested that I work on Colin's area if there was some light work I could do in there. Before my accident it had been a running joke between me and Colin that I was supposed to be working on his evaluation trench, but had been replaced by Bill so I could finish [2084]. So when Clive told Colin that I would be with him in Area six – the area opened around the two small evaluation trenches – he said dryly 'Finally!' **(Diary entry: Monday 31st January 2005)**

Over the remaining ten days of the site Colin asked me to undertake a number of tasks that were physically low-stress, but still productive. For the first few days I drew both the north and south facing sections through Area six that had been provided by a modern pipe trench that ran east through it for 20m. With that completed he asked me to ensure that the context numbers that people were taking out were added to the section drawing where necessary. That also led to me working on the rolling Area Matrix – essentially a schematic representation of all the stratigraphic relationships between the contexts. This was normally an Area Supervisor's job, and ultimately one experienced archaeologist, who was effectively employed full-time in this task, tied the whole site Matrix together. I had drawn many matrices over the years and I always enjoyed the challenge of piecing the jigsaw together. However, working on this particular one for a number of days, while work was still continuing on site and forcing me to rethink various relationships, gave me a unique view of these strings of numbers.

The Area six matrix was at a stage when I felt that I had all the relationships under control and was able to pop onto site every now and then and add new numbers where necessary. Having been staring at this for days now, and become familiar with most of the context numbers, it was almost like I saw the features themselves when I looked at it rather than just a family tree of apparently

random numbers. It's difficult to describe and I wasn't sure if it was because I had subconsciously laid out different types of features in different ways, or whether because left to right was almost a section through the area from east to west. Whatever it was, the string of numbers indicating stratigraphic relationships became, in my mind, almost as clear a graphical representation as the section drawing.
(Diary entry: Friday 11th February 2005)

It also seemed that my efforts were of real benefit to Colin, who had been freed up to concentrate on the actual excavation in this area. This was particularly pleasing as I had been concerned that I would be employed in meaningless tasks when I returned from my time off work. I was clearly happy that I was still able to be a productive part of the team and that this was at least in part due to a certain amount of loyalty I felt towards Colin.

After work I popped to the Crown with Bill – taking a diversion to post a birthday card for Laura on the way. He couldn't stay long as he had band practice, but we had a good chat first. He said that Colin had said to him how 'lucky' my bad back had been because it meant that I was able to sort out the Area matrix. I'm glad that my work has helped Colin out. I've been very lucky on site as Colin and Steve have both been great area supervisors and nice guys as well.
(Diary entry: Thursday 10th February 2005)

My injury had to be reported to the Health and Safety Executive under RIDDOR regulations. The "Reporting of Injuries, Diseases and Dangerous Occurrences Regulations" (HMSO 1995) require that any injury in the workplace that leads to an employee being unable to work for three or more days – the point at which employers require certification from a doctor to that effect for sick pay to continue – should be reported. Table 32 shows the available data held by the Health and Safety Executive on archaeological workplace accidents up to the end of 2005. Because of the way the data is stored it was necessary to request a search of the database for company names with 'archaeol' plus a wildcard. This should pick up the vast majority of commercial units, but may also include academic and amateur organisations. This probably accounts for the inclusion of a 'hot substance' injury to a chef or cook, though the warehouse manager could be employed in an archaeological store belonging to a number of employer types. It is also interesting to note that there are two 'major' (which includes fractures and dislocations) trip injuries suffered by members of the public, probably on archaeological sites. These statistics show that trips account for the majority of the 20 reported accidents, followed by falls and (manual) handling/sprains.

However, I believe that my accident accounts for two of those reports as I recall that Clive Green, when completing the RIDDOR form, put it down as a low fall and 'striking something fixed' (ie the side of the well). It was recorded as a 'major' accident because at the time a compression fracture hadn't been ruled out, though in hindsight it should just have been recorded as 'three days +'. Even taking this into account, the fact that there have been nine 'major' accidents in an archaeological workplace over those nine years, plus ten accidents that led to three or more days off work, is something of a concern given the relatively low numbers employed in the discipline.

Discussion: Camaraderie in adversity

The effects of fatigue on the mind and body, resulting in susceptibility to illness and accident and the increased frequency of errors of judgement, are familiar elements of prolonged periods of exertion. There is no more dramatic an illustration of this than the final weeks of Captain Scott's expedition to the South Pole (Scott 1913; Wilson 1972). Petty Officer Evans, described by Scott himself as a tower of strength and by others as one of the biggest men in the Navy (Gran 1984), injured

Year	Status	Kind of injury	Occupation	Major	Three days+	Total
1997/98	Employee	HANDLING/ SPRAINS	OTHER MANUAL	–	1	1
			OTHER PROFESSIONAL	–	1	1
		STRUCK BY	NATURAL SCIENCE	–	1	1
1997/98 Total				–	3	3
1998/99	Employee	HANDLING/SPRAINS	OTHER BUILDING	–	1	1
	Public	TRIP	PUBLIC	1	–	1
1998/99 Total				1	1	2
1999/00	Employee	HIGH FALL	OTHER MANUAL	1	–	1
	Public	TRIP	PUBLIC	1	–	1
1999/00 Total				2	–	2
2000/01	Employee	COLLAPSE/ OVERTRN	OTHER ASSOCIATE	1	–	1
		HANDLING/ SPRAINS	OTHER PROFESSIONAL	–	1	1
				–	1	1
		MACHINERY	OTHER PERSONAL	–	1	1
		STRUCK BY	NATURAL SCIENCE	–	1	1
		TRIP	OTHER MISC	1	–	1
2000/01 Total				2	4	6
2001/02	Employee	FALL–height unknown	OTHER MISC	1	–	1
		HITSOMETHINGFIXED OR STATIONARY	NATURAL SCIENCE	–	1	1
2001/02 Total				1	1	2
2002/03	Employee	EXPOSURE/HOT SUBSTANCE	CHEFS/COOKS	1	–	1
2002/03 Total				1	–	1
2003/04	Employee	SLIP / TRIP	SOCIAL SCIENCE RESEARCHER	1	–	1
2003/04 Total				1	–	1
2004/05	Employee	FALL – Low	SOCIAL SCIENCE RESEARCHER	1	–	1
		HITSOMETHINGFIXED OR STATIONARY		1	–	1
		SLIP / TRIP	WAREHOUSE MGR	1	–	1
2004/05 Total				3	–	3
GRAND TOTAL 1996-2005				**11**	**9**	**20**

Table 32: RIDDOR reportable injuries where the company name refers to "Archaeol★", as reported to HSE, 1996/97–2004/05. *Data provided by the Health and Safety Executive, Statistics Branch.*

his hand whilst making sledges around January 1st 1912 and it became badly infected (Wilson 1972:230). From this point his decline was the most rapid and shocking, particularly following the discovery by Scott's party, on January 16th, that they had been beaten to the South Pole. By January 23rd he was the first to suffer from a badly frostbitten nose and fingers. At this point, Scott notes, Evans became annoyed with his perceived weakness and his mental strength began to fade. On February 4th 1912 Evans suffered his second fall into a crevasse – which Dr. Wilson believed caused an injury to his brain – and on February 17th having fallen slightly behind the other four he collapsed and then died a few hours later. Tryggve Gran, being in the party that discovered Scott, Wilson and Bower's bodies the following November, draws these conclusions on Evans' death after reading Scott's diary:

> Of our own polar party there is only the most tragic news. I have only glanced through Scott's diary but, from what I have seen, it is clear that misfortune accompanied my dead comrades... Right from the Pole itself they had noticed a great change in this big, strong man, and the fall seemed to take toll of the rest of his vitality. The fact that Amundsen was first to the Pole in a way meant more to Evans than to the rest. Had Scott been first, Evans would have achieved financial independence. But now the future must have seemed uncertain and unattractive.
> **(Gran 1984: 216–7)**

Yet despite this, or perhaps because of it, the abiding image of Scott's Expedition, in the diaries of the survivors and the doomed Polar party, is one of a strong sense of comradeship in extreme adversity.

I do not intend to draw too many parallels between Antarctic exploration and the life of a commercial archaeologist in Britain, but there are certain key similarities. The perils of fatigue, injury and accident are common to all physical occupations, whilst camaraderie exists in any occupation that endures some kind of external adversity, forcing individuals to form close, interdependent relationships. The analysis in this chapter has demonstrated a number of things. Principally, that aspects such as interpersonal relationships, structures, hierarchies and day-to-day activities are all central to the experience of being a commercial archaeologist. Being forced to consider these elements in a new light has revitalised some issues that I had already considered. These include the issue of camaraderie amongst site staff that for many is pivotal to their continued enjoyment of the job despite, or perhaps because of, the adversities they face.

> He had apparently been at the upper incremental stage of the supervisor grade before leaving briefly a year or so ago. He had done painting, decorating and odd jobs for friends, family and anyone else who hired him. He said that he had earned pretty good money doing that – which he'd needed as his ex-wife was after a substantial amount of child support money – but as he was working on his own he really missed the camaraderie of working on an archaeological site.
> **(Diary entry: Thursday 10th February 2005)**

Furthermore the elements highlighted in this chapter have, by summarising the key aspects of that two-month period, painted a picture of life on a large commercial project with all of its highs, lows and vagaries. I am certain that those familiar with these circumstances will recognise instantly the kinds of relationships and situations that I have described. I am equally certain that, for those who are external to commercial archaeology, this chapter has provided something of an insight to the issues with which I am largely concerned in this research. Namely the structure and management of archaeological units and the effects of the current system of tendering; the pay and conditions of employment of junior staff; the formation of relationships and the importance of camaraderie.

CHAPTER SEVEN
The Interviews – Part two: perceptions

THE DOWNSIDE OF WEARING
HI-VIZ VESTS IN HIGH
SUMMER ...

Figure 48: The problem with summer. © *Jon Hall*

Introduction

The methodology employed during the interviewing process has previously been discussed in Chapter Five, but it is worth reiterating that each interview covered a set of pre-determined themes. The extent to which each topic was discussed, and the subsequent foci of the interview, were determined by the participant in what is described as 'semi-structured' interviewing (Burgess 1982, 1984; Breakwell 1990; Mason 1996, 2002; Fetterman 1998). This approach was deemed to be most appropriate for the purpose of gathering data that was often very personal to the participant and sometimes could not be predicted. Whereas the career paths of the participants, as discussed in Chapter Five, were often covered in the early stages of the interview during which the archaeologists provided a great deal of biographical information, their perceptions were scattered throughout the interview. Equally, each participant chose to highlight different aspects and focused more on one area than another. This 'weighting' of topics made it relatively easy to determine which themes each participant considered of greater importance. In this chapter I will discuss the predominant, recurring themes expressed by commercial archaeologists within the interviews, and demonstrate how widespread concerns of falling standards are often mitigated by the camaraderie and an abiding enjoyment of excavation. Some excerpts may appear long and they might not always stick rigidly to the topic. However, it was important when selecting excerpts for analysis that they were not removed from their context, but rather that the personal narrative of each participant should be preserved where possible.

Thematic analysis

Perceived changes in the profession

An approach used in each interview was to ask the participant to consider the changes they had seen in the profession since they started their career. More often than not they would describe how much better things used to be, particularly in relation to the quality of archaeologists employed in commercial archaeology. It is impossible to test the accuracy of these beliefs and it might just be that as they themselves gained more experience they became more aware of the deficiencies of those around them. However, so common were these views that it is hard to rule out the possibility that they hold some truth. P19 suggests that diggers have lost their confidence and ability to fully engage with the archaeology as well as the willingness to use their initiative when necessary. In his opinion it is a combination of poor training and commercial pressures that have brought about this change.

P19–M38–08/2004: *And I would like [current] diggers to have the flexibility that I had when I was a digger in the 80s, to use, you know... diggers are often seen, I mean in your thing... the problem of 'labourers', but they're not just labourers. A labourer digs a hole. An archaeologist digs a hole and thinks about... the number of times I would be thinking 'Why have I got a pit here? What are these post-holes doing? Hey, you know, Curly come across look at this. Have you got these as well? What did you think it was?' There's discussion, there's... now they're like robots, there's automation... I'm appalled... students come out, no offence to students, but they now come out, one here was going he's got two years experience. 'No you don't'.*

Me: *Six weeks.*

P19: *You come out and I'm just thinking, you know, a certain site which will remain nameless, those guys are going to be thrust out into the archaeological field, in contracting archaeology, with no further training and all they know how to do is brush sand away from a pot. That's not going to help them on a watching brief on a road with two JCBs going like the clappers. Where's the training in that? Where's the ability to then go to the management and say 'I need to know this' or 'I think this is happening'?*

Me: *It sounds like, you know, what you're talking about is a complete loss of initiative.*

P19: *An initiative bypass because you're frightened of 'That's my job. If I piss off Unit A then they will not employ me and I need the employment. So I'll keep my mouth shut and grumble in the corner that they should have put trenches over there, that they should have put a trench there but I won't say anything in case I lose my job'…*

P19: *… but in this society, that archaeology is in just now, it's understandable. Don't rock the boat.*

Me: *Yeah, yeah.*

P19: *Don't find archaeology. The classic statement before you're sent out on site 'Remember kids, don't find archaeology'. Or if you do, don't find much…*

Me: *Basically, you're 22 years in the job… your experiences of working on site over those years… How much do you think it's changed, from the point of view of a digger or maybe a manager?*

P19: *Managers I think have got more to manage. A lot more paperwork, a lot more worries. Health and Safety. Risk Assessments. Ooh… whimper, whimper. Spot checks. The digger, strangely for the digger, like we discussed before, diggers… really a lot has not changed, in as much as dreadlocks, ripped clothes, army combats are de rigueur. The one thing that has changed is they don't seem to have the interest and the confidence anymore. Because, again we go back, they come out of university they have not a 'scooby doo' about how to dig a site and they never learn, cos not at any point does a contracting unit have time to say 'heh, this is how we do it' or 'go and learn some blah, blah.' It's 'Can you do it?' 'No.' 'Right forget it. Get him. Can he do it? Yes he can. Right.' …*

P19: *Engage with the past and then you're worth your money. Until then I'm afraid you're a person who digs holes… slowly.*

Similarly P20 felt that the standard of site staff had dropped in recent years, particularly the standard of supervisors on site. In his opinion it was a failure of junior staff to appreciate the value of field experience and that they seemed to feel that the degree and a short period on site qualified them to supervise. Unfortunately the units supported this misconception by promoting people before they were really qualified and this has had knock on effects with regard to the quality of commercial archaeologists.

Me: *So is it the type of people who are working in commercial archaeology or the environment that they weren't able to get that continuous work under their belts?*

P20-M38-10/2004: *I think so. I think you can still do that, I just think people aren't willing to put in the time basically. Sounding like an old fogey… 'In my day…' I don't know, I suppose some of them… I found towards the end of my period in contract* *archaeology [c 2001], people would come in with degrees, maybe do six months or a year digging, that would be their experience, and they'd be looking to get supervisors jobs and they got them as well. That's the thing.*

Me: *Really?*

P20: *Yeah, exactly. Basically I think the expectation is, now, you get your degree and you do your digging… people expect to be promoted on to be supervisors… I don't think… I think the standard of supervision in contract archaeology has dropped massively since 1990.*

Me: *Is that, at least in part, down to the high turnover of staff in contract archaeology. I mean, if people aren't staying in then the ones who stay for 6 months or a year and then apply for a supervisors job have got a crack at it?*

P20: *I don't think so. I think we've always had a fairly high turnover of people… I remember when I started digging there was still a high turnover but the question of… whether you're willing to stick with it or not… I mean pay was even worse when I started… I don't know. It just seemed as though you had to do your time and get your experience and then you can apply for higher positions.*

P28 also stated that the quality of supervisors has dropped since around 1990. His belief was that supervisors played a key role in the training of staff and setting and monitoring of high standards on site. Blaming commercial pressures and restricted timetables he is clearly of the opinion that without a strong and experienced supervisor to monitor their work, site staff were becoming increasingly ill-equipped to undertake an excavation to a sufficiently high standard. Referring again to his early experiences he feels that, despite all the hardships faced by archaeologists in the 1980s and earlier, they realised the importance of accurate excavation and detailed recording and would not have kept their job otherwise.

Me: *What about changes in the quality of the work, have you seen any chance since [1989]…?*

P28-M34-08/2005: *I would say there's much less care. It's like hospitals, they're not being kept as clean as they used to be, archaeological sites are not as precise and clean as they used to be. My first task in field archaeology was hoeing 150 square metres of gravel. 10 by 15 metre square. I had to do it to a very high standard and because of that I found a Neolithic, possible Neolithic early Bronze Age building which was gravel backfilled postholes in gravel with a slight difference in the texture and colour …A lot of times these days they're cleaned to machine standards and not hand cleaned after that. That's I think… oh and the edges of sites were kept immaculately clean. Sections were kept immaculately cut. It was far more labour intensive. Recording was done to a standard and if the standard wasn't… well this was, I'm talking* *about* [county] *Council now, but the recording was done to a standard that was acceptable to the supervisor. The supervisor was usually a university graduate with four or five years of fieldwork behind them and they were expecting, they were looking at reasonably exacting standards. You wouldn't get away with not filling in boxes and certainly in… even as late as 93, 94 I was working for supervisors who would go through paperwork and this was something that used to happen and doesn't really happen anymore as far as I'm aware in commercial archaeology, the supervisors weren't expected to work they were expected to supervise and they would go through every single context sheet and plan as they were delivered into the site hut and if they were found lacking in any way they would ask you to do them again. That simply doesn't happen any more. Most people these days, supervisors, are hacking holes with everyone else and collecting context sheets in a file they don't look at until they get back to the Dig House… not the Dig House, the office. And then where are they? All the information is gone. I'm as guilty as the next person. This is the condition that's been imposed on me by commercial archaeology and the need to do things quick quick. You go back and you think x or y is a good archaeologist, but because he's bust up with his girlfriend or he's been hitting the juice heavily or whatever you find that half his context sheets are gibberish. And, you know, that swathe of archaeology he's been cutting into all month is completely wasted and it's lost any kind of relevance to the site and then of course you start making it up because you have to. Start filling in the gaps and that's not scientific. So, I can't, obviously I have a narrow experience of what life was like before and after, but certainly by 93, 94 and… at* [unit] *you were expected to hand in context sheets that were finished, precise and actually meant something and fitted in, and have all your… I mean cross-referencing was absolutely the number one thing supervisors used to haul you up on. If you hadn't cross-referenced everything you'd be hauled into the dig hut and asked why this and this and this box hadn't been filled in and why you hadn't cross-referenced your plan sheet with your context sheet with your section numbers and why your… everything was cross-referenced and that kind of intensive checking and supervision doesn't happen…*

Me: *You talk about the guys you worked with in the late 80s, the characters that they were, what sort of changes have you seen in the people that now populate contract archaeology? How would you categorise the changes in those people?*

P28:   *Maybe it's because I was young but I felt that in the earlier days we had a real esprit de corps and that we were all in it together. There wasn't as* much bitching about wages. There wasn't as much bitching period as there seems to be these days. There was discontent but people were prepared to put up with more, or maybe as a workforce we've just got older and are prepared to put up with less because we're getting older, but a lot of the guys I was working with, I suppose I was 18 and they were 22, 23, 24 and they were living in appalling conditions and being paid peanuts, but they were having a good time and they knew that what they were doing was worthwhile and they were, there wasn't the movement around... there was a circuit that was dug, but it was a much closer group. There weren't people appearing for one or two years and then disappearing again. Or digging for six months and then becoming a chartered accountant. There wasn't the room for dilettantes and there wasn't the room for... people who didn't work were given short shrift and there's a tendency, I think there's a tendency in modern archaeology to give people the benefit of the doubt which never existed.

Me: *A second chance you mean, when they mess up?*

P28: *Second, third, fourth, fifth chance. I mean, I know diggers that should have been fired a long time ago who are enjoying positions in units. I won't mention any names.*

Me: *I could always blank them out...*

P28: [laughs]

Me: *You mean people working shoddily?*

P28: *I mean people who refuse to work. I mean people who will do twenty minutes of work and then go and talk to somebody for three quarters of an hour on the other side of site. People who continue to do something the wrong way because they think it's the right way, instead of... people who refuse to be supervised should not be allowed on site because often they have far, far less experience than the people supervising them and they think they know better and they don't. They simply do not know. They don't have the overview that somebody who has been working in that area for four, five, six, seven, eight years has. They come in and they want to do something differently. Okay they don't tend to last for very long, but there are people coming into archaeology who are willing to learn, but still don't have the faculty for doing a good excavation.*

In contrast P3 believes that standards have actually improved and that the speed at which features are excavated has increased dramatically. He is not alone, however, in stating that commercial pressures have on occasion meant that he was not able to undertake quite the high standard of excavation that he would have liked. The commercial pressures faced by site staff seem to be blamed by most participants for many of the current problems in the profession.

Me:

So, if you started in 1990 you must have seen most of the major changes in the profession then, since PPG16 and competitive tendering really kicked off in a major way. To your mind what have the major changes been?

P3-M40-04/2003:

Probably it's the speed, the rate at which we work. Or the rate at which, you know, I've learned so I expect people to work on site, I mean sometimes it's much more excessive because of the resources, the resources are so tight, so it's time or money or both, that you really have to work hard and get the crew to work hard to achieve the goals that you've been set in the time allowed and so sometimes it gets frustrating... When I think about what we used to do, what I used to do when I used to work for the city units, like [unit] or [unit], the rate we used to work at is unbelievably slow, almost research sort of...

Me:

Really?

P3:

Yeah. Compared to what is expected now on an average day on an average site I think it was far easier then and you could dig far slower, whereas now you've just got to hack things out unless it's of exceptional value, because that's just the way we work so I just got used to it.

Me:

Do you think we lose anything in terms of the information? Is the archaeology sacrificed to an extent?

P3:

I think sometimes there's lost information because the frantic nature of digging features out really quick, things like finds might go missing, that people used to recover, you know like 'Small Finds' or coins, maybe when people were doing a lot more trowelling and a lot less heavy 'getting the dirt out of the feature', that sort of attitude, there might have been a greater recovery of 'Small Finds' and things like that. I think standards have got better in the sense that there are systematic recording systems in place now. There were then, in 1990, to be fair... I suppose I'm talking about a long time ago when people used to have 'field diaries'... but our recording system has changed. We used to have a physical recording system where physical relationships were recorded, I mean, god knows why because you still had to do a stratigraphic matrix at the end... but there have been times where, I wouldn't say... we had to make a compromise. That would be the polite way to say it, but I wouldn't say we'd done a crap job. I don't think I'd ever... I could never... Put my hand on my heart, I'd admit it if I'd done it and say I'd done a crap job because I wouldn't allow myself or the crew or... I wouldn't be able to live with myself to be honest because that's not what I got into archaeology for. But there have been times when I've been really pushed and so

I've pushed the crew to work… to get something done in an unrealistic time schedule where with what I've got, with the people I've got, it's been unrealistic so I've either… I've usually had to not do things I would have liked to have done in an ideal situation. I would have dug another section through that, or a bit more of this feature, or a bit more of that feature, but I've not done it because there's just not been the time to do it. It would have been like a luxury thing to do, rather than an essential, so it's a lot about prioritising.

It is perhaps obvious that comments such as the ones above only came from archaeologists with enough experience of the profession to have formed an opinion over time. More junior staff rarely expressed an opinion on any perceived changes within the profession, but those who had experienced commercial archaeology before the implementation of PPG16 in 1990 often felt that there had been a clear and obvious downward trend in some aspects of the profession, such as the ability of new staff, and the weakening of the supervisory role. Even P3, despite believing the changes had been positive, hinted at a contradiction in his own thinking. When he said "now you've just got to hack things out unless it's of exceptional value, because that's just the way we work so I just got used to it", the implication is that, rather than seeing it as a positive approach to fieldwork, it is just something that has to be accepted.

The MSC

Almost without exception the experienced staff who felt that standards had dropped in recent years looked back on the Manpower Services Commission as something akin to a golden era, when staff were properly trained, properly supervised and were given an appropriate amount of time to excavate a site. For all of the controversies surrounding some of the MSC schemes, which were discussed previously, and the fact that wages and conditions of employment have improved considerably since then, there is a prevailing opinion that the schemes produced some of the most talented and most dedicated field archaeologists currently working in the commercial sector. P28, having taken a year out before university in 1989, went to work with a local council unit to gain field experience. He was immersed instantly in the archaeological 'counter culture' of the time and it is clear how much respect he still has for the work they did in those days.

P28-M34-08/2005: *And I learnt a lot of lore from those guys and they were all MSC, ex-MSC diggers and, I suppose in 1989 there was still Manpower Services?*

Me: *No, I think that closed down in late 87*

P28: *… and they were hardcore. They were living in [building] which was a derelict country house owned by the county council, with rats in the walls and holes in the roof and they were smoking jam-jar bongs most of the time and getting wasted; having parties; getting laid. You know, it was… didn't really happen again… remember we're talking real dreadlocked crusty, dog on a string kind of archaeology, but proper, no pissing about. They would be digging if it was raining, digging if it was sunny, digging whatever the weather and they were doing a good job by and large. And they*

Me: *Really?*

P28: *Yeah. There'd be, you know, there was quite a big scene, quite a good scene, a counter-culture scene, of which the archaeology was a hardcore minority in [town] at that point and they were talking to people down the pub and when work came and went they'd take them on as basically hired labour, and the county council was quite happy to do that. They just got taken on by the council as hired labour and became morphed into archaeologists, though quite a few of them have now morphed into… hospitals! I haven't seen some of them… I worked with a few of those early crew again back in the mid 90s and the toll had been taken on them. They were, you know, apart from anything the death of county council archaeology had hit them hard, I think, because they were council workmen. They were issued donkey jackets and standard ammunition boots that the road sweepers were issued and those nasty yellow waterproofs with the orange county council writing on the back. But mostly just donkey jackets. They were lucky to get waterproofs at all. And it was all county council issue, and county council vans and they were treated like 'Parks and Gardens'… but with slightly less respect [laughs] but they didn't care.*

P20 also reflects that it was the experience that the MSC diggers were able to accrue that meant that they stood out, but also a realisation that a field archaeologist needed a few years to really learn the skills that would make them a good supervisor. The suggestion is that people may have been staying in the profession at the lower grades for longer, so that by the time people achieved promotion to supervisor they had substantially more experience than is the case currently.

Me: *It's interesting that you say that you felt there was a drop off in the quality of diggers since 1990.*

P20-M38-10/2004: *Not necessarily a drop off in the quality of the diggers. It was more of a change, I felt, in the attitude in diggers. When I… I started in the tail end of the 80s and most of the people I worked with had come up on the Manpower Services Commission schemes and there were… none of them had any formal qualifications but they were all, almost without exception, really good field archaeologists, basically because they were given the time… because money had been there for them to be digging for three or four years continuously and particularly in, like I said, in [county], in [town] in the mid 80s it was a boom time for contract archaeology, especially for*

[unit]. *They even had a small office in [town] they were doing so much work down there and they just built up a massive skill base of really experienced diggers down there and at that time it was generally accepted that you had to do at least three years before you even think about applying for a supervisor's job and if you did apply you were almost laughed down if you had less than that experience.*

In contrast, P3 again states that he feels that standards have improved, citing the point that more diggers have degrees as a principle reason behind this. He then goes on to add that some of the MSC diggers were the best archaeologists employed within his unit, but his language suggests that he favours the more professional and less 'easy going' approach of contemporary commercial archaeology.

P3-M40-04/2003: *I think the professional standards have definitely got better. I think individual diggers feel like they have a much more valid input into what they do. There are a lot more graduates, you know, people who have actually done a degree in archaeology than there used to be. There used to be, almost like social waifs and strays would drift into archaeology and some of them would come in and stay in and were absolutely brilliant you know, that's not decrying their talents. Some of them were the best we've ever had, I mean they were absolutely brilliant... They just drifted in from the old MSC schemes... They just built up such a wealth of knowledge and experience, but with the professionalisation and the number of people doing degrees now it's an employers' market... The attitude of diggers used to be a lot more laid back. Not a holiday camp, but it was a lot more easy going. There didn't seem to be the pressures on you that there are now.*

As has previously been discussed in Chapter Five, archaeologists who can trace their experience back to a Manpower Services placement are often considered, at least by the slightly older staff who are aware of the MSC's role, to have come through a difficult initiation into the profession, but also to have benefited from the kind of extensive, apprenticeship-style training that many currently bemoan the lack of. It is commonplace for commercial archaeologists to refer to ex-MSC staff as the best they've ever worked with and this is largely due to the training they received and the extensive experience that they have subsequently accrued. It is interesting to note that, despite a degree now being almost a prerequisite for employment in commercial archaeology, the qualification that says the most about someone's skill and experience is that they were long-term unemployed in the 1980s and were given a Manpower Services Commission placement.

Perceptions of fieldwork

It was quite common, particularly amongst younger staff, for participants to express the sheer pleasure they got from the physical aspect of fieldwork. For many this seemed to depend as much on the labour involved and being outdoors as on the excavation of archaeological remains. P14 is quite clear in his perception of archaeology being in opposition to normal office-based jobs and takes a great deal of pleasure from his feeling that he is somehow different.

P14-M25-04/2004: *I do really enjoy archaeology, it's just the pay and conditions are poo... and the complete lack of advancement opportunities.*

Me: *So, you said you enjoy the process of excavation... of archaeology... do you think it's just... is it just being outside but also the...?*

P14: *Manual labour I like.*

Me: *...manual labour.*

P14: *I like manual work.*

Me: *Shifting dirt?*

P14: *Yeah, I think I'd get really fat if I didn't do that to be honest. Manual work, I've always loved manual work. I grew up on farms and stuff. You know, I feel fiddly if I sit in an office for more than two weeks. I feel fat and sluggish and horrible... and weak... pathetic... and [quietly] I like having a tan...*

Me: *Which is not so great in this country!*

P14: *Well, it can be if you work outside. You can get a tan from this time of year onwards. You've got a good tan by summer. By the time all the pink office people come out and lobsterise themselves on the beaches... get cancer on their butt.*

The response of other participants when questioned about their perceptions of fieldwork was markedly different. P20, with considerable experience of commercial and academic excavations, felt very strongly that excavation was not given the same status as other specialist skills, despite being the bedrock of the discipline. A number of participants also expressed this feeling, suggesting that this devaluing of the skill of excavation was a direct result of commercial pressures, the drive for an increasingly professional image and the low value placed on it by many university courses.

P20-M38-10/2004: *I haven't said anything about digging in commercial archaeology, but I think in commercial and academic archaeology there's a very low opinion within the powers that be of the actual skill of excavation. I mean, I've worked on training digs for [unit] where they've deliberately brought in experienced supervisors so there is some recognition there that it is an important skill that some places lack, but there is still a very entrenched attitude that it's not a specialisation at all, that it's something that anyone can do and I think that it's very prevalent in both commercial and academic archaeology. I think it's a reflection of why students expect to be promoted earlier now because they don't see it as an important skill or something that you might have to take time to learn. So... it's only something you can learn by doing it, to be honest. And that's why I was saying earlier on, you needed a minimum of three years digging before you were experienced enough to start supervising really. I think that holds true today … There's also an attitude in academic archaeology that it's not a specialist skill either. In archaeology you might have someone with four weeks field experience and then goes on to do an MA or a PhD and sits in a library for four years and then applies for British Academy funding and gets to run a fieldwork project… and what have they got? Four weeks. If that! People with Classics degrees… running these big projects… [laughs]*

Me: *Surely there has to be some sort of quality control you'd have thought. I mean…*

P20:   *I find the idea that someone can go and do, lets say maybe a minimum of six years as an archaeologist in a Higher Education establishment and not actually do any archaeology, but they can still apply for funding and end up running a fieldwork project absolutely hilarious… I find that astounding…*

Me: *It's not right is it?*

P20:   *No. Not at all. I mean, the usual bail out clause is to employ some minion who actually knows what they're doing to do the excavation and then…*

Me: *Take the credit for it…*

P20:   *Take the credit for it, yeah, when they get to the publication process… mentioning no names. [laughs]*

Lucas, himself employed in commercial archaeology at the time he was writing *Critical approaches to fieldwork*, also describes the absence of respect for the excavators that has been a common theme throughout the previous chapters of this study.

> *Currently, each excavator (or 'site assistant' as they are often called) can be responsible for the whole process from digging to recording a feature on a site and the director/ supervisor merely co-ordinates; this gives the impression of democratic digging – yet the excavator's focus is very narrow and the level of interpretation minimal (for example, 'this is a pit'). This is not to denigrate the skill involved, but it is an illusion to think that the average excavator of today has necessarily any more power on a site than had the labourer of a century ago.*
> **(Lucas 2001a: 8)**

There is a sense, as was often expressed in the written submissions discussed in Chapter Four, that junior site staff are not treated as archaeologists. They are, instead, simply the people who excavate the archaeological features and recover the artefacts so that a real archaeologist can then interpret the site. There is genuine frustration that the process of excavation is rarely considered to be a skill that takes time to become proficient in and the current paucity of practical training opportunities does tend to support that view.

The other side of the coin, so to speak, is the often expressed enjoyment of the sheer physical nature of the engagement with fieldwork. P14 was one of a number of participants to describe their love for archaeology as 'manual work' situated outside, in the fresh air and in stark contrast to most 'normal' jobs. There seems to be a perception, also present in P14's words, that it is a healthy job in that respect, unlike offices which are often described as stifling, oppressive and unnatural. I believe that this represents more than an enthusiasm for physical activity borne out of the release of endorphins during exercise, though this may indeed play a part in the associated feelings of well being. Archaeologists in the field for months at a time often describe how they have never been healthier, or that they haven't even caught a cold for months or years. A further, and perhaps more profound reason almost certainly lies in the psychological separation of archaeology from 'normal' jobs. To 'be' an archaeologist, as has been discussed previously, is often about the rejection of what most people regard as normal, or at least advisable. In this sense, commercial archaeology represents old-fashioned physicality in a largely virtual world.

Public perceptions of archaeology

There was an almost universal feeling amongst the participants that the public did not fully understand archaeology, let alone the peculiarities of the commercial sector, despite its remarkable popularity. A number of participants blamed inaccurate portrayals of the discipline in the media and a sense that the 'documentary' nature of television programs such as Channel Four's 'Time Team' meant that the audience were inclined to take it at face value. Those involved with 'Time Team', however, assert that their audience realise that it is as accurate a portrayal of archaeology as 'The Bill' is of the Metropolitan Police and that it is 'just good telly' (Tony Robinson, pers comm). A number of participants felt that this misunderstanding was, in part, the root of the poor pay in the profession, often focusing on the perceptions of developers towards archaeology. P10 and P11 certainly believed that without greater understanding of the work undertaken it would continue to be undervalued.

Me:	*So in terms of the perception of the profession from the public and from developers, do you think they understand…?*
P11–F50–02/2004:	*No. I don't think they do at all. I don't think… even the 'Time Team' thing we've had has helped people to understand. It gives a very glorified idea of archaeology. You know, there's lots of money and you can do almost anything… Yeah, okay they do it within three days, but then again that's a bit of an artificial thing… timescale to place on it. You get two reactions when you tell people you're an archaeologist. They either think it's a complete waste of time or they think it's interesting. [laughs]*
Me:	*Do you think that's part of the problem with pay and conditions? That people don't understand what we do…?*
P10–M50–02/2004:	*It's not valued is it? If people don't understand it then they can't value it. I suppose the flip side of the coin is that the more mysterious it is possibly… especially the process of archaeology… the more mysterious they are, the more you can charge. I don't know. I think it's more the other way, that they don't understand what you're doing and they don't value it.*

It is interesting to note that P4 and P5 feel similarly to P10 and P11 that television coverage of archaeology, though generating interest, gives a false impression of the majority of fieldwork and leads to a greater misunderstanding of, specifically, commercial archaeology. They then go on to describe a site in which the developers would not let the archaeologists advertise or even discuss the project openly with members of the public for fear of a negative commercial impact.

Me:	*So how do you think people outside the profession perceive us?*
P4–F26-02/2004:	*Bunch of weirdoes and…*
P5–M24-02/2004:	*Yeah!*
P4:	*Pissheads!*
P5:	*When you have a haircut and they ask what you do it always starts with the whole conversation about….*
P4:	*There's massive interest…*
P5:	*There is…*
P4:	*General public interest…*
P5:	*It ranges from… I've had people going 'Oh, that means you go to Egypt a lot', it's like, ermm… 'No.' [laughs]…*
P4:	*And then there's the whole "Time Team" aspect…*
P5:	*There's all "Time Team", "Horizon", all that kind of stuff… A lot of the time the general public don't realise we're on building sites do they? … A lot of the time it's "Oh, you do research digs". They all think you work for universities and you're out doing…*
P4:	*They don't know anything about the development side of it…*
P5:	*No. I think that needs to… yeah, people should emphasise it more… the actual, real-world commercial… entity, and that we get out there like builders do…*
P4:	*I think it would benefit… be beneficial to the developer as well especially… on [city], the site we did for the Friary, we wanted to advertise… we had a public notice board up with all the information and stuff, but they were going to make more of a thing about it within the actual building they were going to put up there, so they were going to encourage the knowledge of what they were living on, in the flats, but they're not…*
P5:	*Well, because of the burials…*
P4:	*They toned it down a hell of a lot…*
P5:	*When we had visitors… we had an open day… lots of, quite a few people came round… more like the local people that had been looking in on site going 'What are they doing?'… seeing random walls appearing… and the local archaeological society… We weren't allowed to mention burials..*

P4:	*No… In the end they said 'If they ask, you can'.*
P5:	*Yeah, if they ask, but we weren't allowed to say 'Oh, there was this burial there…'*
P4:	*And these are the prospective buyers, you know, they were always really interested in that land…*
Me:	*The 'Poltergeist' effect..?*
P5:	*Yeah, a lot of time it is…*
P4:	*They were just scared of people being haunted by…*
P5:	*I think so. Well, because we did leave quite a few in as well. [laughs]*
P4:	*Yeah, but you know we could say about the burials and then say there's none left…*
P5:	*What they ended up doing on open days was say 'Yes, but we've taken them all out where the building is going to be'. Which we did…*
P4:	*That's the point isn't it…?*
P5:	*We just didn't tell them that where the gardens are…*
	[laughter]

P3 had an interesting insight into public perceptions of archaeology, having given up his previous career to retrain as an archaeologist in his late twenties. Clearly his brother did not see archaeology as a good career move, perhaps correctly, but P3 was clear that it was about doing something he enjoyed rather than the amount of money he could earn. It seems likely that in justifying his decision he is also criticising his brother's choices and setting himself up in opposition to accepted career norms.

P3-M40-04/2003:	*But I did get quite a lot of support from them [his parents] and my friends. Some thought I was, you know… my eldest brother, he was a bank manager, thought I was a nutter. He said 'Why are you throwing away a good career to do something weird like that?'*
Me:	*But it's fairly priceless to actually do something you enjoy isn't it?*
P3:	*That's it. It sounds cheesy but it's true, if there's something you enjoy doing and you can get paid to do it… who can ask for more? Or would you rather do a job you hate where you get paid tonnes of money, but you only get four weeks a year to do something you like? I say, a bad day's archaeology is 100 times better than a good day in engineering.*

The prevailing suggestion is that archaeology, particularly commercial archaeology, is misunderstood, mysterious and far outside the experience of most of the population. Although some participants indicated a feeling that this might be part of the problem in terms of low pay within the profession, and others demonstrated frustration with the situation, there is an over-riding sense that many of them rather enjoyed the idea that most people did not understand what they did. This follows on from an aspect of the previous theme, that there is something distinctly contradictory to normal society in the process of archaeological

HERITAGE RESEARCH SERIES NO. 1

fieldwork. Somehow pursuing a career in commercial archaeology is not only a rejection of a number of social norms, but it also appears that it occupies a slightly liminal position in society because of the mystery that is attached to it.

Money

Unsurprisingly the wages paid by commercial units were an issue that was covered in great detail by many of the interview participants. For a number it was an issue of great concern. For some it was a concern that they could postpone until they started thinking about mortgages or families, but it was still something that they were aware of all the time. For some, however, their wage was an inconsequential aspect of the job. P19 begins by describing the situation he found himself in several years ago when he was struggling financially, but goes on to state that he does not think that the pay is that bad. In his opinion the biggest problem is the difficulty in maintaining full-time employment, which means that some commercial archaeologists actually earn very little.

P19-M38-08/2004:   [unit] *really wasn't a company, it was just a way of having a self-employed status, I'm still [then] on about, believe it or not, about twelve grand a year, so much time without any work, times were hard still. I'm back to living with my mother and this is no longer a nice option, you've got no money in the bank, I'm four grand overdrawn, I'm living in the back-room of my mother's house… I think the pay thing, I mean, I'm not one to say that diggers are whiners… the pay actually is not that bad. It's not good, but it's not that bad. What's wrong is the conditions. If, if you offer me 13 grand to dig a, dig some holes outside, and someone's telling me where to dig them and yeah, okay I've got to work out, you know, if I'm interested in finds, thinking about this, and I'm just being pointed in the right direction, set off, 13 or 14 grand is fine. What's not fine is that the, at the end of the year, you're only taking home seven, eight grand, cos how do you get a house, as I discovered at the age of 30. No house, no car and living with my mum. A laughing stock. [laughs]*

However, P19 goes on to summarise the situation as he sees it. Implicit in his views are the idea that low wages are one of the sacrifices that one has to make in order to 'be' an archaeologist, and that those who are determined enough will eventually be rewarded.

P19-M38-08/2004:   *But it has to be said you're not going to get rich as an archaeologist. It's a lifestyle choice. Doesn't mean you have to be underpaid to do it, but be realistic. There are only so many counties in Britain. There are only so many units in Britain, so there are only x amount of jobs. It cannot expand exponentially. It's at saturation point as it is, so I would say to the 85% of diggers, you know, accept it. Enjoy your three or four years as a digger, five years as a digger. Use it, have a good life, smoke lots of drugs, drink lots of drink, get off with either women stroke men or both. Go abroad. And then get a proper job. If you're lucky and really want to be an archaeologist for the rest of your life then you'll make it. I mean, twenty two years I waited to get where I am and who knows how long I'll be an archaeologist. I mean I'm never going to give it up. Absolutely not.*

In contrast, P3 chose a job in commercial archaeology over completing his PhD precisely because it offered the opportunity to earn a regular wage (which, he seems to agree with P19, is not too bad under the circumstances). In his opinion, at the time, commercial archaeology was far more reliable and predictable, and therefore a safer bet, than an academic career.

P3-M40-04/2003: *Whilst I was doing [a part-time PhD] I was a toilet cleaner and porter at [Hotel] … but I got paid a crap wage so after about a year and a quarter, year and a half I was so skint that I started borrowing money off my girlfriend, whose now my wife. My mum had lent me a thousand quid … and my elder sister even gave me three hundred quid. And I just thought, my personal ethics, I thought this isn't on. I'm a 31 year old bloke borrowing money off my family … So I wrote down on two bits of paper, on my girlfriend's suggestion cos that's how she used to make big decisions, and you write down all the pros and cons of one argument and all the pros and cons of another. And when I put all the pros of being a field archaeologist against the pros of being an academic it was totally skewed. You know, cos you could actually go and earn a wage so you wouldn't be poor. The chances of getting employment were a lot more than doing a PhD. You're getting close to the top of that pyramid, you know, where everyone starts off doing the undergraduate, masters, PhD … Some of those people get to be academics and others just fall by the wayside, a very small percentage get the academic status that they want. You know I've got friends who have got all the way to the top and did post-doctoral fellowships and then they just couldn't get that last bit cos they got too specialised so they ended up doing all sorts of weird things, doing adult education classes or leaving archaeology all together which is a waste really cos there was so much investment, not only their own personal investment, but the financial investment by taxpayers into their doing well and they got all those skills and that knowledge that they built up and then its not used. It's a disgrace really. So, that made my decision up for me and the first job that came along, after I'd made that decision in March 94, was a dig came up in [county] and it was a massive excavation.*

Of the younger staff hoping to maintain a career in archaeology, P26 reflects the widely held concern that low wages will become a barrier to greater stability as they get older. He does also raise the issue of comparing wages with other professions employed on large sites. This was a feature of a number of the interviews. Clearly for many staff it serves to highlight the apparent disparity in pay across the development sector.

Me:	So how do you see your future then? Do you see a long term future for yourself in…?
P26-M25-12/2004:	I would like to think so. The only concern for me… I mean, absolutely love doing my job… Really love it… but the only concern is, well, it hasn't been so much of a concern, but it's becoming one is obviously the money and whether I can sustain… a life… on a digger's wage…
Me:	How old are you now?
P26:	I'm 25… I'm expecting a supervisor position to come up. Well, hoping. Hoping for about a year and a half now, but… that's the next step…
P26:	…at [site], because there were 3,000 people working there or whatever, and there were all these reports on the news and in all the papers that they were taking on immigrants, or non-skilled workers at a base rate of 32 grand to do whatever, and then we're up there… we're earning 12, 13 grand and you talk to the digger driver and… There was a site newspaper. It was like a whole town up there. There'd be articles about the archaeology, sort of explaining to all the workers what we're actually doing, and it says like 'specialists' and 'experts' and he was like 'How can you carry on like this?' He was really surprised, because we were talking about money and I just had this perception about how much a digger driver earns and I was wrong and he was very wrong about me.

P1 also touches on the issue of pay as being something that was increasingly a concern, and suggests that she does not anticipate that the increase in pay with promotion will be sufficient to improve the situation. She does reflect, however, that she has known people to achieve a certain level of stability in their lives and that it is achievable.

Me:	You strike me as someone who's in the job for the long haul, that's your, as you said in your [written] submission about wanting to work your way up, so you obviously see it as a career.
P1-F23-04/2003:	I would like to see it as a career yes. Definitely. It's what I'd like to do, but long haul is definitely the right words for it.
Me:	[laughs] So, do you think that the money and the conditions of the job… do you think that's a basis for a career or are you prepared for the sacrifices?
P1:	Well that's the problem really, that you know on what I earn now there's no way I could ever get a mortgage on a house and even if I make it up to Project Officer the wages are so horrifically low that I mean you can't afford to live and you certainly can't afford to live around [town] which is where, you know, the [unit] offices are based.
Me:	Yeah.
P1:	It's difficult because you have to have a car and you're burning more money or at least as much

	money as you earn. I don't know. Money is a bit of an issue at times… like when the rent's due.
Me:	*Yeah, yeah. Absolutely… What about, obviously some time in the future, but, what about having a family or whatever?*
P1:	*Erm…*
Me:	*Or does that not figure in your plans?*
P1:	*I think that having a family and being an archaeologist can be combined. I think it can be done. I know people who have done it, as long as you work for a company that… is large enough and flexible enough.*

Very few of the participants went so far as to suggest a reason behind the low pay in the profession, aside from a widely held belief that competitive tendering – combined with the traditionally low pay scales in archaeology – was the root of it. P28, having read some of my early research, had clearly given the issue some thought and expressed in great detail the economic process that he felt was responsible, starting with the origins of the demise of County Council units.

P28-M34-08/2005:	*Generally speaking, the Housing crash [c 1992] killed off… it stripped back staffing levels to a point where commercial archaeology could take them on and it froze wages, importantly, it froze wages and made people, it actually cowed people into the jobs, they were afraid of losing their livelihoods. And that's a malleable workforce. And it was on the back of that… PPG16 came in [1990] and set it in stone that basically you look out for yourself because central funding is drying up. Think they gave us three years of grace, you know, but they were saying, I remember talking to my friends and they were saying 'We've basically been given three years of grace but at the end of those three years we're expected to be standing on our own two feet.' It was in those terms.*
Me:	*From the council?*
P28:	*From the government. Government was centrally funding, was giving the money to the councils. The government was putting the squeeze on the councils and the councils were putting the squeeze on the archaeology units and the archaeology units decided to leap, mostly, instead of being pushed … they were pushed to the point where they decided to jump. To begin with they were hopelessly… developers were outraged that they had to start paying. I got kicked off several sites by developers who just simply refused to do anything…*
P28:	*…one of those private units was the [unit] and that was a closed down district council unit. And that was what basically happened. A lot of them got sold off. Sold on and changed… nominally part of the council but in practical terms entirely commercially viable, or meant to be commercially viable though more often than not the councils were bailing them out to the tune of umpteen*

HERITAGE RESEARCH SERIES No. 1

tens of thousands a year, simply through bad management and poor practice and that's really I suppose another heart of the bad wages we have. Archaeological units couldn't pay people decent wages because the money was being squeezed and at that point as well, and this is another big point, at that point, at the point of the crisis in archaeology when the building slump in 91, 92 hit the county council units jumped out of the county council pay scheme. That's the only way they could prevent… that's the only way they could squeeze wages and that lost you a number of important benefits. It lost you council health insurance, council pension, it lost you privilege of tenure and it lost you perks, various perks came with the job. It also lost you most importantly a yearly increase in wages, a guaranteed increase in wages. And I think from 91 to 95, 96 archaeological wages were frozen to the actual point that they are behind national wages now. If there was a time when… because I'll point out now that I've read your research, some of your research into the wages, and I think that's the point at which they were frozen. They got hammered as well in the transition from county council to commercial, because they were squeezing wages, but it was actually the pulling out of, effectively council workers from the council pay scheme and guaranteed labour wages that started to depress.

In the modern, western world, one's capacity to earn money is all too often a significant factor in the way we are perceived, and the image we project. Over recent years there have been increasing demands for an increase in archaeological wages, supported by the argument that a graduate job demands a graduate wage. In many ways, however, it seems that this argument is counter-productive in the sense that any claim for an extra £11,000 a year (roughly the amount required to bring archaeological wages in line with the average for recent graduates) will always be treated scornfully. The truth is that commercial archaeology is not a typical graduate career and many of those employed in the profession are far more realistic about their wages. As P28 points out, it was the freezing of wages during the early 1990s that have really hit staff hard and if wages were to be increased by that amount now it would make all the difference. This point was also observed in conversations during the period of participant observation (see Chapter Six).

> *We agreed that the pay isn't ideal, but in every other aspect it can be a really great job. It's not even as though we wanted much more money, but we both agreed that an extra £3,000 a year – roughly what you'd get for London weighting – would make all the difference if you're working anywhere in the south of England.*
> **(Diary entry: Thursday 18th January 2005)**

There is, however, another point to be made here, which is that part of the sense of 'being' a commercial archaeologist is that there are certain sacrifices one has to make. As P19 stated, "it has to be said you're not going to get rich as an archaeologist. It's a lifestyle choice. Doesn't mean you have to be underpaid to do it, but be realistic." It is common for commercial site staff to go straight to the pub after work, wearing their high-visibility jackets and steel-toed boots almost as a badge of honour, whilst other construction industry trades get changed into clean clothes that conceal their occupation. It is, perhaps, a curiosity in the modern world that many commercial archaeologists choose to advertise what they do, rather than what they earn.

IFA/union membership

A large number of participants expressed a feeling that neither the Institute of Field Archaeologists nor the Trades Unions were really doing enough to represent ordinary archaeologists. P19, though broadly of the opinion that commercial staff should participate more fully in order to highlight their current plight, had lost faith in union membership since they had been unable to prevent 'sharp' employment practice some years ago.

Me:	*What about the role of Prospect then? Is the IFA not doing what it could?*
P19-M38-08/2004:	*I think it has to be a pronged attack. Prospect has really got to beef itself up. I've never been a real fond favourite of unions ever since there their fabled 'It's alright lads, we'll sort this out. It's alright lads, actually we couldn't sort it out because they said they'd get new people in.'*
Me:	*Where was that?*
P19:	*That was at [unit]. We demanded sickness pay and holiday pay because they would sack us every three months and employ us again on the Monday and so we wanted, well, rights. IPCS came in, I think that's pre-Prospect. The Institute of Professional Civil Servants? IPCMS?*
Me:	*It was IP... IPMS*
P19:	*IPMS!*
Me:	*Institute of Professionals, Managers and Specialists or something.*
P19:	*That's the buggers. And they went in to the meeting and they came out and just said 'Right, I'm afraid unfortunately they said that they'd sack all of you and get new people in. So there's nothing we can do for you.' And right then I stopped my union dues, cos hey, you know, it is a pint a week.*

P28 was one of a number of archaeologists to express a feeling that the IFA represented the interests of unit managers over the majority of staff in commercial archaeology – ie those that are site-based. He also suggests that the IFA's self-proclaimed role of 'setting standards in archaeology' has not been entirely effective either.

Me:	*I think, depending on the length of tape I reckon we've got about five minutes or so left, but...*
P28-M34-08/2005:	*I still haven't answered your question, as to how I'd make things better*
Me:	*No...*

P28: *I've been bitching for the last…*

Me: *[laughs] You have a little bit. How would you make things better?*

P28: *How would I make things better? In short I'd strengthen the IFA and make it more representative of the actual number of people working in archaeology. I would up standards and expect the developers to pay for it, ie I would charge them more money for doing a better job. Not a job they would consider to be better, but a job which archaeologists would consider to be better and hope that they would take it on good faith that the job that was getting done was to the best… they would expect the same of plumbers. They wouldn't expect a plumber to do a crappy job. They would expect a plumber to do the best job they could. Or a bunch of bricklayers, whatever. And they'd expect to pay for them. And I think that there's a lot of, and I would say that part of the problem we have is unit managers do not think that the job that people are doing is to the best quality and they're not, therefore not tendering to the sort of quality that they should be doing. A chicken and egg question. I think that unit managers are cynical buggers who know that their supervisors are hatching, cobbling stuff together left, right and centre and dealing with everything on a daily basis and the work isn't good, but it's, it's less than brilliant, but it's getting done and they think 'Fine. At least the reports are coming out on time'. Everything is to the least, everything is to the lowest common denominator and because they know that their supervisors can keep delivering, to a certain standard, they're happy to tender to that standard. They're not happy to up the process, up the standards.*

Me: *You're basically saying that the big change that you've noticed is the standard to which work is done…*

P28: *I think shortcuts have been found. I still think there's a lot of good work being done, but it's being couched in not very good methodology and I think a lot of stuff slips through that could be more interesting. How would I deal with it? I'd get the IFA to pull their finger out and start squeezing developers.*

Me: *So you think it needs to be more of a regulatory body than it is currently?*

P28: *Yeah. It's supposed to be maintaining standards in archaeology. All it's done is facilitate the worst decline in standards since Mortimer Wheeler started banging on about them in 1930. Basically. And it's done that by, because it represents the unit managers and unit managers only want to hear what they want to hear. They're dealing with units on a day-to-day basis and they want to see*

*files on developers' shelves, because that's their pay
cheque and that's all they're f**king interested in.
And if they can't, if they don't have the vision or
the integrity to demand a good job is done then
they're certainly not going to demand it of the
developer. They're not going to demand the money
to be able to do a good job from the developer,
even if they thought it was a good idea. You know,
they need to, unit managers need to change their
perceptions as well. As far as I can see they're a
bunch of chancy buggers, who are realise they're
onto a good thing and most of them are... 25, 28,
30 thousand pounds, as opposed to 14 thousand
for a supervisor.*

P28 went on to suggest that one of the ways the IFA could begin to improve standards would be to ensure that only suitably qualified archaeologists were able to become members. The 'Practitioner' grade he refers to is traditionally that to which the majority of junior site staff in the IFA belong and is the lowest corporate grade of membership – ie that with voting rights in elections and at the AGM.

P28-M34-08/2005: *I think the IFA needs to tighten up its acceptance procedures for candidates. I don't think you should have 'Practitioners' with less than 3 years field experience... Six months [the current requirement]? You can't learn anything in six months even if you're being taught every day!*

Aside from scepticism of the effectiveness of the IFA and the Trades Unions another significant factor was general apathy towards them. For all of their heartfelt complaints I know that P19 is now a union member once more, and P28 has since joined the IFA in order to get more involved in its policy-making. P4 and P5, perhaps because they have spent most of their short careers with one unit in more or less stable employment, have never felt a need to be part of either organisation, although P5 admitted that he had joined the IFA at the non-corporate, student grade thinking it would help him get a job and has never bothered to update his membership.

Me: *Are you guys in the IFA, or Prospect?*

P4-F26-02/2004: *No...*

P5-M24-02/2004: *The IFA, but not Prospect...*

P4: *No. I want... I'd consider joining Prospect, mainly because of the whole... they want to encourage all units to charge the same and then get developers, they'd be forced to pay more. And... I haven't done it yet....*

Me: *Just haven't got round to it?*

P4: *Yeah, mainly, and the IFA I've never seen the point of... They don't do enough, really...*

Me: *Really?*

P4: *I don't think so...*

P5: *The only reason I joined the IFA was to get a job. I joined it before I was at [unit] and then I got a job and haven't updated my membership or anything... just left it at the minimum level...*

Me: *Yeah...*

P4: *You're still paying as a student aren't you?*

[laughter]

P5: *Yeah, looks like I've been a student for a long time now!*

It is clear that opinions within the profession remain divided on the merits of membership of the IFA and Trades Unions, though for different reasons. There is a perception that the IFA does not do enough to improve the working conditions for commercial archaeologists, that it represents the interests of unit managers over junior staff and that the subscription is not good value for money. These views, right or wrong, prevail despite repeated attempts by the IFA to attract more members from the large number of junior site staff. A recent initiative has seen the establishment of the Diggers' Forum. This is registered as an IFA, 'special interest' group, similar to those that have long been established to cover Building Recording, Finds, Maritime Archaeology and regional interests. The Diggers' Forum is an attempt to allow non-IFA members a voice on issues that affect them, without requiring them to become full IFA members (Diggers' Forum membership is free to members of the Institute and currently only £5 a year for non-members). The IFA hopes, ultimately, that junior site staff will appreciate the merits of IFA membership if they understand some of the less-publicised work that the Institute does. The Diggers' Forum committee hope that, in time, enough of their members will also be in the IFA and will be able to stand for election to the IFA council. It is felt that greater representation of site-based staff on the council will go a long way to encouraging more junior staff that it is worth joining the IFA.

The Trade Unions, in particular Prospect, have had some success in recruiting commercial archaeologists, particularly within the larger units where they have a more established presence. There is, however, some frustration that Prospect has not delivered any substantial improvement in pay and conditions and many staff express the feeling that their own union is more concerned with representing other high-profile professions, such as engineers and scientists employed in the defence and energy sectors. The other main union representing commercial archaeologists is Unison, the public services union. Similarly, archaeologists are a small, low-profile group within county councils and unitary authorities. However, they are invariably employed on standard pay scales and Unison, the largest trade union in the UK, has had some success in improving pay. This tends to have knock on effects across the profession and generally encourages wages to rise slightly, though not at the rate many would like.

Camaraderie

A number of participants referred to the camaraderie in archaeology as being a major factor in the pleasure they got from their job. In fact this has been one of the significant themes to come out of my research, being already highlighted in the participant observation study, the online survey data and the written submissions. There is a real sense that the perceived adversity of low pay, poor conditions of employment, bad weather or even badly run excavations forges a strong bond of camaraderie amongst staff already united by their interest in archaeology having prevailed over practical, often financial, considerations. For P26 the camaraderie on his first site made the difference between him staying in archaeology or leaving straight away. Had he gone straight to his second site it seems doubtful whether he would have stayed in the profession.

P26-M25-12/2004:	*To be honest I've got no real gripes with working for [unit]. I think they're probably one of the better people to work for. I've heard some horror stories from other people, but I think I've been quite lucky there.*
Me:	*You were saying you worked for [unit] for a couple of weeks and that's obviously a name that springs to mind when people think of cowboy units…*
P26:	*[laughs] …Yeah. That two weeks was… It was just a bit of an eye-opener, because I'd worked for [unit] and I'd stopped for about two or three months and was working at Asda because I couldn't get a job … but it was just little things like reusing finds bags and sort of, having one huge great big piece of permatrace, drawing tiny things on and boxing them off and then you couldn't draw because someone else had the plan… there was only four of us there, but the PO who was in charge was just a complete tosser. He was… I couldn't even tell you his name… well, it's probably best not to… anyway, he just completely ruined everything for everybody. It was just a really bad atmosphere. It was a really crappy site. It was just big holes with nothing in.*
Me:	*It does seem like, from what a lot of people have said, and from my own experience as well, I think it's the case that having a dodgy PO, manager, supervisor on site makes things difficult for the staff…*
P26:	*Some sites, like you say… First site I worked on was really good for me, because the people were so nice and they would go out of their way to help me and we'd go down the pub after work. It was really nice. They were all friends anyway because they used to drive in together from [town] and a lot of people took me under their wing, but I'm sure if it was the opposite I wouldn't be sat here today… I'd probably have gone 'Oh, this isn't for me at all' and sort of go off and do something else…*
Me:	*Yeah, it's a support network isn't it?*
P26:	*Exactly.*
Me:	*It's one of the few things that can make a shitty site bearable.*
P26:	*That's the thing. You either get a good crew or a good site. You rarely get them together.*
Me:	*Yeah, it brings out the best in people sometimes.*
P26:	*… I was up in [town] over Christmas and that was a reasonable site with really good people, but when you're all sort of… the camaraderie… in the trenches, slogging it out and working in snow, or being made to work in snow which is just completely ridiculous. Most stupid thing I've ever done in my life. Scraping snow off the site.*

P26 effectively summarises the importance of camaraderie within the profession, but P28 provided an interesting insight into inter-departmental camaraderie within a county council set-up at the start of his career. This highlights the parity archaeology had with related departments and goes some way to explaining why the pay and conditions of today's archaeologists are so similar to professional gardeners, as was discussed in an earlier chapter.

P28-M34-08/2005: *I mean it's all relative, because field archaeologists at that point were being paid the same or less than road sweepers on a sort of par with gardeners anyway so it wasn't... I mean we used to borrow tools off the gardeners I remember and vehicles and stuff and vice versa and there was always a camaraderie between the two groups, and the highways and byways guys as well, the same, doing similar sorts of jobs out in the countryside digging holes in stuff, well they were fixing fences but we were digging up fences.*

The theme of camaraderie through adversity and through shared experiences was discussed in Chapter Six. It is interesting to note how much more explicitly it was raised in my own observations than in the interviews. However, reading through all the interview excerpts in this Chapter and in Chapter Five it is inescapable that camaraderie is implicitly referred to all the time by commercial archaeologists. Yarrow notes that volunteers on an archaeological dig responded positively to the feeling of 'community' that was fostered through a sense of equality.

As one volunteer commented: "The best thing about archaeology is the people you meet". In a similar way people often fondly recounted memories of past years of excavation in terms of particular characters or social occasions and many of the volunteers told me that the "social life" was a big part of the reason for their participation. Part of the "good social life" was put down to the "equality" that existed amongst different volunteers and the way in which it was therefore possible to meet "people that in ordinary life you might not". **(Yarrow 2006: 25)**

It is undoubtedly true that the 'social life' also reinforces the camaraderie amongst commercial archaeologists, but largely there is a real sense that it is adversity that forges it in the first place. The 'equality' that Yarrow describes on a training excavation becomes, in the context of commercial archaeology, an equality founded on shared adversity.

Age and physical effects

On a number of occasions participants referred to recurring injuries or the cumulative effects of years of site work. Obviously these were more prevalent amongst participants over 30. As P19, and the data from the online survey, suggests this is often the age at which site staff are forced to evaluate their 'career'.

P19-M38-08/2004: *And then, I still go to places, go to Yemen, started to get fat and drink too much and the spiral started because, you know, suddenly you realise you have been digging, you're now 30 and where the hell's it going? What happened to all that time and your body can't do it any more. Panic begins to set in. So I think that's the time that most diggers* *really realise that if you're not director of a unit or a lecturer or a county, then you are f**ked matey boy. So yes, I was a fine figure of a blobby pile of shit. No self respect anymore.*

For those site staff that are starting to find that they can no longer physically excavate one of the routes open to them is to specialise. This is precisely what P28 was planning.

P28-M34-08/2005:   *From 2002 I left... 2003, 2004, 2005 yeah nearly three years I left commercial archaeology to gain experience in the building trade, various types of... well, all sorts of stuff I did ... in preparation for doing a Masters in Historic Buildings Conservation. To get some experience... I went back with the [unit] about six months ago ... and I'll start the Masters hopefully at Christmas and start a new phase of my career. I'm not going to make such a cut from archaeology as I have done, but I've got to do something less physical because my back is playing me up and I need the money.*

There is no doubting the fact that archaeological fieldwork is physically demanding and, for site staff in commercial archaeology, it is an all year round occupation. Inevitably, problems with backs and knees are very common and some staff find themselves unable to continue to work manually. They are forced to move into an office-based specialism or revaluate their plans for the future and leave archaeology completely.

The Future

In terms of their future plans, the responses of participants generally fell into one of three categories. They either intended to remain in commercial archaeology for as long as they could (ie as long as they could find work), or they were planning to retrain in order to specialise within archaeology (primarily for financial, physical or career advancement reasons), or they were planning to leave the profession altogether. A fourth, and slightly vaguer category, was the one in which participants enjoyed their job, but were becoming aware that it would not support a stable, familial lifestyle should they want that in the future. Almost invariably those participants were in their mid-twenties to early-thirties and were beginning to realise that they might have to make a choice between the job they loved and the desire to start a family eventually. P21 had recently got married and her husband's job was also not highly paid (though it was non-archaeological). Despite a clear desire to work her way up the career ladder her thoughts were also turning to the prospect of supporting a larger family in a few years time.

P21-F26-12/2004:   *Personally at the moment I think I'd be quite happy staying here for... indefinitely... I'd like to be able to work here long term, to build up my career, to build up my experience. To be able to become a manager one day and run projects and be part of it, but I don't see how practical that's going to be for somebody who wants to have children and start a family as well. So... you get the same... I mean archaeology's one of the few careers where you get the same if you were a man. I mean, women have always had this 'oh, she wants babies' and stuff, but I don't know very many men who work for us,*

for example, who are able to support a family …
Particularly for diggers.

Both P4 and P5 intended to stay in the profession for the next few years, but had clear plans to specialise through postgraduate courses. P5 was at that time planning to study part-time so that he could retain the job with his current unit, though I heard subsequently that he was laid off when the unit hit financial difficulties in 2005.

Me:	*Do you see your future with [unit]?*
P4-F26-02/2004:	*I do at the moment… definitely.*
P5-M24-02/2004:	*Yeah for the next…*
P4:	*At least five years.*
P5:	*Yeah, I would say the next three or four years.*
Me:	*Do you have any plans for the long term or do you not look that far ahead?*
P4:	*You've got plans. You've got better plans than I have. [laughs]*
P5:	*I'm going to start my PhD in September…*
Me:	*In [university]?*
P5:	*No, in [university], doing an animal bone, a PhD on animal bones, but I'm going to do that part time and work with [unit] part-time as well so it's going to take me…*
P4:	*That's what I'm hoping to do with a Masters at some point, but I haven't yet… I was applying for a Masters every year since I left, up until, well, last year I didn't because they didn't do the course I wanted to do. I wanted to do it down here so I could still work.*

For P19 these choices boiled down, in essence, to how much people wanted to stay in the profession. To his mind it was clear that if you want to stay in it, then you would find a way, whether that be by accepting that your career might not advance at the rate you would like, or that it might be necessary to specialise in order to achieve greater financial stability. In hindsight I would have been interested to ask him whether having no children at the age of 38 was his solution to some of the problems faced by commercial archaeologists, but it is a delicate and very personal issue that I really had no right to raise during the interview unless it was already broached. It is equally true that many couples are waiting till later in life to start families these days, so that both have an opportunity to establish a career first etc, and it is not a trend specific to archaeology.

Me:	*You think then that people should resign themselves to the situation?*
P19-M38-08/2004:	*Not resignation, not resignation at all. It's… accept the fact that, you know, if you look at the construction industry, not every brickie is going to own a brickie company.*
Me:	*Yeah.*
P19:	*Not every spark is going to be having their own construction company. There's no reason you can't*

	do it for as long as you want and enjoy it, enjoy that lifestyle. If you have the drive that you want to continue doing it then fair enough, go for it. Because you'll succeed, because you want to, but you make sure you care about the archaeology and not the money.
Me:	*Yeah sure*
P19:	*If you just want to have a damn good time, then do it for that. Enjoy the archaeology and then get yourself a nice job and join up a local group, because how lucky would a local group be to have a professional archaeologist who can help them do weekend digs, or go and record graveyards, get the local community involved. Then you have the best of both worlds. You have money coming in. It's not resignation, it's just accepting the fact that there are 129 county archaeological jobs. There are maybe 120 unit manager jobs. There are maybe 200 project manager jobs, 250 project manager jobs. And then of course if you want to go into heritage, things like English Heritage, Historic Scotland, the [Royal] Commission, there are these options. Have a skill. If you want to be a digger fine, but if you want to… as a digger you could maybe learn how to be a surveyor. Join a surveying company. If you can get into GeoPhysics, join a Geodata company.*

Conclusion

When considering the perceptions of commercial archaeologists, as expressed by the participants in my interviews, it is hard to ignore an overwhelming sense that despite many advances and improvements in the profession since 1990, the predominant trend has seen a reduction in the standard of site-based work. With the exceptionally high turnover of staff, which has long been a feature of field archaeology - though perhaps now reaching new and problematic levels – the experience and skill of supervisors does not seem to be as high as it used to be and, in some cases, they are perhaps below what one might reasonably expect. To further compound this the role of supervisors has changed. Ten to fifteen years ago a supervisory role was just that. In the modern climate, with commercial pressures forcing apparently negative shifts in project management, site-based supervisors often simply do not have the time to monitor the work of their staff, particularly the preparation of records, to the level that they would like. If, as some of my participants suggest, the skill, dedication and initiative of many recent graduates is also becoming weaker then clearly the profession needs to allow for the sort of 'on the job' training, supervision and appraisal that was, for many of them, a feature of the 1980s and early 1990s.

CONCLUSION

The portrait of contemporary commercial archaeology presented in this study has been generated through an historical analysis and three major sets of primary data including a quantitative survey (which also produced a wealth of qualitative submissions), detailed observations made during a period of employment and a series of lengthy, semi-structured interviews. The end result is a comprehensive assessment of the state of commercial archaeology in Britain that examines the great variety of opinions, backgrounds and experiences, whilst picking out the key themes that are shared by the majority of those within commercial archaeology. Throughout this research the problems facing the profession have been analysed from the perspective of their impact on those employed within it. Conclusions drawn, and the recommendations made below, should be seen in this context. This approach, however, represents a unique opportunity to assess the direct impact of contemporary developer-led archaeology on its workforce and their ability to perform their duties to a satisfactory level.

Chapter One outlined the historical developments in planning and ancient monument legislation that led up to the publication of PPG16 in 1990, demonstrating how, for all of its perceived failures, PPG16 provided significantly greater protection for archaeological remains than anything before it, despite being non-statutory. Alongside this there was a background to the growth of commercial archaeology. There was consideration of its roots in purely research-led fieldwork, through the period of under-funded, often frantic, 'rescue' work ahead of development, to the establishment of commercial, developer-led archaeology during the 1980s, later enshrined by PPG16. Through this chapter it became clear that commercial archaeology had evolved from the efforts of a predominantly, volunteer workforce trying to record as much as possible before archaeological remains were lost forever, and had ultimately found itself thrust into a commercial marketplace to which it had to adapt.

In Chapter Two the focus was on those who work in commercial archaeology, particularly the junior site staff most often referred to as 'site assistants' or 'diggers'. In examining the use of labourers on early archaeological sites, it became apparent that the relationship between a contemporary digger and a project manager or unit director is uncomfortably similar to the relationship between a labourer and the antiquarian of old (Everill 2007b).

The analysis of the survey data in Chapter Three allows a greater insight into the world of commercial archaeology and the estimated 2,100 staff employed in that sector in 2003 (rising to an estimated 2,300 in 2006, and perhaps approaching 2,900 before the recent economic crisis led to widespread redundancies). Male dominance of the profession was confirmed in this survey, though it was possible to demonstrate that the under 25s were predominantly female. Among the significant data to come out of this chapter was the indication that it might not be the low pay and poor conditions of employment that are driving people out of the profession. In trying to find significant 'push' and 'pull' factors it was noted that those intending to leave the profession did not seem to be identifying motivating issues, but that they did score significantly lower in identifying 'the archaeology' as something they loved about commercial archaeology. It can be intimated from this that it is only when staff lose their love of archaeology that they seriously think about leaving the profession. It was also noted that 76.6% of respondents felt that the profession was either already in crisis, or would be if nothing was done to change the current system.

Chapter Four presented a thematic analysis of excerpts from the written submissions, which many respondents included as an optional component of the online survey. A significant number of these themes had already been discussed in previous chapters, such as the need for increased professionalism and organisation – which has been a concern for 30 years; the negative effects of the system of competitive tendering on the quality of work; low pay and poor conditions of employment; and the sense that site staff felt that they were not treated as specialists, but often merely as labourers.

Many of these themes were expanded upon in Chapter Five, during which the semi-structured interviews were thematically analysed. The focus here was on the background, experiences and career paths of the participants. It was noted that a number of participants had discovered an early pleasure in excavation and discovery, or had experienced archaeological remains and historic sites during family holidays or day-trips with their school. On the other hand, some had not considered archaeology as a career until they came to choose their university course, and concerns were expressed regarding the quality of practical training at university and whilst working for commercial organisations – particularly when compared to the apprenticeship-style training experienced under the MSC in the 1980s. The concept of 'being' an archaeologist was discussed, along with the largely masculine overtones implicitly expressed when considering the nature of fieldwork and the associated social life. Throughout this chapter it was demonstrated that there was an over-riding sense that pursuing a career in commercial archaeology required a large number of sacrifices to be made, and this seems to be an accepted part of the profession. It is possible to go even further and suggest that this self-sacrifice represents an initiation into the discipline, in which dedication, luck and hard work combines with a natural talent for excavation to make a career possible. Those who are seen to succeed without these elements are regarded scornfully.

Chapter Six presents an opportunity to examine some of these themes still further, during the analysis of the participant observation study. The Project and Site hierarchy is considered, as are the conditions of employment and the process of establishing friendships with co-workers. Camaraderie, which has been implicitly mentioned in the preceding chapters, comes to the fore as a major element in day-to-day relationships on site. The hardships involved in working in winter, and on a demanding urban site, take their toll on the site assistants leading to a spate of injuries, accidents and illnesses towards the end of the project.

However, it is perhaps this adversity that creates a strong bond between many of the archaeologists on the site, particularly those who are staying in 'Bed and Breakfast' accommodation during the week.

The perceptions that commercial archaeologists have of themselves and their profession are also examined in Chapter Seven. In this, the second part of the analysis of the semi-structured interviews, the major themes addressed were: changes in the profession; perceptions of fieldwork; pay; public perceptions; future plans; the IFA and trade unions; and Camaraderie. Participants who started work in commercial archaeology in the late 1980s or early 90s tended to be of the opinion that standards in fieldwork had declined since then. Largely this was put down to a change in the role and the standard of site supervisors, who were no longer always expected to have several years experience and who were not allowed the time to monitor or train the site staff appropriately. The sense that excavation was not treated as a specialism was also expressed as a contributing factor in the decline of standards and relates to the feeling that 'excavation is labouring' as expressed elsewhere.

At the outset of this research I had hoped, even expected, that the conclusion would consist of a series of recommendations to improve the situation in contemporary commercial archaeology. As the study took shape it became apparent that many of the problems within the profession are also the things that define it, and even attract people to it. One need only listen to a conversation in a pub after work on site to hear how diggers seem to revel in the retelling of how they once worked on a site where it was even colder/wetter/dustier than today, or how terrible the managers/supervisors/diggers were at a previous unit. Adversity like that not only forges a remarkable camaraderie between diggers, but it also defines them in opposition to what they often perceive as 'normal' jobs. For many of them archaeology is a lifestyle choice, but it is one that stands in stark contrast to the choices made by the majority of people in the UK. Diggers choose to work outdoors in all weather, earning half the average graduate wage, doing a job that very few others really understand or value, with little realistic prospect of promotion. It seems hard to comprehend if you are not an archaeologist yourself. Those that are just accept that there are sacrifices you have to make in order to pursue your vocation.

There are, however, some points to emerge from this research that should be considered as recommendations to ensure the future development of the profession. It seems that the only way of guaranteeing a high standard of fieldwork, post-excavation work and publication across the UK, as well as ensuring that national pay scales and job grades, 'continuing professional development', sick pay, holiday entitlements and pension schemes are available equally across the profession, is to create a 'National Archaeology Service'. This could be operated on a regional basis and funded by a 'developer tax' rather than paid directly by developers to each unit. It seems likely, however, that the opportunity to establish such a body was lost in the 1970s and so the following five points represent changes that are still achievable, and would represent significant progress within the profession.

1. University-based training

The majority of archaeologists employed in the UK are employed within the commercial sector, yet universities are almost invariably failing to adequately prepare their students for this sector (see Croucher et al, 2008, for a detailed discussion of this issue. This has knock-on effects both for commercial archaeology, but also for those who choose to remain within academia and may ultimately find themselves trying to run a fieldwork project with little experience. If the first year of a degree was substituted for an HND or equivalent in fieldwork and practical skills – with the course content determined, monitored and supported by local employers and the IFA – then students would have the option to remain within the university to pursue a degree for a further two years, or to seek employment after completing the HND element. An alternative might be for students to complete an NVQ in Archaeological Practive alongside an explicitly 'practice-led' degree. This would provide a quality assurance for potential employers from whom a university degree is no indication of practical ability.

2. Work-based training

Employers also need to be more prepared to offer 'on the job' training, or time off to attend courses. There is currently a fear prevalent in the profession, especially among smaller units, that staff will take their new skills and go to a competitor. This is, however, short-sighted and represents an under-investment in the skills of staff. The IFA is currently formulating a system to encourage each unit and each employee to consider and act upon 'continuing professional development' targets. If this is accepted across the profession one can only hope that site staff will have the opportunity to broaden their skills, or to specialise within their current employer.

3. Management training

Even though the paucity and disorganisation of archaeological management was identified three decades ago little seems to have changed in that time apart from within the larger units - though not always even then. There needs to be some way of ensuring that those entering into a management role are capable of undertaking all the tasks required of them, as there are currently no restrictions. It cannot be assumed that field experience qualifies someone to manage and there should be some kind of business management qualification, perhaps run through the IFA as a distance-learning course, which helps prepare a candidate for that role. Successfully obtaining this qualification should be a requirement for all managers within units that are IFA 'Registered Archaeological Organisations'.

4. Adequate supervision

If site staff were to receive better training within a few years the quality of supervisors would also improve. However, there needs to be a recognition within the profession that a supervisor needs time to actually supervise the staff below him/ her. An aspect of the commercial pressures on units has been the gradual abandonment of traditional supervisory roles. Supervisors today are expected to work on site, excavating features alongside site assistants, answering questions and giving advice when asked. What is needed, in reality, is not just 'another body' on site, but someone who is allowed the time to organise and maintain the site archive as it develops, and to effectively monitor the work of the site assistants – both on site and in the paperwork as it is submitted. It is an indictment of contemporary commercial archaeology that a site supervisor is often perceived as little more than a 'foreman' of archaeological labourers, when in fact they are pivotal figures in the process.

5. Pay and conditions of employment

One of the biggest complaints of those employed within commercial archaeology, particularly those at the bottom of the system, are the low wages and the unpredictable nature of employment. First and foremost the practice of employing staff on a 'self employed' basis should be banned in professional archaeology. A few units still do this and, for some reason, it is currently most prevalent in Scotland. Staff may feel that they are benefiting as their 'take-home' wages are higher, but they still have to pay income tax and National Insurance contributions. Furthermore, being self-employed leaves staff with no holiday entitlement or sick pay. It is, in essence, a way for employers to dodge their responsibilities.

Without altering the system by which projects are tendered for it is difficult to envisage an end to employment on three month contracts, with the possibility of extension if there is sufficient work. However, there is no reason why units can not cooperate with each other and subcontract or loan staff to another unit, rather than making them redundant. This does occasionally happen, but it is very rare. A regional, or national, archaeology service would make it possible for staff to transfer between regions without losing their accrued holiday entitlement, sick pay and other benefits.

The wages for archaeological staff seem to have been frozen for a few years in the early/mid 1990s and this, combined with competitive tendering – which has largely held back the rise in wages beyond that of inflation – leaves commercial archaeologists substantially underpaid. It is not realistic to demand that wages be brought into line with other 'graduate' jobs (currently *c* £24,000 a year), but staff should reasonably expect to be paid at least £17,000 a year – around £2,500 to £3,000 more than the current average for new staff. This would represent a pay rise of between 18% and 21%, and a recent IFA pay 'benchmarking' exercise has demonstrated that archaeological salaries are between 13% and 53% behind comparable sectors (Price and Geary 2008). Despite the best intentions of the IFA, however, moves to begin to raise wages in 2009 look likely to be affected by the global financial crisis. This has already resulted in a sudden and crippling fall off in developer-led archaeological work and widespread redundancies.

It is not thought likely that many of the above five points will be acted upon, despite much of it being common sense that has repeatedly been raised over the last thirty years. That leaves us to wonder what will become of the 'Invisible Diggers' over the next thirty years. Assuming planning legislation and guidance does not move away from the protection of archaeological remains – in which case commercial archaeology as we know it may have ceased to exist – it seems likely that little will have really changed. New technologies and methodologies will undoubtedly be introduced in that time, but I have a strong feeling that field archaeologists will actually be much the same. Hopefully better paid, better trained and, dare I say it, more 'Visible', but also still enjoying the physicality of excavation, the thrill of engaging with the archaeological remains and the camaraderie that define the experience for many today.

APPENDIX

Catalogue of Recorded Interviews

P	Career Stage	M/F	Age	Interview	Date	Duration	Place
1	Project Assistant	F	c 23	1	?-4-03	1 hr	Car
2	Project Assistant	M	c 24	2	?-4-03	1 hr	Pub
3	Project Officer	M	40	3	30-4-03	1 hr	Site
4	Supervisor	F	26	4	3-2-04	1 hr 15m	Pub
5	Supervisor (Finds)	M	24				
6	Unit Director	M	c 40	5	4-2-04	1 hr	Pub
7	Unit Director	M	c 55				
8	Site Assistant	F	c 23	6	4-2-04	1 hr	Office
9	Site Assistant	F	c 23				
10	Unit Director	M	c 50	7	12-2-04	1 hr	Pub
11	Unit Director	F	c 50				
12	Supervisor (Finds)	M	c 25	8	12-2-04	1 hr	Pub
13	Site Assistant	M	c 25				
14	Supervisor	M	c 25	9	14-4-04	1 hr	Site
15	Unit Director	M	c 45	10	22-4-04	1 hr	Pub
16	Unit Director	M	c 40				
17	Archaeological Officer	F	c 30	11	6-5-04	1 hr	Office
18	Assistant " " "	M	c 25				
19	County Archaeologist	M	38	12	17-8-04	1½ hrs	Airport
20	(Ex) Project Officer	M	38	13	5-10-04	1 hr	Office
21	Project Assistant Maritime)	F	26	14	10-12-04	1 hr	Office
22	Assistant Supervisor Finds)	F	c 40	15	10-12-04	1 hr	Office
23	Assistant Supervisor (Enviro)	F	c 28	16	10-12-04	1 hr	Office
24	Project Officer	F	c 30	17	10-12-04	1 hr	Office
25	Project Assistant	M	c 40				
26	Assist. Supervisor	M	25	18	10-12-04	½hr	Office
27	Project Officer (Maritime)	M	29	19	10-12-04	½hr	Office
28	Supervisor	M	34	20	21-08-05	1hr	Abroad

REFERENCES

Addyman, P. 1974. York: The anatomy of a crisis in urban archaeology. In Rahtz, P (ed) *Rescue Archaeology*. Harmondsworth, Penguin Books Ltd: 153–162.

AIP (Archaeological Investigations Project) Website 2006. http://csweb.bournemouth.ac.uk/aip/aipintro.htm.

Aitchison, K. 1996. Working in field archaeology and the IFA. *Assemblage* 1: 17–20.

Aitchison, K. 1999. *Profiling the Profession: a survey of archaeological jobs in the UK.* York, London and Reading; CBA, EH and IFA.

Aitchison, K. and Edwards, R. 2003. *Archaeology Labour Market Intelligence: Profiling the Profession 2002/3.* Bradford, Cultural Heritage National Training Organisation.

Aitchison, K. and Edwards, R. 2008. *Archaeology Labour Market Intelligence: Profiling the Profession 2007/8.* Reading, Institute of Field Archaeologists.

Andrews, G., Barrett, J.C. and Lewis, J.S. C. 2000. Interpretation not record: the practice of archaeology. *Antiquity* 74: 525–30.

Anon 1994. The female anthropologist's guide to academic pitfalls. In Nelson, M.C., Nelson, S.M. and Wylie, A. (eds) *Equity Issues for Women in Archaeology*. Archaeological Papers of the American Anthropological Association No. 5: 5–6.

Anon 1998. Crisis of conscience: archaeology and development. *Rescue News* 74: 2–3.

APPAG 2003. *The Current State of Archaeology in the United Kingdom – First Report of the All Party Parliamentary Archaeology Group.* London, APPAG.

Barker, P. 1974a. The scale of the problem. In Rahtz, P. (ed) *Rescue Archaeology*. Harmondsworth, Penguin Books Ltd: 28–34.

Barker, P. 1974b. The Origins and Development of RESCUE. In Rahtz, P. (ed) *Rescue Archaeology*. Harmondsworth, Penguin Books Ltd: 280–285.

Barker, P. 1977. *Techniques of Archaeological Excavation.* London, B.T. Batsford Ltd.

Barker, P. 1987. Rescue: Antenatal, Birth and Early Years. In Mytum, H. and

Waugh, K. (eds) *Rescue archaeology – what's next? : Proceedings of a Rescue conference held at the University of York, December 1986.* Department of Archaeology, University of York Monograph 6: 7–9.

Bateman, J. 2005. Wearing Juninho's shirt: Record and negotiation in excavation photographs. In Smiles, S. and Moser, S. (eds) *Envisioning the past: Archaeology and the image.* Oxford, Blackwell Publishing Ltd: 192–203.

Benjamin, R. 2003. Black and Asian representation in UK archaeology. *The Archaeologist* 48: 7–8.

Biddle, M. 1994. *What future for British Archaeology?* Archaeology in Britain Conference 1994. Oxbow Lecture 1. Oxford, Oxbow Books.

Blackhall, J. C. 2000. *Planning Law and Practice: 2nd Edition.* London, Cavendish Publishing Ltd.

Boyle, R. 1772. *Works. (Volume 2).* Edited by T. Birch. London.

Bradley, R. 2006. *Bridging the two cultures: commercial archaeology and the study of British prehistory.* A paper presented to the Society of Antiquaries, 12th January 2006. http://www.sal.org.uk/downloads/Bridging-Two-Cultures.doc.

Braidwood, L. 1959. *Digging beyond the Tigris: A woman archaeologist's story of life on a 'dig' in the Kurdish hills of Iraq.* London, Abelard–Schuman Ltd.

Breakwell, G.M. 1990. *Interviewing.* Leicester and London; The British Psychological Society and Routledge Ltd.

Breeze, D. J. 1993. Ancient Monuments Legislation. In Hunter, J. and Ralston, I. *Archaeological Resource Management in the UK: An Introduction.* Stroud, Alan Sutton Publishing Ltd: 44–55.

Burgess, R. 1982. The Unstructured Interview as a Conversation. In Burgess, R. (ed) *Field research: a sourcebook and field manual.* London, Allen & Unwin: 107–110.

Burgess, R. 1984. *In the Field: An introduction to Field Research.* London, George Allen and Unwin.

Cane, C. 1994. Women in Archaeology in Britain: Three Papers. In Nelson, M.C., Nelson, S.M. and Wylie, A. (eds) *Equity Issues for Women in Archaeology.* Archaeological Papers of the American Anthropological Association No. 5.

Carman, J. 1996. *Valuing ancient things: Archaeology and law.* Leicester, Leicester University Press.

Carver, M. 2006. Thinking Allowed. *Rescue News* 100.

Chadwick, A. 2000. Taking English archaeology into the next millennium – a personal review of the state of the art. *Assemblage* 5. http://www.shef.ac.uk/assem/5/chad.html.

Champion, S. 1998. Women in British Archaeology: visible and invisible. In Diaz-Andreu, M. and Sorensen, M.L.S. (eds) *Excavating women: A history of women in European archaeology.* London, Routledge: 175–197.

Colt Hoare, Sir R. 1810. *Ancient History of Wiltshire, Volume 1.* Privately published.

Cooper-Reade, H. 1998. Competitive tendering: Is it time we stopped complaining? *Rescue News* 75: 2.

Crewe, Sir G. 1843. *A word for the poor, and against the present Poor Law.* Derby.

Croucher, K., Cobb, H. and Brennan, A. 2008. *Investigating the role of fieldwork in teaching and leanring archaeology.* Liverpool, Higher Education Academy Subject Centre for History, Classics and Archaeology

Crump, T. 1987. The role of MSC funding in British Archaeology. In Mytum, H. and Waugh, K. (eds) *Rescue archaeology – What's Next? Proceedings of a Rescue Conference held at the University of York, December 1986.* Department of Archaeology, University of York Monograph 6: 41–46.

Cumberpatch, C. and Blinkhorn, P. 2001. Clients, contractors, curators and archaeology: who owns the past? In Pluciennik, M. (ed) *The responsibilities of archaeologists: archaeology and ethics.* Lampeter workshop in archaeology 4. Oxford, Archaeopress: 39–45.

Cunnington, R. 1975. *From Antiquary to Archaeologist: A biography of William Cunnington 1754–1810.* Aylesbury, Shire Publications Ltd.

Daily Mirror 2003. *We're 3-time Losers: Pension plans in crisis.* http://www.mirror.co.uk/mirrormoney/mirrormoney/tm_objectid=12557299%26methond=full%26siteid=94762-name_page.html.

Darvill, T. and Russell, B. 2002. *Archaeology after PPG16: Archaeological Investigations in England 1990-1999.* Bournemouth University School of Conservation Sciences Research Report 10. http://csweb.bournemouth.ac.uk/aip/ppg16/index.htm.

Denison, S. 1999. Want to be an archaeologist? Read this. *British Archaeology* 48: 15.

DoE (Department of the Environment) 1990. *Planning Policy Guidance Note 16: Archaeology and Planning.* London, HMSO.

Drake, J. 1987. Management – Field Archaeology's Worst Failure. In Joyce, S. M. Newbury and Stone, P. (eds) *Degree, digging, dole our future? Papers presented at YAC '85 Southampton.* Southampton, Southampton University Archaeology Society: 47–53.

Edgeworth, M. 2003. *Acts of Discovery: An ethnography of archaeological practice.* BAR International Series 1131. Oxford, Archaeopress.

English Heritage 1991. *The management of archaeological projects (second edition).* London, English Heritage.

Everill, P. 2003a. Invisibly Digging: Outline of a new research project. *Rescue News* 90: 5.

Everill, P. 2003b. Tales of the Invisible Diggers: An Update. *Rescue News* 91: 7.

Everill, P. 2007a. A day in the life of a training excavation: teaching archaeological fieldwork in the UK. *World Archaeology* Vol. 39(4): 483–498.

Everill, P. 2007b. British Commercial Archaeology: Antiquarians and Labourers; Developers and Diggers. In Hamilakis, Y. and Duke, P. (eds) *Archaeology and Capitalism: From ethics to politics.* One World Archaeology Series: 54. Walnut Creek, California, Left Coast Publishing.

Fahy, A. 1987. Job Satisfaction Doesn't Pay the Rent: The Problems of Short Term Contracts. In Joyce, S., Newbury, M. and Stone, P. (eds) *Degree, digging, dole our future? Papers presented at YAC '85 Southampton.* Southampton, Southampton University Archaeology Society: 20–27.

Fetterman, D. 1998. *Ethnography: step by step – 2nd edition.* London, SAGE Publications Ltd.

Fitzgerald, C. 2003. Why choose horticulture as a career? *The Garden: Journal of the Royal Horticultural Society* 128 (Oct): 796–7.

Flannery, K. 1982. The Golden Marshalltown: A Parable for the Archaeology of the 1980s. *American Anthropologist* 84: 265–78.

Gero, J. 1994. Excavation Bias and the Woman at home ideology. In Nelson, M.C., Nelson, S.M. and Wylie, A. (eds) *Equity Issues for Women in Archaeology.* Archaeological Papers of the American Anthropological Association No.5: 37–42.

Gerson, K. and Horowitz, R. 2002. Observation and interviewing: Options and choices in qualitative research. In May, T. (ed) *Qualitative Research in Action.* London, SAGE Publications: 199–224.

Gilchrist, R. 1994. Women in Archaeology in Britain: Three Papers. In Nelson, M.C., Nelson, S.M. and Wylie, A. (eds) *Equity Issues for Women in Archaeology.* Archaeological Papers of the American Anthropological Association No.5.

Gold, R. 1958. Roles in sociological field observation. *Social Forces* 36 (3): 217-23.

Goodfellow, S. 1990. Undercutting the excavators. *History Today* 40: 6–8.

Gran, T. 1984. *The Norwegian with Scott: Tryggve Gran's Antarctic diary 1910-1913.* London, H.M.S.O. for National Maritime Museum.

Graves-Brown, P. 1997. S/he who pays the piper… archaeology and the polluter pays principle. *Assemblage* 2. http://www.shef.ac.uk/assem/2/2gb2.html.

Green, F. 1987. MSC: Their Involvement in Archaeology. In Joyce, S., Newbury, M. and Stone, P. (eds) *Degree, digging, dole our future? Papers presented at YAC '85, Southampton.* Southampton, Southampton University Archaeology Society: 28–34.

Hardy, A. 1997. Someone else's problem? An inquiry into fieldwork training. *The Archaeologist* 29: 8–9.

Hawkes, J. 1982. *Mortimer Wheeler: Adventurer in archaeology.* London, Weidenfeld and Nicolson.

Hinton, P. 1996. Good archaeology guaranteed: standards in British Archaeology. *Field Archaeologist* 26: 7–11.

Hinton, P. 1997. IFA: future directions. *The Archaeologist* 30: 7–8.

Hinton, P. 1998. The role of the IFA. *Assemblage* 3. http://www.shef.ac.uk~assem/3/3hinton.htm.

Hinton, P. and Aitchison, K. 1998. Profiling the Profession: a new survey of archaeological employment in the UK. *Rescue News* 74: 3.

HMSO 1995. *The Reporting of Injuries, Diseases and Dangerous Occurrences Regulations 1995.* Statutory Instrument 1995 No. 3163. http://www/opso.gov.uk/si/si1995/Uksi_1995193_en_1.htm.

Hobley, B. 1986. The Archaeologists' and Developers' Code of Practice – a great leap forward. In Mytum, H. and Waugh, K. (eds) *Rescue archaeology – What's Next? Proceedings of a Rescue Conference held at the University of York, December 1986.* Department of Archaeology, University of York, Monograph 6: 35–40.

Hobley, B. 1987. The Need for Professionalism and Modern Management in Archaeology. In Joyce, S. M. Newbury and Stone, P. (eds) *Degree, digging, dole our future? Papers presented at YAC '85 Southampton.* Southampton, Southampton University Archaeology Society: 41–46.

Hodder, I. (ed) 2000. *Towards reflexive method in archaeology : The example at Çatalhöyük by members of the Çatalhöyük teams.* British Institute of Archaeology at Ankara Monograph No.28. Cambridge, McDonald Institute for Archaeological Research.

Howe, L. 1995. Living on the edge: working on short-term contracts in archaeology. *Field Archaeologist* 23: 27–28.

Hunter, J. 1987. Field Perspectives on Student Training. In Joyce, S., Newbury, M. and Stone, P. (eds) *Degree, digging, dole our future? Papers presented at YAC '85 Southampton.* Southampton, Southampton University Archaeology Society: 13–19.

Hunter, J., Ralston, I. and Hamlin, A. 1993. The Structure of British Archaeology. In Hunter, J and Ralston, I. (eds) *Archaeological Resource Management in the UK: An introduction.* Stroud, Alan Sutton Publishing Ltd: 30–43.

IFA 1995. Quality of work/life survey. *Field Archaeologist* 24: 7–11.

IFA 2006. *Institute of Field Archaeologists Yearbook and Directory 2006.* Reading, IFA.

Jones, A. 2002. *Archaeological theory and scientific practice.* Cambridge, Cambridge University Press.

Joyce, S., Newbury, M. and Stone, P. (eds) 1987. *Degree, digging, dole our future? Papers presented at YAC '85 Southampton.* Southampton, Southampton University Archaeology Society.

Knight, M. 2002. *Camera Obscuring: Representing excavation in the photographic age.* Paper presented to the Cambridge University Archaeological Field Club. Unpublished.

Lawson, A. 1993. English archaeological units as contractors. In Hunter, J and Ralston, I. (eds) *Archaeological Resource Management in the UK: An introduction.* Stroud, Alan Sutton Publishing Ltd: 149–157.

Lucas, G. 2001a. Destruction and the Rhetoric of Excavation. *Norwegian Archaeological Review* 34: 35–36.

Lucas, G. 2001b. *Critical Approaches to Fieldwork: Contemporary and historical archaeological practice.* London, Routledge.

McFadyen, L., Lewis, H., Challands, N., Challands, A., Garrow, D., Poole, S., Knight, M., Dodwell, N., Mackay, D., Denny, L.,

Whitaker, P., Breach, P., Lloyd-Smith, L., Gibson, D. and White, P. 1997. *Gossiping on people's bodies*. Unpublished paper presented at TAG 1997, Bournemouth.

Mason, J. 1996. *Qualitative Researching*. London, SAGE Publications Ltd.

Mason, J. 2002. Qualitative Interviewing: Asking, listening and interpreting. In May, T. (ed) *Qualitative Research in action*. London, SAGE Publications Ltd: 225–241.

Miles, D. 1978. *An introduction to archaeology*. London, Ward Lock Limited.

Millet, M. 1986. Universities and the future of Archaeology in Britain. In Mytum, H. and Waugh, K. (eds) *Rescue archaeology – What's Next? Proceedings of a Rescue Conference held at the University of York, December 1986*. Department of Archaeology, University of York Monograph 6: 29–34.

Moloney, R. 1998. Practitioner survey 1997. *The Archaeologist* 32: 15–16.

Morris, E. 1991. Women in British archaeology – the equal opportunities working party report 1991. *Field Archaeologist* 15: 280–282.

Morris, E. 1992. 1990/1 *Equal Opportunities in Archaeology working party report: Women in British Archaeology*. IFA Occasional paper 4. Reading, IFA.

Morris, E. 1994. Extracts from "Women in British Archaeology". In Nelson, M.C., Nelson, S.M. and Wylie, A. (eds) *Equity Issues for Women in Archaeology*. Archaeological Papers of the American Anthropological Association No. 5: 203–212.

Morris, R. 1994. Taking archaeology into a new era. *British Archaeology News* 18: 9.

Morris, R. 1998. Riding down the road to regional chaos. *British Archaeology News* 37: 15.

Morris, R. 1999. An abiding faith in archaeology's worth. *British Archaeology News* 45: 15.

Moser, S. 1995. *Archaeology and its disciplinary culture: The professionalisation of Australian archaeology*. University of Sydney. Unpublished PhD thesis.

Moser, S. 1998. *Gendered Dimensions of Archaeological Practice: The Stereotyping of archaeology as fieldwork*. Paper presented at the School of American Research Conference, 'Doing Feminist Archaeology' April 1998. Unpublished.

Noel Hume, I. 1969. *Historical Archaeology*. New York, Alfred Knopf.

Philp, B. 1974. Kent, Dover, and the CIB Corps. In Rahtz, P (ed) *Rescue Archaeology*. Harmondsworth, Penguin Books Ltd: 73–78.

Philp, B. 2002. *Archaeology in the front line: 50 years of Kent rescue 1952–2002: discovery – excavation – publication – preservation – presentation – education*. Published on behalf of the Kent Archaeological Trust by Kent Archaeological Rescue Unit, Dover.

Piggot, S. 1975. Reviews. *Antiquity* 49 (195): 238–239.

Pitt Rivers, A. H. L. 1892. *Excavations in Cranborne Chase, Volume III: Excavations in Bokerly and Wansdyke, Dorset and Wilts. 1888-1891*. Privately published.

Price, F. and Geary, K. 2008. *Benchmarking archaeological salaries report.* Reading, IFA http://www.archaeologists.net/modules/icontent/inPages/docs/Benchmarking%20report.doc.

Pugh-Smith, J. and Samuels, J. 1996. *Archaeology and the law.* London, Sweet and Maxwell.

Rahtz, P. 1974. Rescue Digging Past and Present. In Rahtz, P (ed) *Rescue Archaeology.* Harmondsworth, Penguin Books Ltd: 53–72.

Robbins, B. 1993. *Secular vocations: Intellectuals, professionalism, culture.* London, Verso.

Scott, Captain R.F. 1913. *Scott's Last Expedition. Volumes I and II. Arranged by L. Huxley.* London, Smith Elder & Co.

Sellers, M. 1973. The secret notebook for the practicing archaeologist: With preliminary notes toward an ethno-science of archaeology. *Plains Anthropologist* 18 (60): 140–148.

Shapin, S. 1989. The Invisible Technician. *American Scientist* 77: 554–563.

Shortland, M. 1994. Darkness Visible: Underground Culture in the Golden Age of Geology. *History of Science* xxxii: 1–61.

Snell, K. 1985. *Annals of the Labouring Poor: Social change and agrarian England, 1660–1900.* Cambridge, Cambridge University Press.

Somerville, A. 1852. *The Whistler at the Plough.* Manchester.

Sparey-Green, C. 1995. Which side of the fence? The dilemma of archaeology and development. *Rescue News* 67: 3 and 6.

Spoerry, P. 1991a. Structure, funding and legislation in British Archaeology: The RESCUE Report. *Rescue News* 54: 1.

Spoerry, P. 1991b. Structure and funding in British Archaeology: some points raised by the 'RESCUE' questionnaire. *Rescue News* 54: 2.

Spoerry, P. 1992. *The structure and funding of British Archaeology: The Rescue Questionnaire 1990-1.* Hertford, RESCUE.

Spoerry, P. 1997 The Rescue Survey 1996: some preliminary results. *Rescue News* 72: 6–7.

Sturt, G. 1907. *Memoirs of a Surrey Labourer.* Firle, Caliban Books.

Sturt, G. 1912. *Change in the Village.* London, Gerald Duckworth & Co. Ltd.

Sturt, G. 1941. *The Journals of George Sturt.* London, The Cresset Press.

Thomas, C. 1974. Archaeology in Britain 1973. In Rahtz, P (ed) *Rescue Archaeology.* Harmondsworth, Penguin Books Ltd: 3–15.

Tilley, C. 1989. Excavation as theatre. *Antiquity* 63: 275–80.

Turner, R. 1996. Jobs in British archaeology 1995. *Field Archaeologist* 25: 8–9.

Turner, R. 1997. Jobs in British archaeology 1996. *The Archaeologist* 29: 6–7.

Turner, R. 1998. Jobs in British Archaeology 1997. *The Archaeologist* 31:12–14.

University of Southampton 2004. *Flyer for Archaeology 'Open Day', School of Humanities.* Unpublished.

Wainwright, G. 2000. Time please. *Antiquity* 74: 909–943.

Walker, J. 1996. Let us have franchises in archaeology. *British Archaeology* 20: 11.

Wheeler, Sir M. 1954. *Archaeology from the Earth.* Oxford, Clarendon Press.

Wilshire, B. 1990. *The moral collapse of the university: Professionalism, purity and alienation.* Albany, SUNY.

Wilson, E.A. 1972. *Diary of the Terra Nova Expedition to the Antarctic 1910–1912.* London, Blandford Press.

Wood, J. 1991. Professional training in archaeology: what do the professionals think and do? *Rescue News* 53: 6.

Woodbridge, K. 1970. *Landscape and Antiquity: Aspects of English Culture at Stourhead 1718 to 1838.* Oxford, Clarendon Press.

Woolley, Sir L. 1930. *Digging up the Past.* Harmondsworth, Penguin Books Ltd.

Yarrow, T. 2003. Artefactual Persons: The relational capacities of persons and things in the practice of excavation. *Norwegian Archaeological Review* 36 (1): 65–73.

Yarrow, T. 2006. Sites of knowledge: different ways of knowing an archaeological excavation. In Edgeworth, M. (ed) *Ethnographies of archaeological practice: Cultural encounters, material transformations.* Oxford, Alta Mira Press: 20–32

Zeder, M.A. 1997. *The American archaeologist: A profile.* Walnut Creek, AltaMira in cooperation with the Society for American Archaeology.